BUSINESS ECONOMICS

K. RAJAGOPALACHAR

ATLANTIC
PUBLISHERS & DISTRIBUTORS (P) LTD

Published by

ATLANTIC

PUBLISHERS & DISTRIBUTORS (P) LTD

7/22, Ansari Road, Darya Ganj, New Delhi-110002
Phones : +91-11-40775252, 40775214, 23273880, 23275880
Fax : +91-11-23285873
Web : www.atlanticbooks.com
E-mail : orders@atlanticbooks.com

Branch Office: Chennai
Phones : +91-44-48531784, 28291383
E-mail : chennai@atlanticbooks.com

Printed & bound in India by Atlantic Print Services

Dedicated
to
Miraculous Infant Jesus
for
All the Good things that I am Bestowed upon,
To B.S.S. that Driving Force,
and
To Prof. K.V.G.
Who Taught me Most,
To Prof. R.V. Swamy who got me jobs
While I learnt
From American Professors such as
Dr. Jones and Dr. Adams

Preface

Though this book is prepared in accordance with the syllabus of Business Economics for First Year B.Com. of the Bangalore University, it caters also to the needs of Business Economics of all universities of Karnataka and B.A. students and C.A.I.I.B. and I.C.W.A. courses. Keeping these courses in view I have prepared the Second Part of 'The Business Economics'.

There are many books of standard on Managerial Economics but they cater to only a part of the syllabus of Business Economics. As such, a sincere attempt is made to make this book wholesome.

The topics are treated in a simple but lucid manner without compromising on quality and standard. The language is simple and style of presentation is scientific. Footnotes are given wherever necessary.

Certain topics such as Demand Forecasting, Profit Policy, Price Policy and Cost-Output Relations are simplified and illustrated diagramatically, numerically and tabularly for quick perception by students of average I.Q.

It was felt that the work would be incomplete without topics on International Financial Institutions and the R.B.I. and S.B.I. These topics, it is hoped, would enhance the utility of the book to one and all.

I hope that this book would also be a useful addition to the Reference Section of any library.

I have drawn richly from the works of many great economists in preparing this book. My greatful thanks are due to all these great economists.

I am especially thankful to my colleague Sri. D.Vasudeva Rao, Department of Commerce, A.P.S. College of Commerce, because of whose moral and financial support I could write this book.

I am grateful to all my colleagues who encouraged me to prepare this book.

I acknowledge with happiness and pride my son Anoop Rajgopal's sincere support in preparing this book. Last but not least, I am lovingly grateful to my wife Shashi and my daughter Amitha who stood by me like none in completing this book.

I unmincingly thank M/s. Atlantic Publishers & Distributors and their team for their timely and fine execution of this work.

I crave the indulgence of my colleagues and students for their useful suggestions without which no work can be made more useful. Such suggestions may please be addressed directly to the author.

K. Rajagopalachar

Contents

PART I

PART II

PART I

1

Meaning and Objectives of Business Economics

Lord Keynes rightly pointed out that '*The study of Economics is mental gymnastics*'. Business Economics is a logic of choice. Business Economics is the study of the art of decision-making in a firm or undertaking. In business, a firm is beset with numerous alternatives. Its resources being scarce, they have to be used in the best alternative. Decision-making is not an easy task. Thus, Business Economics comes in handy at this stage.

Indeed, Business Economics is the economics of business decision-making. It is the "*Study of the allocation of resources available to a firm and other unit of management among the activities of that unit,*" according to Hynes and others.

In other words, Business Economics is basically concerned with the allocation of resources among alternative uses. Whether it is a society of saints or a firm; the basic problem is that of '*Economising*' of resources. Business Economics is the art and science of economising. In other words, it enables the firm to make a rational or correct choice of resources and to gain maximum returns. The returns must not only be maximum but they must be obtained with minimum resources and effort. This is made possible only when the selection of choice or decision-making is '*the best*' among the various alternatives open to the firm.

Business Economics integrates the basic principles of Economic Theory with that of the practice of business. Thus, the subject-matter of Economics of Business relates to economic analysis of *business problems, policy-making and business planning.*

A fruitful study of Business Economics involves mastering of the basic principles, contents and logicity of Economics. It involves the exposition of the student to the '*Micro*' and '*Macro*' economic principles

THE ROLE AND RESPONSIBILITIES OF A BUSINESS ECONOMIST

It should be worthwhile to remind the student to remember that it is neither desirable nor feasible to apply the theory of Economics or the tools of Economics to the practice of business. To be able to do so one must be fully equipped with the basic trends of Economics and of Business Economics in particular.

Thus, the role and responsibilities of the '*Business Economist*' are dynamic and varied. He cannot afford to be theoretical. Nor can he be too rigid in his decisions. For, he has to re-make his decision as per changing business circumstances or trade environment. Incidentally, the business environment is rigorously subject to changes in market forces viz. '*supply*' and '*demand*', '*cost*' and '*price*' and so on.

The 'Role' of the business economist is that of the '*Charmer*'. Like the charmer, he has to offer suggestions to his firm according to the strength and depth of the changing business conditions. If the crowd of problems circumventing the firm are dwindling, he has to change his suggestion to the problem.

The '*Responsibility*' of the Business Economist is different from his 'Role'. The 'Role' of the Business Economist can be compared to the Role of a pair of bullocks drawing a cart. *Like they move at a co-ordinated speed and in the same direction and carrying equally shared weight, the Business Economist of a firm has to move in the same direction as the objective of the firm, give the suggestions to the project of the firm (according to its short and long-run objectives), hold himself responsible for the failure of his suggestion equally with the proprietors of the firm and above all he must assume responsibility and feel one with the successes and failures of the firm.*

For the sake of easy memory we may list the 'Role and Responsibilities' of the Business Economist or the Managerial Economist as under:

1. To fore-warn the firm of imminent risk of losses when he foresees it.
2. To advise the firm on matters of purchase of raw-materials, plant and equipment.
3. To honestly advise the firm on matters of finance, procurement of raw-materials, etc.

4. To strongly recommend or denounce the way in which the administration of the '*Marketing Section*' of the firm is organised or functioning.
5. To suggest ways and means to expand the markets for the product or products of the firm.
6. To explore possibilities of opening up new venues for the use of the by-product if any.
7. To recommend to the 'Research and Development Department' of the firm to find out 'New' techniques to reduce cost of production and increase the competitive strength of the product of the firm.
8. To have a close and fruitful rapport with the 'Employees' and 'Boss or Bosses' of the firm so that what he says will have the required weight and honesty and earnestness.
9. Above all, he must be dedicated to the firm and offer timely and valuable, feasible and workable help to the firm true to his capacity as the Business Economist or Managerial Consultant.

Thus, a Business Economist forms the core of the firm. He must act as a friend, a philosopher and a guide of his firm. He is both a 'pessimist' and an 'optimist' in short and in one.

He is like a '*Shot-put Ball*' which is rolled into one and which consists of a number of particles but still carries weight. *He is the root and stem of the firm to which he belongs.*

Apart from these responsibilities, he has to perform some '*Specific Functions*' according to K.J.W. Alexander and Alexander G. Kemp. They are:

(a) forecasting sales on the basis of market information;
(b) aid and conduct extensive and objective industrial market research relevant to the product;
(c) intensively dig into the pricing problem of his industry or firm;
(d) analyse the market for shares, debentures and securities related to raising capital;
(e) offer useful advice on public relations; and
(f) foretell business environment by acting as a barometer of '*Business Shocks*'.

2

Consumption

CONSUMERS' SOVEREIGNTY

It is said theoretically that the consumer is the king or the sovereign of the market under capitalism. '*The Sovereign*' means '*the King*'. Hence, 'Consumers' Sovereignty' means that the *consumer is the one who dictates or determines what the producer will or has to produce and can sell in the market.*

The point is; how can the consumer be at the dictating end of a capitalist market!

Theoretically, the consumer is the one who decides what to produce but practically there are a number of constraints against the consumer. These constraints make the consumer '*a virtual slave than a sovereign of the market*'.

***Why is the Consumer called a Sovereign*:** The consumer, in a purely capitalist system of conduct of business or production, is really the sovereign or the king. He commands the producer or the businessman.

The way in which he 'is thought to command the producer' is easy to understand. The 'Key' is the consumer's tastes, fashions and habits. All these will change and so the demand will also change. Then the product has to change too. For instance, you cannot sell 'Bell-bottom pants' now because the fashion of the youth has changed.

Obstacles to Consumers' Sovereignty

The consumer is obstructed from exercising his monarchy by a few factors under the Free Enterprize System. The basic obstacle to the consumer's sovereignty is the advertisements. In the wake of advertisements the consumer becomes an object slave rather than the king of the market.

The advertisments have a tremendous influence on the consumer's behaviour or pattern of purchases. He is made to buy what is produced and marketed.

Especially, the audio-visual advertisements, have a telling impact on the demand for a firm's product.

Further, the sales techniques like discount sales, exhibition sales, prize schemes, etc., also tempt the consumers to buy what they did not intend to buy.

Even the 'demonstration effect' has its impact on the pattern of consumption. We often consume a commodity simply since it is consumed by the neighbour or by the people of another country or community. Prof. Dusenberry has successfully proved this fact. Hence, it is, known as the 'Dusenberry Effect'.

The introduction of 'substitutes' also influences the consumption pattern. The finest example is the availability of innumerable kinds of tooth-pastes and toilet-soaps with newer and newer fragrances and lathers.

Even the 'trade marks' have their own influence on the consumer's sovereignty. There are consumers who have stuck to the LifeBuoy soap or Colgate tooth paste for over a number of years though many other too have come into the market.

In substance, the consumer is no longer a 'sovereign' but only a 'slave' (a slave of his own making; a slave of choice, of influence).

CONSUMER'S BEHAVIOUR

The Importance of Consumption: Consumption is the basic purpose of great bulk of economic activity. It is the be-all and end-all of activity. Even the construction of a steel plant is motivated by the needs of the consumers, since steel will be incorporated in consumer goods or in factories that make machines which produce consumer goods. Except in the case of defence and prestige activity the ultimate pay-off and purpose is in the realm of consumption. According to Francis Hutcheson "The greatest happiness for the greatest number is the broad goal of an economy. Firms altogether must produce things that the consumers require. This is made possible by expression of consumers' wants. The wants induce the firms to produce. In effect the consumers vote with money when they buy goods. The fundamental problem of allocation of scarce resources is such that more of everything wanted by the consumers cannot be produced. Therefore, the consumers must be induced to express the relative urgency of their wants.

According to Robert Dorfman, "Each consumer must be made to confront in miniature the great choices that the economy as a whole has to confront." This is done through awarding inçome to the consumers. Each consumer then divides this income among things he wants according to his relative urgency.

Thus, the consumer is compelled to make choices which are replicas of the choices of the economy. This chapter is concerned with consumers' decisions, their importance and the factors that influence these decisions. It is a complex phenomenon. We can at best discuss how a consumer's purchases convey information about his tastes and desires. Reciprocally (also how these decisions are influenced) by the price or cost of production and the scarcity of the products. We can do this by taking the example of a hypothetical consumer as is done by Dr. Alfred Marshall.

The Cardinal Utility Analysis

The utility analysis or the Theory of Demand seeks to examine the demand behaviour of the consumer and how he seeks to maximise the satisfaction from a given commodity and reaches equilibrium. In short, it deals with the factors that cause the Law of Demand. In effect, the I theory of consumers' behaviour analyses why consumers tend to buy more when the price of a commodity falls and less when the price rises.

Broadly speaking, there are two ways in which we can approach the theory of consumers' behaviour. They are: (1) The Marginal Utility approach of Marshall or the '*Cardinal*' approach and (2) The Indifference Curve analysis or the '*Ordinal*' approach of Hicks and Allen.

In the 19th century three contemporary economists developed the concept of '*utility*' independently of each other (Jeavans, Menger and Walras). In 1890 Alfred Marshall gave perfection to the concept in his celebrated work 'Principles of Economics'.

The 'Marshallian Approach', as it is popularly called, is based on three important concepts, *viz.*:

1. The concept of Marginal Utility or its cardinal or numerical measurement,
2. The Law of Diminishing Marginal Utility, and
3. The Law of Equi-marginal Utility.

This is a Neo-classical analysis of consumer's behaviour which is also associated with A.C. Pigou and others. It rests on '*Hedonism*' and '*Utilitarianism*' by philosophy.

'*Utility*' is an introspective and relative term. It denotes want-Satisfying capacity of goods and services. Whether the commodity is injurious or poisionous or helpful to health it may be said to have utility as long as it satisfies a want. Be it liquor or food, it has utility.

Utility is a '*relative*' term and not an '*absolute*' term. It is related to the habits, tastes, fashions and prices of the goods in question.

The Cardinal Marshallian Utility analysis assumes that utility is measurable in numerical terms. Marshall coined the term '*utils*' to express the quantum of utility of a commodity. It depends on the intensity of the urge or desire or want of the consumer - how badly the consumer wants it. An unsatisfied want and highly urgent commodity gives more units of satisfaction than a less urgently needed commodity or '*already satisfied want*'.

Utility is not only measurable but it is also 'additive' or addable. The measurability of utility is based on the assumption that:

1. the consumer is rational enough to calculate, choose, measure and compare the utility of different units of the commodities so that he maximises satisfaction,
2. the consumer is aware of the choices of commodities available to him,
3. the choice he has made is certain,
4. the commodity in questions is not influenced by the prices of other commodities,
5. there are no substitutes to the commodity under consideration;
6. the utility is measurable in terms of money-price the consumer is prepared to pay, and
7. the 'Marginal utility of money' will remain constant—*i.e.*, as the consumer spends his fixed income on further units of the commodity he will not hesitate to spend the diminishing stock of money.

THE LAW OF DIMINISHING MARGINAL UTILITY

With these basic assumptions Marshall went on to say that "All enjoyments tend to fall if repeated".

In other words, according to Mithani and Gharat, ".... when a want is being satisfied in the process of consumption, it tends to become less intense than before" other things being given.

This tendency is described as Diminishing Marginal Utility. According to Marshall, "The less we have of a commodity the more we want of it; and the more we have of a commodity the less we want of it."

In other words, human tendency is such that more of anything in succession will reduce the intensity of the subsequent units of it.

Way back in 1871 Carl Menger of Austria formed this law when he wrote thus: "Value is a judgement of mind; not a property of the thing or an independent entity". Thus, he anticipated the theory of Marginal Utility of which Alfred Marshall wrote on later.

Jeavons of England expressed the '*First Law of Gossen*' thus when he said, "The magnitude of one and the same satisfaction, when we continue to enjoy it without interruption, continually decreases until satiation is reached."

However, it must be noted that it was Marshall who coined the term 'utility' and till then it was known as 'Enjoyment satisfaction' or 'final degree of satisfaction' and so on in the earliest works of Herman, Jeavons and Gossen. They founded the law of Diminishing Marginal Utility but Marshall perfected it and used it as the basis of his '*Theory of Value*' which we know today as the '*Dual Theory of Value*'.

The Law of Diminishing Marginal Utility is best understood with the help of the following diagram:

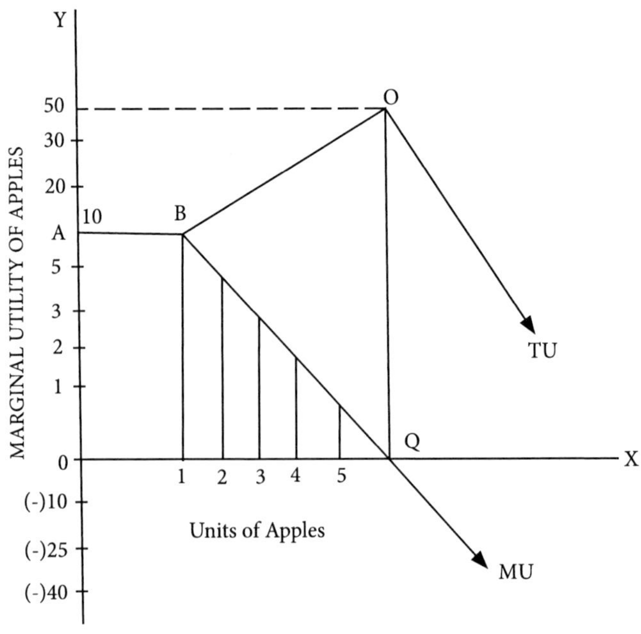

Fig. 2.1. Law of Diminishing Marginal Utility

It may be observed that in Fig. 2.1 the 'Total Utility Curve TU reaches its maximum height at the point O. Further, the 'Marginal Utility Curve MU reaches its maximum height at B and then onwards begins to drop till it intersects the OX axis at the point Q. As long as the Marginal Utility is 'positive' the Total Utility is positive too. However, at the point Q, Marginal Utility becomes Negative as shown by the 'Minus' sign below the OX axis. At this point the Total Utility is maximum at O. The Marginal Utility being negative (Disutility) Total Utility also begins to fall after the point O.

Thus, as long as TU curve rises so long will the MU curve fall. When TU curve reaches maximum height the MU curve will become negative at Q where Marginal Utility is 'Zero' or after Q the Marginal Utility makes Total Utility also to decline.

Thus, the total utility of apples in the diagram is the increasing function of its quality. 'The Marginal Utility of it is the net addition made to total utility as a result of consumption of one more unit.'

In other words, MU is the incremental increase in total utility caused by consuming an additional or 'Marginal' unit of the apple in our example.

The Marginal utility goes on 'diminishing' as the imaginary consumer goes on adding to the quantity of its consumption.

It can also be defined as, "The difference between the utility of the total units of the stock of consumption of a given commodity *minus* that of consuming one unit less..." according to Mithani and Gharat.

Therefore, in our example, MU determines the rate at which TU rises or falls. Thus:

$$\text{MU of `x'} = \frac{\text{dU of x}}{\text{dQ of x}}$$

[Read as: MU= Marginal Utility, dU = an incremental or small change in demand or utility, dQ = Incremental change in the quantity and x = apples]

Illustration of the Law of D.M.U. (Tabulated)

The law can be hypothetically illustrated in a tabular form with the help of the following utility schedule No. 1. It is an imaginary utility schedule prepared through the introspective method.

From the schedule 1 it is apparent that the marginal utility of each successive unit of commodity x diminishes. At the 5th unit it becomes *Zero* as Total Utility is constant. It is the point at which the want is fully satisfied and the intensity of the want has become zero.

SCHEDULE 1

Utility Schedule

Units of Consumption of X	Total Utility (TUx)	Marginal Utility (MUx)
1	30	30
2	45	15
3	53	8
4	56	3
5	56	0
6	52	– 4

From the given schedule it is also clear that the Marginal Utility varies *inversely* with the stock of the commodity; the variation is not necessarily *proportionate* and uniform and if it is, it is just a coincidence. It is also observed that any further addition to the stock of commodity x after the 5th unit will cause *Disutility* as shown by a *minus* sign which is (–)4 at the 6th unit.

If you view the schedule in the *ascending order* you can notice that as the stock of x decreases its marginal and total utility increases.

Mathematically, the *Total utility* is a function of the number of units of the commodity x. Thus:

$$TUx = F\ (Qx) \text{ where } \frac{\Delta\ TUx}{\Delta\ Qx} > 0$$

(Read as: Total utility of x is the increasing function of quantity of x, TUx is the total utility of x, F is the functional relation, Qx is the quantity of x and D (delta) is the incremental increase or decrease.)

Similarly, there is a diminishing functional relationship between Marginal utility of x (MUx) and the quantity of x (Qx). Thus:

$$MUx - F\ (Qx) \text{ where } \frac{\Delta\ Ux}{\Delta\ Qx} < 0$$

[Read as: > = less than, Δ (delta) = a small change in utility or quantity of x.]

We may also represent the MU curve diagrammatically. In Fig. 2.2 (MUx is the Marginal Utility curve of) the hypothetical consumer for commodity x. The M.U. is measured on OY axis, while the units of the commodity is measured on Ox axis.

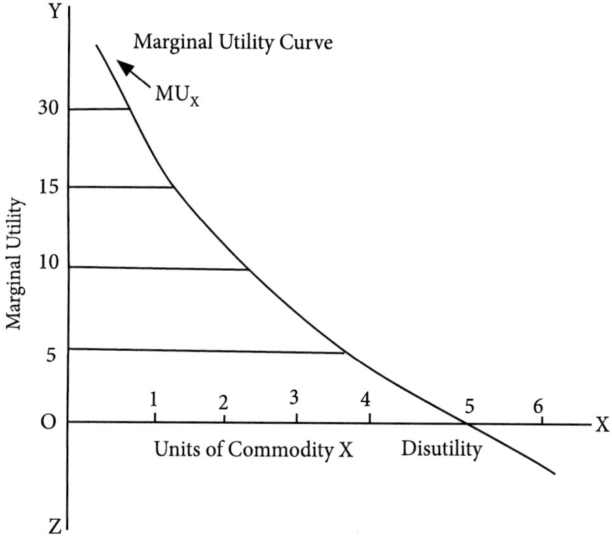

Fig. 2.2

As per Fig. 2.2 The MUx is the Marginal Utility Curve which slopes from left to right downwards like the demand curve. Up to the 4th unit MU is positive. It shows that the want is still not satisfied fully. At the 5th unit satiety is full and complete. Hence the MUx is '*zero*'. If the 6th unit is consumed '*Disulity*' equal to—6 will set in. The disutility is measured on the OZ axis. Note that the MUx curve intersects the Ox axis at the 5th unit.

According to Dr. Marshall the demand curve can be easily derived from the Law of Diminishing utility. This is because the utility of a commodity determines how much the consumers wish to purchase at a given price.

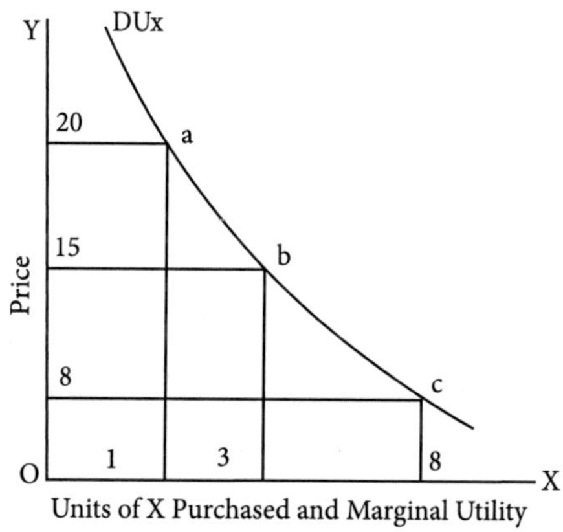

Fig. 2.3

The demand varies inversely with the price just as utility varies inversely with price and quantity of the goods. In simple terms if you join the points of different Marginal utilities you derive the demand curve as shown in Fig. 2.3.

As observed the DUx is the demand curve of x at different prices and different Marginal utilities. Thus, when price is 20 rupees the marginal utility is low at one '*util*' and the demand is only for one unit. If the price falls to ₹ 15 the MU rises to 3 *utils* and so also demand to 3 units. If the price falls further to ₹ 8 per unit the MU rises to 8 and so demand expands to 8 units. If we join a, b, c and so on a downward sloping curve is formed and that is the demand curve.

Consumer's Equilibrium Condition Under Cardinal Approach

The attainment of equilibrium under Marshall's cardinal utility analysis is based on certain assumptions. Marshall's cardinal analysis is a *Single Commodity Model*. The consumer in this model can buy either spending his income on x at given prices or keep it unspent and sacrifice his want. As a rational consumer, he will spend his income and buy a certain quantity such as to maximise satisfaction. Therefore, 'rationality' implies that he compares the MU of x to its price every time he buys some more of it—willing to pay a higher price for earlier units and lower price for later or additional units (since successive units yield lower MU).

In the case of earlier units and till MU becomes zero the consumer gets surplus satisfaction, *i.e.*, utility is greater than the price paid for the unit-which Marshall calls '*Consumer's Surplus*'.

Thus, the consumer reaches equlibrium when he no longer wishes to buy any more of the commodity x. In other words, equilibrium is attained just when price paid is equal to its MU.

Mathematically, if the price of x is ₹ 10 for the 5th unit and the MU of the 5th unit is considered as just worth its price,

Then, MUx = Px

(Read as: MUx = Marginal Utility of commodity x and Px = Price of commodity x.) And this is the condition of equilibrium. In fact, as long as Total Utility increases by consuming the successive units so long, the consumer's equilibrium is not reached. Technically, it is attained just when Total utility becomes *constant*. At the point of equilibrium the consumer does not mind buying that unit and no more.

HYPOTHETICAL NATURE OR LIMITATIONS OF THE LAW

Like all *Economic Laws* the Law of Diminishing Marginal Utility is hypothetical or conditional. It necessarily begins with *prefix 'ceteris paribus'* or that *other things being equal*—such and such a tendency will follow. Therefore, it is worthwhile to know the assumptions on which the law is based.

The Assumptions of the law

The chief assumptions of the law are:

1. That the Consumer has a fixed income.
2. That the consumer is rational.
3. That his tastes, fashions and preferences do not change.
4. That the commodity in question is a *normal* commodity and not a *necessity* or a prestige symbol commodity or a habitual commodity like liquor and so on.
5. The price of the commodity is constant.
6. That there is no time gap in consuming.
7. That the different units are *homogeneous* or identical in quantity and quality.
8. That the *Marginal Utility of Money* remains constant even as the fixed stock of money decreases when spent.

Limitations of the Law

The Law of Diminishing Marginal Utility is a psychological law. It is valid in the case of social or artificial wants. The greatest weakness of this law is its unrealistic assumptions which we have just now observed. Like any other economic law, the law of DMU is hypothetical and holds good only when the assumptions are given. If we relax these assumptions one by one the law becomes invalid. Thus:

1. The units of consumption must be *homogenous* in quality, size, taste, etc. If this homogeneity is violated it is likely that the successive units will yield increasing utility.

2. There must be *continuity* in consumption at a given time. Thus, the different units must be consumed without break of time. If there is a time interval in consuming different units the utility may be more from the successive units.

3. The units of the commodity must be of a reasonable size. Taking tea in spoonful is one thing and taking it in cupful is another. If the size is too small then the utility of the subsequent units will increase.

4. The price of different units of the commodity must be constant. Similarly, the prices of substitutes must be constant too. Otherwise the MU of the commodity will not diminish.

5. The consumer should be *rational* and an 'Economic Man' and not abnormal. For instance, a drunkard may go on consuming more and more of liquor as it gives more and more intoxication to him.

6. The law does not hold good in case of *indivisible* consumer's goods like motor cars, television sets etc. Nobody buys a number of units of such goods nor can they be bought in parts.

7. The law also does not hold good in case of *hobbies* like collection of rare coins,'stamps, antiques etc. The more one collects them the greater will be the pleasure of collecting them. However, this cannot be treated as a true limitation because nobody collects the same stamp or coin each time but a different one.

8. In case of *misers* also the law does not operate. As more and more money is accumulated one becomes greedier and greedier. Thus, in the case of money the marginal utility does not decrease. Further, it is said that a miser is not rational and hence this cannot be a valid objection.

9. In the case of finer things like music, reading novels etc. the law does not operate. In such cases reading of more and more novels gives more utility.

However, if one reads the same novel many times or hears the same song many times it bores the person. Thus, The law may be said to operate.

10. The law assumes constant Marginal Utility of money which is most objectionable. Just as the marginal utility of an apple increases when the stock of apples decreases so does the MU of money increase when the stock of his income decreases when he spends his fixed income. For instance, if you have ₹ 10 with you, you spend liberally the first rupee but when you are left with ₹ 2 you certainly hesitate to spend one more rupee. This hesitation shows that the MU of the 9th Rupee is higher than that of the previous Rupees spent. Hence, the assumption of constant MU of money is unreal.

11. The law assumes that the consumer consciously measures and compares the MUs of different units like a calculating machine. In real life the consumer is either too busy to try to do so or he is unable as he is buying not one commodity but many more. It is practically impossible.

12. The assumption of measurability of utility is severely criticised by Prof. R.G.D. Allen and J.R. Hicks. According to them utility is like a 'Hill'; if three persons are standing at different heights of a hill and if you are asked to say who is at what height from a distance you will only say that Mr. A is above Mr. B., Mr. B is below Mr. A and Mr. C is below Mr. A and so on. You cannot say by how much above or below any one is from each other.

Thus, from the adjecent diagram we can say that 'A' is above 'B' and 'C' and so he is at the highest level from a distance. Or we can say that B is above 'C' and below 'A' but we cannot say what is the height of A, B and C. Similarly, utility of one unit can be '*compared*' to the other units and cannot be quantified cordinally and numerically as, so many 'utils' as imagined by Marshall. Moreover, 'Utils' has no definite scale of measurement. Utility is the experience of the mind; it differs from time to time, place to place and consumer to consumer. It may even be different for the same consumer at different times and places. Utility is, therefore, '*Ordinal*' and not '*Cardinal*' *i.e.*, it can be arranged in order of preference of the goods and utilities of these goods.

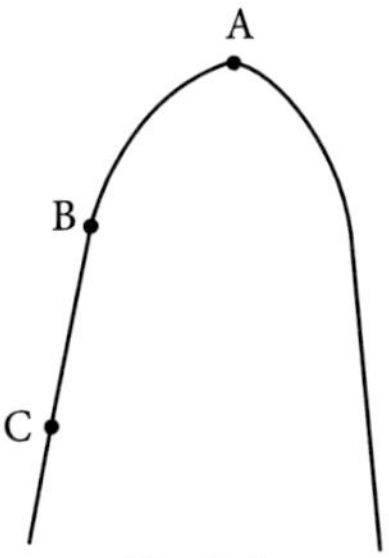

Fig. 2.4

13. Lastly, Marshall has derived the concept of 'consumer's surplus' on the basis of this law. The concept is as vague as the law itself.

Practical and Theoretical Importance

It must be noted that the law of DMU is not altogether worthless or nonsense. It is true that utility is *subjective* and immeasurable, but it is only ordinal. It is equally true that further and further consumption of the same commodity yields lower and lower satisfaction. Only its measurability is untrue but fundamentally the Law of DMU is useful in theory and practice.

Theoretical usefulness: Its theoretical uses are invaluable. They are:

1. Though it is a 'Single Commodity Model' it has succeeded in explaining the consumer's behaviour and equilibrium, *i.e.* in the sense, that it says that the consumer's total satisfaction from a single commodity is maximum when he feels that it is not worthwhile to buy any further units of it.
2. The law cannot be treated as 'little better than nonsense'. It still remains a fact that utility is measurable ordinally if not cordinally. In fact, this is why Marshall's concept of utility is considered as his greatest contribution to economic theory.
3. It has provided the theoretical basis for the theory of Indifference Curve Analysis of Hicks and Allen.
4. It proves that each want taken separately can be satisfied fully.
5. The Law of DMU has succeeded in solving the famous '*Diamond-Water Paradox*' of value. Thus it shows why though water is in

plenty its value-in-use is high but the *value-in-exchange* is low. At the same time, the diamond would still have a great value-in-exchange but no value-in-use whether it is lying in a pit or worn by you. It shows that MU determines value-in-exchange

Practical: The practical significance of the law of DMU is equally great:

1. Firstly, with its knowledge the producer or seller can know that the sales of his product can be raised by reducing the cost of production and the price It is the first advice that a business economist must offer to his firm to increase the profits and maximise the turn-over.
2. The 'policy of taxation' of a Government has much to learn from this law: it shows that higher percentage of taxes can be levied on the incomes of the rich than on the middle class incomes. It helps to distribute the *burden* and *effect* of taxes equitably.
3. It shows that redistribution of wealth from the rich to the poor is beneficial in the long-run to the underdeveloped countries.
4. It is a direct guide to Indirect Taxation since it shows that necessities should not be taxed heavily as their MU is always very high.
5. In a monopoly market the businessman can raise the price upto the level of MU and Maximise profits if he knows the Law of DMU.
6. It has formed the basis of *Socialism* which argues for the poor and the working class.

Thus, the Law of DMU and Marshall's concept of '*Utility*' is rightly acclaimed by many great economists as the greatest of contributions to the '*Theory of Value*' in Economics.

In this context let us know what some of them say:

Keynes, when Marshall died in 1924 said, "The greatest economist in the world for a hundred years."

Prof. Harrey acclaimed him thus: "Alfred Marshall will stand in history of economic thought as one who made more progress toward a united and consistent theory of value and distribution than any predecessor."

Thus, Marshall is rightly regarded as the leader of second generation of the Marginal Utility School.

CONSUMER'S EQUILIBRIUM UNDER THE LAW OF EQUI-MARGINAL UTILITY (EMU)

The law of Equi-marginal Utility states that 'other things being equal (*ceteris paribus*), a consumer gets maximum satisfaction by allocating his fixed income among many goods so that the Marginal utilities of all goods are equal to each other and to their prices'.

Gossen was the first to state this law which is called 'Gossen's Second Law'. Gossen vaguely stated the law of EMU thus:

> 'Each man spends his income/money on different commodities in such a way that the amounts of all enjoyments are equal'.

Gossen thought that maximum '*enjoyment*' (later Marshall substituted the term Enjoyment with the term 'Utility) will result from a uniform level of satisfaction.

Marshall developed it into a perfect law *viz.*, the law of EMU. He based it on three characteristics of human wants viz. *Competitive, Substitutable* and *Complementary*.

The law is based on the assumptions that:

1. Consumer's income is fixed.
2. Wants are many and hence they are arranged in order of importance.
3. Consumer is rational.
4. The prices of what he buys are fixed.

Given these conditions the consumer attains equilibrium under the law of EMU when he has spent his fixed income in such a way that the MU of commodity X and its price are equal to the MU of Y and its price and these two MUs and their prices are equal to the MU and Price of Z and so on.

Symbolically,

$$= \frac{MUx}{Px} = \frac{MUy}{Py} = \frac{MUz}{Pz} \quad \text{... and so on}$$

is the condition of equilibrium of the consumer under the law of EMU.

However, if the price of any one of the goods (of X or Y or Z changes) then the '*Equilibrium*' will be disturbed. Then, the consumer will reallocate his income in such a way that he buys more of that which is now cheaper and buy more of some other commodity to re-attain equilibrium.

The Law of EMU is therefore said to have indirectly hinted the '*Income Effects*' and '*Substitution Effects*' for the use of the Indifference Curve Approach of Hicks and Allen.

THE INDIFFERENCE CURVE TECHNIQUE OR THE ORDINAL APPROACH TO UTILITY

The student is now aware of the basic defects of the Marshallian *Cardinal* analysis of utility and he is now better prepared to understand the ordinal approach to utility. Incidentally, it is my duty to warn the student to glance through Marshall's Cardinal Approach before attempting to go through this section for a clearer understanding of this section.

Introductory Remarks

The 'Indifference Curve Technique' or the 'Ordinal Utility Analysis' was first casually introduced by Edgeworth in 1881. An Italian economist, Pareto refined Edgeworth's concept. It was perfected by Profs. J.R. Hicks and R.G.D. Allen of the Cambridge University in 1934. It had no widespread recognition until Prof. J.R. Hicks wrote about the Ordinal Analysis in his celebrated book '*Value and Capital*' in 1939.

Basically, the ordinal approach considers 'utility' as a 'level' and not as a '*quantity*'. The new approach considers the case of a consumer who consumes a number of combinations of (two goods and not on commodity) (and which can be extended to any number of commodities later). Further, the ordinal approach begins with the assumption that the MU of money is subject to changes in terms of its stock and prices of the goods.

However, for the sake of convenience it begins with a Two-commodity Model, fixed prices and fixed income of the consumer. It later explains the effect of changes in prices and income of the consumer also.

It retains the *rationality* of the consumer and constancy of tastes and preferences of the consumer to begin with.

Above all, it accounts for the *preferences* and *indifferences* of the consumers on the amount of goods or services a business firm can sell and what determines the indifference or preference of the firm's customers.

It shows how a trading firm has to and can guard against such changes in preferences of tastes of and incomes of customers. It is but natural that some consumers will attain a higher level of income after some time. It is also possible that new *substitutes* have arrived with lower prices and better quality. Finally, it is possible that there is also a 'demonstration effect' of others on the consumer. The '*New Approach*' warns the business economist and his firm against all such possible changes beyond its control.

It calls upon the producer and the seller to invent new '*selling techniques*' and to promote his firm's product—which is known as '*Research and Development*' in selling and producing and the two aspects are turns of the same profession.

It is a guide to all firms engaged in production or trade, agency and transportation of goods, stocks and shares, lending and borrowing and all others who are aids to commerce and trade in the modern world of dynamism, in the techniques of all these aspects of business. In short, it clearly guides the adviser on business about what is expected of him by his firm.

The Basis of Ordinal Utility Analysis in Some More Detail

The economists after Dr. Manshall rejected cardinal measurement of utility as impossible and unrealistic. The alternative approach *viz.*, the Indifference Approach was developed based on the '*scale of preferences*' or *consumer's choice or choice of priorities.*

The *scale of preferences* is defined as a set of alternative combinations of a number of goods from which the consumer has to choose the ideal combination. He choses that combination which gives the maximum '*level*' of satisfaction. Such a combination will have the largest quantity of the goods. Other cambinations are either rejected or the consumer is '*indifferent*' towards them.

To understand more easily the Indifference Curve Technique let us take an illustration:

Let us assume that Mrs. Sheela has decided to go and buy 2 commodities in the market and has ₹ 100 in her purse. If she spends more on commodity 'X' she will have less to spend on commodity 'Y'. We want to know how much of X and Y she will buy with her fixed income and fixed prices of X and Y.

By the 'axiomatic method' we can find out how she chooses the best combination. This requires some assumptions. The assumptions are:

1. *The axiom of completeness:* It refers to which combination of X and Y Mrs. Sheela will choose. She can be indifferent between any two combinations of X and Y.

Indifference' is a condition when the two combinations which yield her same level of satisfaction at the recost. If she chooses combination 'A' instead of 'B' she is said to '*prefer*' A to B. If she does not mind A or B she is said to be '*indifferent*'.

2. *Non-satiation:* This axiom is that 'more is better than less'. In other words, if there are two combinations with the same quantity of X but one of them has more of Y then Mrs. Sheela *prefers* the one with more of Y.

3. *Consistency:* Consistency is an axiom or assumption that if there are three combinations A, B and C and if Sheela has to either prefer 'A to B' or 'B to C' or 'A to C'. Simply, it is the problem of choosing, when there is no transitivity among many combinations of two goods.

4. *Substitutability:* Suppose there are two combinations 'A' and 'B'. Suppose also that 'A' and 'B' are equal in their level of satisfaction but 'A' has more of X commodity than 'B' Then, if we add more of commodity Y to combination 'B' after reducing commodity X in it Mrs. Sheela will be *indifferent* between combinations 'A' and 'B'

TABLE 1

Indifference Schedule

SI. No.	Commodity (X)	Commodity (Y)	Marginal Rate of Substitution (MRS)
A	1	15	Nil
B	2	10	5:1
C	3	7	3:1
D	4	5	2:1
E	5	4	1:1

On the basis of these four assumptions we can go on to examine the consumer's behaviour under the Indifference Curve Approach. To begin with let us take an imaginary schedule of combinations of goods X and Y.

Indifference Schedule

An Indifference schedule is a group of a number of combinations which give equal level of satisfaction to the consumer. While preparing an indifference schedule we assume that the consumer's income and the prices of the two goods are constant.

According to D.S. Waston "An indifferent schedule is a list of combinations of commodities, the list being So arranged that a consumer is indifferent to the combinations, prefering none of any other."

Table 1 is an imaginary indifference schedule of various combinations of X and Y goods. As per the table the consumer is assumed to have a fixed income and fixed prices of X and Y goods.

Thus, the consumer is indifferent whether he is given combination A with 1Y + 15Y or combination C with 3X + 7Y or combination E with 5X

+ 4Y since all combinations yield equal satisfaction. The point is, why do they yield equal satisfaction? They yield equal satisfaction for this reason: If the consumer 'gives up' (or technically '*substitutes*') 5 units of Y to get 1 more unit of X in combination B he no doubt loses some satisfaction but the loss is compensated by getting 1 more unit of Y. Thus, 1 unit of X is considered equally significant as 5 units of Y which he has sacrificed. It is so in the case of all combinations. This is the basis of indifference of the consumer.

DMRS

The Indifference Schedule reveals one more important aspect *i.e.*, the rate of substitution of x for y goes on dimnishing from one combination to the other. This is because the stock of 'y' goes on decreasing and the stock of 'x' goes on increasing due to substitution of x for y. Naturally, the significance of that which is decreasing is more and the significance of that which is increasing is less. So, the Marginal rate of substitution (MRS) goes on decreasing. This tendency is called the law of 'Diminishing Marginal Rate of Substitution' (DMRS)

The Law of D.M.R.S. forms the foundation of the indifference Curve Approach.

What is an Indifference Curve

We have seen what an indifference schedule is and what is the law of substitution. Now, it is easier to understand the Indifference Curve.

An Indifference curve is nothing but the various combinations of two commodities with equal satisfaction represented diagramatically. In other words, it is the indifference schedule translated into a diagram.

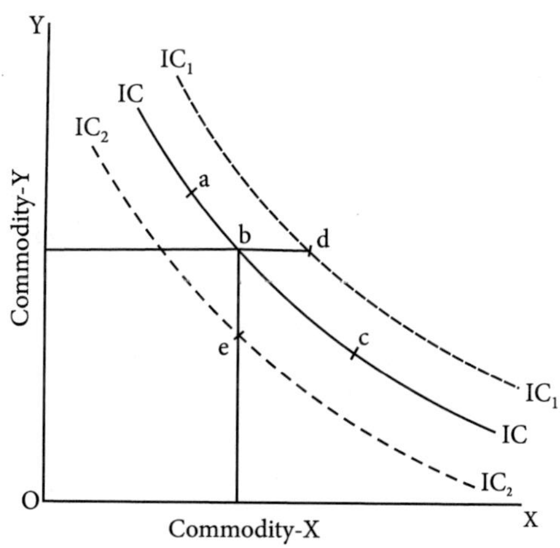

Fig. 2.5

In Fig. 2.5 IC, IC_1 and IC_2 are three indifference curves of different levels of satisfaction. On IC you find three combinations a, b and c. They give the consumer equal satisfaction.

But on IC_1 you find combination d which has the same amount of 'Y' but more of X than in combination 'b' on IC. So, the consumer prefers 'd' to a, b and c combinations. Combination 'e' is on IC_2 which is below IC. So, it has less of both X and Y goods. So he chooses the larger combination.

If a number of indifference curves representing different levels of satisfactions or larger and smaller combinations are plotted on a single diagram one above the other it is called an '*Indifference Map*'. Thus, Fig. 2.5 is an *indifference map*.

Assumptions of Indifference Curve Approach

The *ordinal* analysis retains some assumptions of the *cardinal* approach of Dr. Marshall but has introduced some of its own. It later releases some assumptions and explains what will be the situation then.

The basic assumptions of the *Ordinal Approach* are:

1. *Rationality:* The consumer acts in such a way that he maximises satisfaction. So, he prefers a larger combination to a smaller combination. It also implies that then the M.R.S. will diminish.
2. *Two-Commodity Model*: There are only Two goods X and Y and not one. The consumer buys them in different quantities each time.
3. *Fixed Income*: The consumer has a fixed income which he has to allot between the two goods. Thus, if price increases he has to reallocate his expenditure. This condition is also necessary so that he has to reduce the quantity of X to get one more unit of Y. *i.e.* technically, only then the MRS will diminish and the shape of the indifference curve will be *concave* to the origin.
4. *Constant Tastes, etc.*: The consumer's tastes, habits and preferences are constant.
5. *Scale of preferences*: The consumer has a set of combinations from which he has to choose. This condition enables the consumer to say whether he prefers one to the other or he is indifferent between a set of combinations.
6. *Transitivity*: The transitivity condition is that if the consumer prefers combination A to B and B to C then he must prefer A to C because A is a larger combination than retain B and C.

PROPERTIES OR CHARACTERISTICS OF INDIFFERENCE CURVES

The indifference curves are drawn on the basis of the assumptions that we have already noted. Therefore, the Indifference Curves (ICs) exhibit some universal characteristics. The chief of them are discussed here.

1. An IC is always Convex to the Origin

The *Convexity* of an IC shows that the MRS will diminish as the process of substitution goes on. This is seen in Fig. 2.26

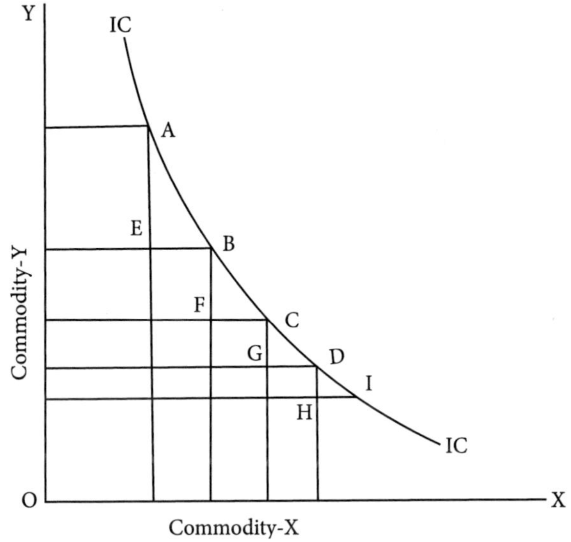

Fig. 2.26. Convexity of IC

An IC sloping negatively from left to right downwards as in Fig. 2.6 gives us a DMRS. Thus, in combination-B the consumer has BF of commodity Y and FC of commodity X. In combination C the consumer gives up ABF of commodity Y to get GD of X. In combination D he gives up CG of Y to get HI of X. Note that BF is less than AE, CG is less than BF and DH is less than CG. Note also that EB = FC = GD = HI. Thus, the MRS diminishes from A to B, B to C, and C to D when the IC is convex to the origin 'O'.

An IC cannot be either vertical or horizontal or concave shaped for the above reason. Let us see what happens if it is so shaped.

In Fig. 2.7 IC is *vertical* to the OX axis. A and B are two combinations on it. In combination-A the consumer has OM of X and OD of Y. If he chooses combination-B the quantity of X remains OM but that of Y increases to OC of Y. This means that, combination-B is preferable to combination-A. However, since all combinations on the same IC must give equal satisfaction there should be indifference. Therefore, an IC cannot be vertical in shape. It is absurd.

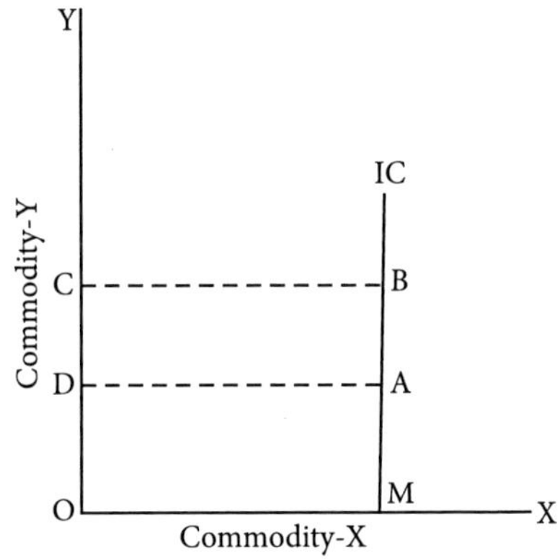

Fig. 2.7

In Fig. 2.8 the IC is *horizontal* to the OX axis. For the same reason as in the case of a vertical IC this is also absurd and violates the principle of substitution.

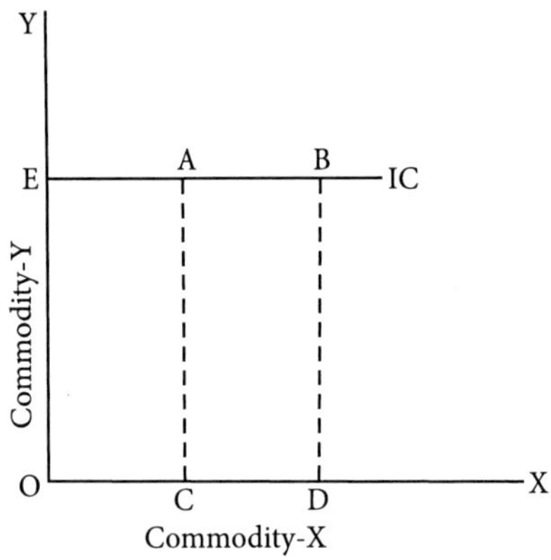

Fig. 2.8

In Fig. 2.9 the IC is *concave* to the origin. A, C and E are three combinations on IC. It can be observed from triangles ABC and CDE that AB is longer than CD. It means that to get 1 more unit of X he is prepared to sacrifice more of Y. However, this means Increasing Rate of Substitution which is irrational behaviour of the consumer. It violates rationality condition and the principle of DMRS. Hence, an IC cannot be concave to the origin O.

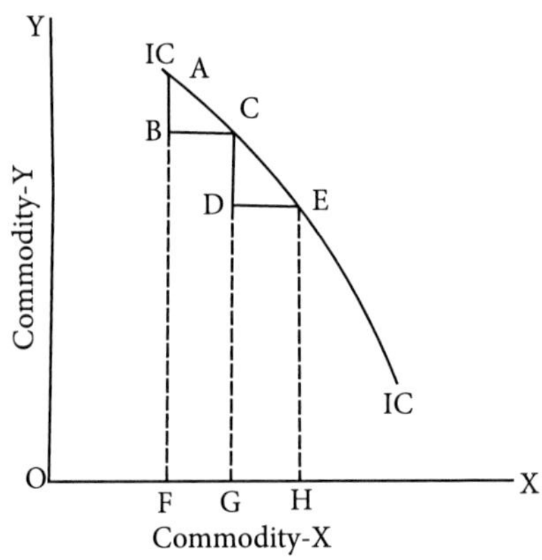

Fig. 2.9

Therefore, the IC is always convex to the origin.

2. Two ICs cannot intersect each other

No two indifference curves should intersect according to the IC approach. If they intersect each other the point of intersection will be a common combination to both the ICs. This point means that the same combination on the IC sometimes gives more, sometimes less and some other times equal satisfaction. This is unscientific because different ICs must give different levels of satisfaction. This is demonstrated in Fig. 2.10.

In Fig. 2.10 the two indifference curves IC and IC_1 intersect at the point E. It is the common combination to IC and IC_1. It lies on both. Take combinations A and B first. Combination-A is on the higher IC_1 and is a larger combination than B which is on lower IC. So, the consumer prefers A to B.

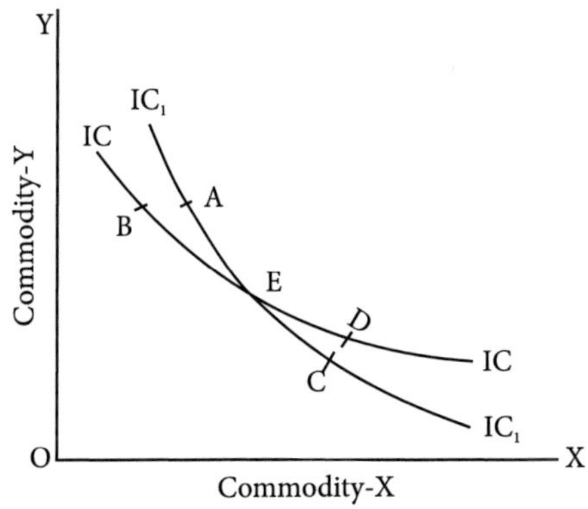

Fig. 2.10

Now, take combinations A and C. They are on the same indifference curve IC, but below the intersecting point E. The IC_1 is below IC. Hence, the consumer prefers D on IC to C on IC_1.

Thus, if two ICs intersect each other combinations which are on the same IC will yield different levels of satisfaction. This is also absurd. Hence, two ICs cannot intersect each other.

3. Higher ICs represent higher levels of satisfaction than lower ICs

If an IC is above another IC it means that the quantity of the two goods in any combination on the higher IC is always larger than that of the lower IC. So, the consumer prefers combinations on the higher IC to those on lower IC. This is proved in Fig. 2.11.

In Fig. 2.11 IC is the original indifference curve and 'A' is a combination on it. Suppose the consumer has more income. Then he will be able to buy more of X and Y goods. Therefore, he will have a new set of combinations larger than on IC. Another indifference curve appears as IC_2 now. 'B' is a combination on the higher IC_2. The combination is 15y + 3x. It is preferable to A which has 10y = 2x.

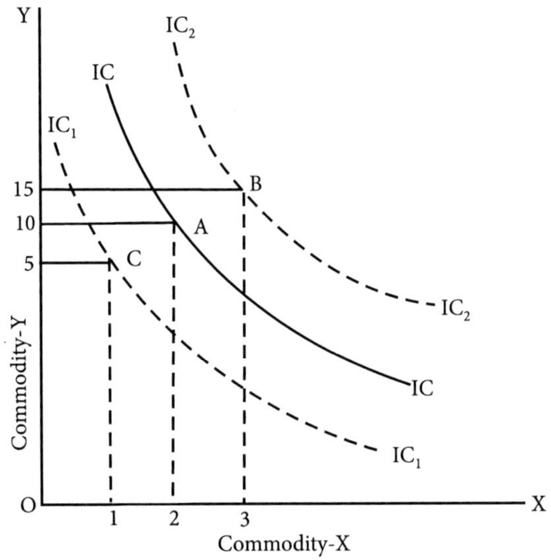

Fig. 2.11

Similarly if there is another Indifference curve below IC (because his income decreases) IC the consumer is 'worse-off, on it than before. Take combination-C on IC_1 which is below IC. In 'C' there is 5y + 1x which is a smaller combination than A and B. It certainly represents a lower level of satisfaction.

4. Indifference curves may or may not be parallel to each other

The ICs in an indifference map may not always be parallel to each other. If two ICs are parallel to each other the increase or decrease in the size of combinations on them will be proportionate, if not, they will be unproportionate.

In Fig. 2.12 IC_2 is parallel to IC and in the rate of increase in combinations of X and Y commodities on IC_2 is proportionate. IC_1 is not parallel to IC and therefore the decrease in the size of combinations is disproportionate.

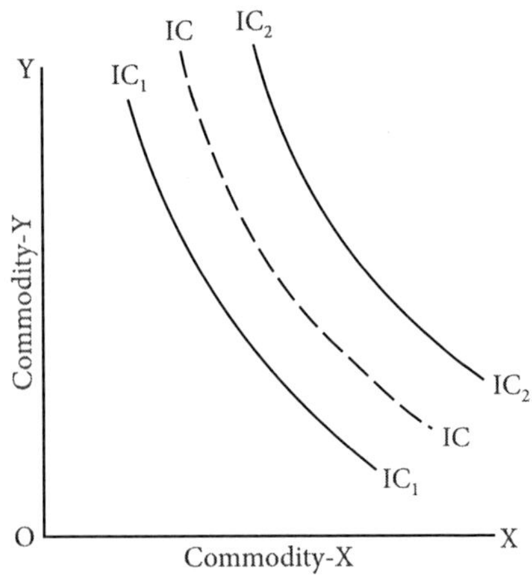

Fig. 2.12

EQUILIBRIUM OF THE CONSUMER

The '*Equilibrium*' of the consumer is a position where the consumer achieves the most ideal combination with the given income and prices or the two goods.

Before we try to analyse the equilibrium of the consumer we must understand what is a '*Budget Line*' or a '*Price Line*'.

A budget line or price line shows how much of his income is allotted for each of the two commodities. In simple terms, it shows the quantity of two goods bought at their fixed prices.

A Budget Line is constructed by plotting different possible ways of spending the income (on two goods X and Y) on a graph sheet. When the different points on OX and OY axes are joined a straight line sloping downwards from left to right will be formed. That line is the 'Budget Line'. It is called the 'Price Line' also since it reflects the prices of the two goods on the basis of which the income is allocated.

In Fig. 2.13 AB is the Budget Line. It is drawn by assuming constant income of the consumer and constant prices of X and Y measured on OX and OY axes respectively. The slope of AB represents the ratio of expenditure on X and Y at fixed prices.

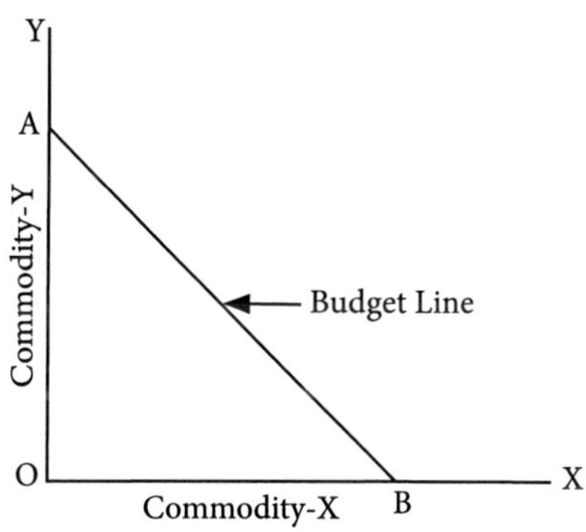

Fig. 2.13

The point 'A' represents the point where the whole income spent on Y will bring OA of Commodity X to the consumer. The point 'B' represents the point where the whole income spent on Commodity X will bring OB of X to the consumer.

However, since he has to rationally spend on both X and Y he allots some money to X and some money to Y. Then, the other points on the budget line will represent the ratio of income spent on both X and Y commodities.

Now you are fully equipped to understand the way in which the consumer attains equilibrium under the IC approach.

There is one more thing you must remember now: The equilibrium is based on two assumptions. They are: (1) The income of the consumer is constant and (2) The prices of the two goods are constant.

I. Equilibrium at Constant Income and Prices

The consumer attains equilibrium or maximum satisfaction with constant income and prices when the Budget Line is 'tanget' to the IC. The point of 'tangency' is the most ideal combination. At this point the consumer has 'optimum' quantity of both X and Y goods. Anywhere else on the IC there is either too much of X and less of Y or too much of Y and less of X.

We may demonstrate this with the help of Fig. 2.14:

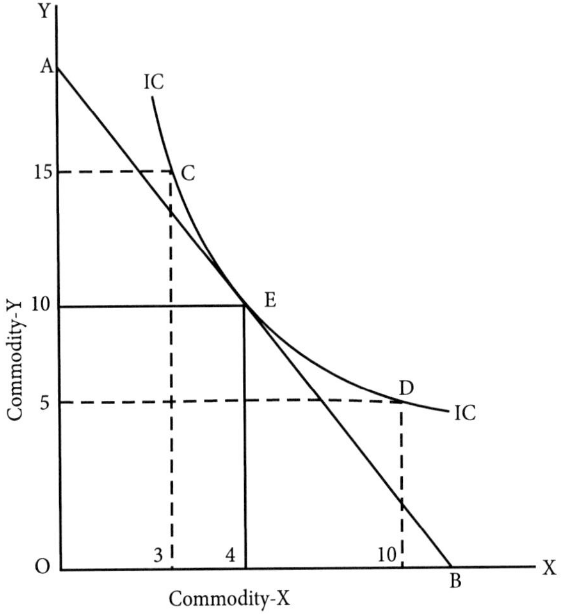

Fig. 2.14. Equilibrium of Constant Income and Prices

In the Fig. 2.14 the Budget line AB is drawn on the basis of what is already explained; so also the indifference curve.

The Budget line AB is *tangent* to IC at E. At the point of equilibrium (E) the combination has 10Y + 4X.

Compare it to combination-C. Here, he has 15Y + 3X. So there is comparatively too much of Y and less of X. At this point (C) above the Budget line the consumer can still re-allocate his budget. As long as reallocation is possible he is not in equilibrium.

Now, compare E to D. Here, he has 5Y + 10X. So, there is comparatively too much of X and less of Y. For the same reasons as in the case of combination-C he is not in equilibrium. The only difference is that at D the combination is beyond his reach. The reason is: the price of X is such that if he buys 5 units of Y he cannot buy 10 units of X but a little less than 10 units. That is why combination-D is not the equilibrium point.

It should be therefore concluded that in this illustration 'E' is the only point of maximum satisfaction or point of equilibrium.

II. Equilibrium with constant prices but change in Income [The Income Effect]

The IC approach is superior because it analyses how the consumer's equilibrium will be disturbed and re-established (though at a higher or lower level than before) when income or price of the commodity or commodities is/are disturbed.

For the present, let us see what happens to the consumer's equilibrium when prices of X and Y are constant but the income of the consumer changes (Income Effect).

Before that, let us know what is '*Income Effect*'. 'The income effect is the effect of changes in income of the consumer (increase or decrease when prices are constant) on the equilibrium of the consumer.'

Thus, the income effect is of two types *viz:*

1. Positive Income Effect, and
2. Negative Income Effect.

The income effect is '*Positive*' or advantageous to the consumer when income increases at constant prices. Then the consumer will be '*better-off*' with higher equilibrium level.

The income effect is '*Negative*' or disadvantageous when income decreases at constant prices. Then, the consumer is 'worse-off at a lower level of equilibrium.

Now, we can go on to demonstrate the Income Effect diagramatically with Fig. 2.15.

In Fig. 2.15 the consumer is in equilibrium at constant income and prices. Suppose: The income increases. Then he can attain larger combinations of X and Y at constant prices. So, there will be a new budget line A_2 B_2 which is tangent to IC_2 at E_2. Here, he is 'better-off'. Therefore, Both the budget line and the IC shift upwards to the right of IC.

If the income decreases and Prices remain constant the two curves shift *downwards* to the left of IC *i.e.*, to A_1 B_1 and IC_1, respectively. Here, the consumer is at a lower level of equilibrium *i.e.*, at E_1 (the point of tangency of A_1 B_1 to IC_1).

If you join the several points of new equilibria with the original equilibrium point you get the ICC curve as shown in Fig. 2.15. It is called the 'Income-Consumption Curve'. It rises upwards.

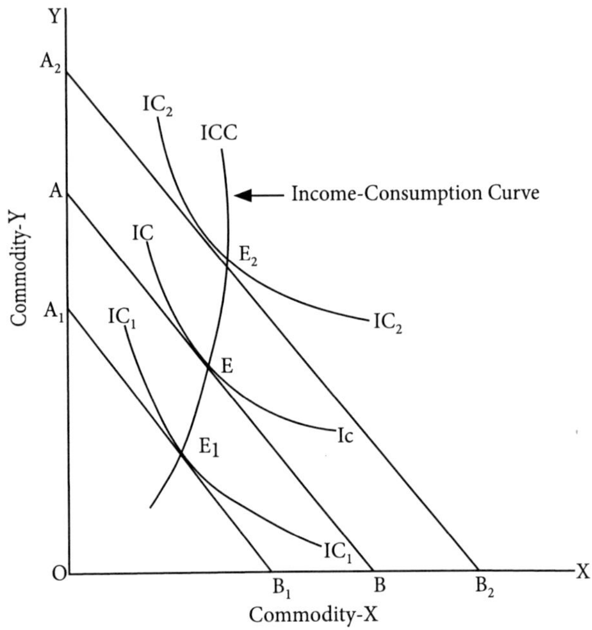

Fig. 2.15. Income Effect

The ICC shows the degree of change in consumption of X and Y due to a rise or fall in income when prices of X and Y are constant.

III. Equilibrium with a change in price [Price Effect]

The Indifference Curve Approach also traces the effect of price changes on the consumer's equilibrium. The 'price effect' maybe defined as:

"Other things remaining constant, the consumer's reaction to a change in price of one of the commodities or of both."

Thus, the price effect traces the effect of a change in price on the demand or on the pattern of consumer's expenditure on the two goods.

Just as the income effect, the Price effect can be either positive or negative. It is positive when the price falls and negative when the price rises. Further, a rise in price makes the consumer worse-off and a fall in price makes the consumer better-off. Moreover, a fall in price shifts the original budget line to the right and a rise in price shifts it to the left of the original budget line.

It should also be observed that the price effect is a combination of both Income Effect and Substitution Effect. Thus:

$$Pe = Ie + Se$$

Where:

Pe denotes price effect

Ie denotes Income effect and

Se denotes substitution effect.

The substitution effect is always positive as the consumer will substitute the relatively cheaper commodity to the dearer commodity.

The price effect is demonstrated in Fig. 2.16. AB, AB_1 and AB_2 are the different budget lines which are tangent to indifference curves IC and IC_1 at E, E_1.

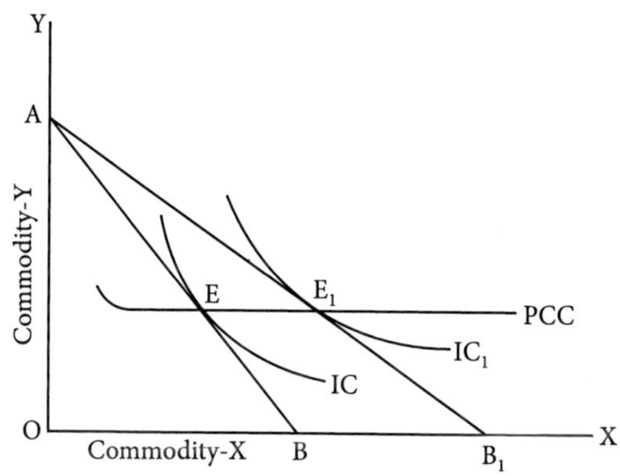

Fig. 2.16. Consumption as a result of change in Price

The slope of the PCC also depends upon the nature of the two goods *i.e.*, when one of them is *inferior* or *superior* to the other. In Fig. 2.18 X is a *superior* commodity and Y is an *inferior* commodity. When the price of X falls the consumer reduces the quantity of Y (though its price has not raised) to buy more of X. So the price effect is negative on Y but positive on X. In other words, Y is a 'inferior Commodity'.

Substitution Effect

With a fall in the price of one of the two goods the consumer will substitute the relatively cheaper commodity to the other whose price may be constant or has increased. Thus, if the price of X falls the consumer reduces the quantity of Y and buys more of X. However, he remains on the same Indifference Curve *i.e.*, only the content of the combination has changed.

This is shown in Fig. 2.16 when the prices of X and Y are constant the consumer is in equilibrium at E on the Indifference Curve IC.

In Fig. 2.16 the consumer is in equilibrium at E where the price line or budget line AB is tangent to the Indifference Curve IC. This equilibrium is established on the assumption that both income and prices of commodities X and Y are constant.

Let us suppose that the price of X falls and that of Y remains constant. Let us also suppose that the *money income* of the consumer is also constant. Then the consumer will be able to buy more of X with the same amount. Hence the budget line shifts upwards to the right of AB and the consumer reallocates his income between X and Y. So, a new Indifference Curve is formed *viz.* IC_2. The new Budget line AB_2 is tangent to the new higher Indifference Curve IC_2 at E_2. The point E_2 is the new equilibrium point with a larger combination. Now the consumer has a *positive price effect* and therefore he is *better-off* than before.

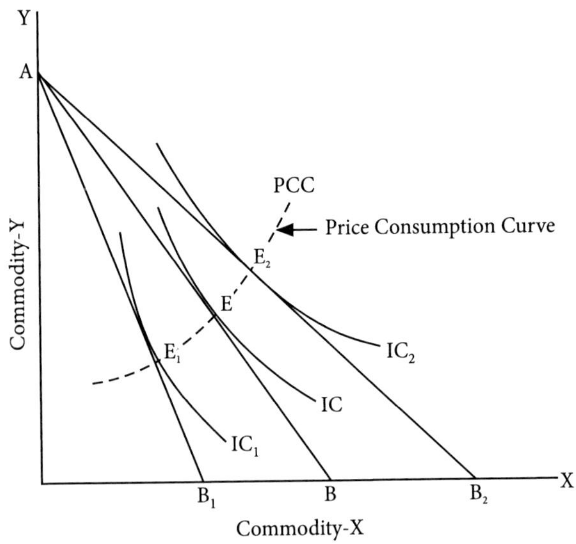

Fig. 2.17. Price Effect when Price of X falls

In the Fig. 2.17 the price effect is that of a fall in the price of Y. The analysis remains the same. The only difference is that the Budget lines originate from B on the OX axis.

Further, when the price of X of Y increases the budget line shifts downwards to the left of the original budget line. This leads to a decline in the level of satisfaction and a lower level of equilibrium at E_1 in Figs. 2.16 and 2.17. Therefore, the consumer is worse-off and the price effect is negative.

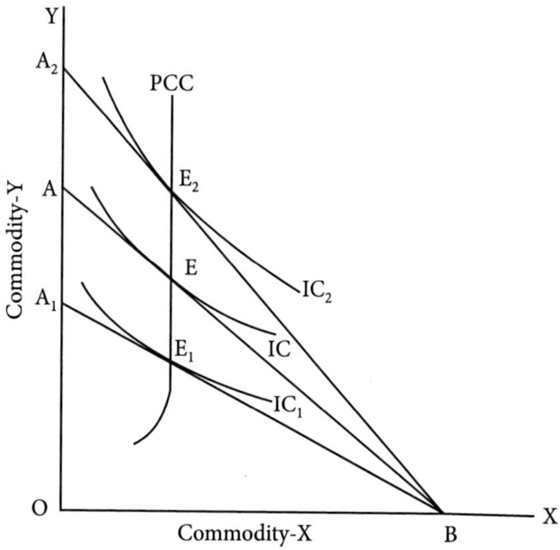

Fig. 2.18. Price Effect when Price of Y falls

When the different points of equilibria are joined the price consumption curve PCC is formed. Its slope determines the rate of change in consumption due to a change in the price of one of the commodities.

SUPERIORITY OF IC APPROACH OVER MARGINAL UTILITY APPROACH

The exponents of the IC approach claim that it is superior to Marshall's cordinal analysis and say that it is a break-through in demand analysis. The plus points claimed on behalf of it are:

1. *It is ordinal:* The IC approach is ordinal while the utility approach is *cardinal.* The former believes that satisfaction or utility cannot be quantified since it is a psychological factor with no definiteness. There is no scale as such. It is unscientific and arbitrary to attempt to measure utility. At best, satisfaction of one commodity can be compared to another and the consumer's preference can be arranged in order of importance. Hence, it is said to be more realistic as ordinal analysis.

2. *Replaces 'Utility' with scale of preferences* and makes demand theory more sensible. The consumer in the real world is guided by his

tastes, habits and likes and dislikes while making decisions on what to buy or how much of which to buy. He is independent of Income here. The consumer simply cares for what would be the relative level of utility and not what is the exact quantity of utility of the commodity.

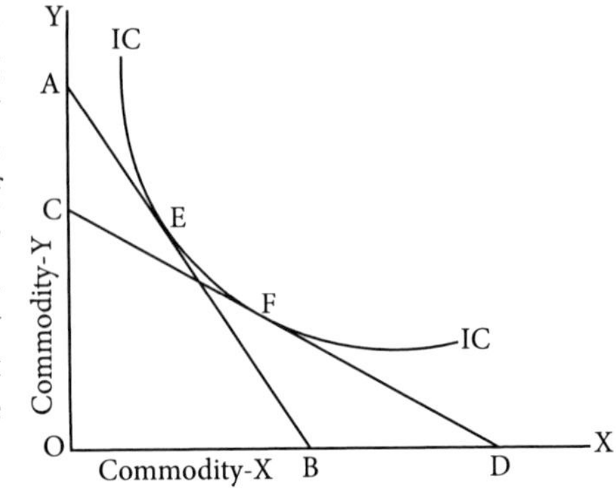

Fig. 2.19. Substitution Effect

3. *Does away with constancy of MU of Money.* Unlike the Marginal Utility analysis, it is nearest to truth that in practice as the stock of money decreases the consumer becomes thrifty in spending.

4. *Two-commodity model.* Unlike the unrealistic single commodity model of Marshall the ordinal approach is a Two-commodity model which can be extended to any number of goods which the consumer purchases in real life.

5. *The Law of DMRS.* The ordinal approach is based on the principle of DMRS while the cardinal approach is based on the Law of DMU which is very hypothetical. The principles of DMRS is practical and hence the IC approach is an improved approach.

6. *The measurability of equilibrium condition.* The condition of equilibrium under ordinal approach is measurable and practicable while it is impracticable and immeasurable under cardinal approach. Moreover, the ordinal approach is highly comprehensive since the quantity of X bought depends on the price of X as well as the price of Y and Z and so on.

7. *Added advantage of income effect and substitution effect.* The IC approach demonstrates all the three effects on consumer's equilibrium *viz.*, income effect, price effect and substitution effect. The cardinal approach has no such method. Hence, the demand theory of Marshall is meaningless in practice.

8. *Satisfactory explanation to Inferior goods case.* The IC approach offers an acceptable explanation to the question of demand for *Inferior Goods* or inferior commodities. But, Marshall's ordinal analysis assumes away such a case conveniently. Hence, the former approach is broader and more precise than the latter approach.

9. *Logical and conclusive.* It is claimed that the IC approach is logically true and conclusive. It is also universal since all consumers are guided by the scale of preferences, prices of other goods and the nature of the goods and their quality. The Utility analysis does not take these real factors into account.

SHORTCOMINGS OF THE IC APPROACH

The indifference curve technique, superior as it may appear to be, is not free from criticism. Profs. Robertson, Armstrong and others have found fault with this technique. Thus, the new ordinal approach 'is the same thing as what Marshall wanted to convey in his exposition....' and he was only laying down the foundation upon which Hicks and Allen built their superstructure of Indifference analysis.

The chief criticisms may be stated thus:

1. Old wine in new bottles: The IC approach is but old wine in new bottles. The logic is that of Marshall but terms are different. It is Hicksian analysis grafted on the trunk of Marshallian analysis; preference in the place of 'utility', 'ordinal' in the place of 'cardinal' and MRS in place of DMU.

2. Determinate and indeterminate at once: The ordinal approach to demand is both *determinate* and *indeterminate* at the same time. The consumer cannot have perfect knowledge of alternatives of combinations just as much as he cannot consciously compare MU of various goods. In a given situation he may express his preference but in a hoast of situations he will find himself perplexed.

3. Self-criticism: The ordinal approach has lent itself to criticism by accepting as its assumption what it itself criticised as the weak-link of cardinal analysis viz., the DMU of goods in the indirect form of DMRS.

4. Intransitivity and Discontinuity: The assumption of *transitivity* and *continuity* is unreal and impossible in certain cases according to Prof. Armstrong. It is possible only in the case of very close points on an IC and not always.

5. Not extendable to Multiple goods: Geometrically it cannot be extended to combinations of more than two goods in practice as it claims.

It may be concluded that though the ordinal approach is somewhat absurd and lacks empirical test, it has been received well by theoreticians of Economics.

CONSUMER'S SURPLUS

The concept of consumer's surplus was not totally Marshall's own concept. It was the '*still born child*' of Mr. Dupuit. Marshall refined the concept and gave it to us in a new clothing in the Third edition of the '*Principles of Economics*' in 1895.

Marshall stated the concept thus:

> "The excess of the price he (consumer) would be willing to pay rather than go without the thing, over that which he actually does pay, is the economic measure of this surplus satisfaction."

Very often we pay less for a commodity than what we are prepared to pay. We get an extra satisfaction over and above the price we have paid. This extra satisfaction is called by Marshall as '*consumer's surplus*'.

According to Marshall the consumer's surplus is very high in the case of matches, salt, postage etc. He considers consumer's surplus as *conjectural* or that it is due to the situation of the consumer.

This can be numerically examplified thus: Suppose the consumer is willing to pay ₹ 5 for a Kg of potatoes. On inquiry he comes to know that the Market Price is only ₹ 4 and pays that price. Therefore, the consumer's surplus is equal to ₹ 1. *i.e.*:

₹ 5 – ₹ 4 = ₹ 1

Cs = Ps – Mp

Where Pp is potential price the consumer is prepared to pay,

Mp is market price paid, and Cs is consumer's surplus.

The consumers' surplus is tabulated in Table 1 below.

TABLE 1: Consumer's Surplus

Units of X	M.U. of X or Potential Price	Market Price	Consumer's Surplus
1	₹ 10	₹ 8	₹ 2
2	₹ 8	₹ 8	₹ 200
3	₹ 12	₹ 8	₹ 4
4	₹ 20	₹ 8	₹ 12
5	₹ 2	₹ 8	₹ 6

In the above table the consumer is ready to pay ₹ 10 and buy 1 unit of X to begin with. Then, according to the formula of consumer's surplus the surplus is equal to the difference between potential price (Pp) and Market Price (Mp). The consumer has paid a Mp of ₹ 8. Hence, the Cs = ₹ 2. *Secondly*, the consumer is prepared to buy 2 units of X at a Pp of ₹ 8 but the Mp is also ₹ 8. Therefore 8 – 8 = Zero Cs per unit. *Thirdly*, the consumer is prepared to pay ₹ 12 per unit of X and buy 3 units but pays a Mp of ₹ 8 again per unit. So, the Cs = 12 – 8 *i.e.* ₹ 4 per unit (Total Cs of 3 units bought = 4 + 4 + 4 = 12) and so on.

It should be noted that the Mp is constant as per the table. If the Mp increases then the Cs will fall.

The Pp column also represents the Marginal Utility of X which is equal to the Pp.

The concept of Cs can also be geometrically illustrated as in Fig. 2.20.

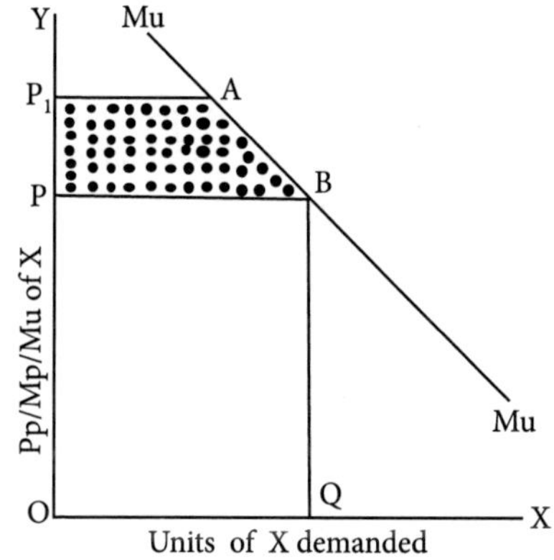

Fig. 2.20. Consumer's Surplus

In Fig. 2.20 the consumer is prepared to pay ₹ OP_1 price per unit of X and buy OQ quantity. However, he pays only OP Market Price. The curve MU is the Marginal Utility curve of the commodity X.

At OP_1 Potential price and OP market price the consumer's total surplus of OQ quantity of X is equal to P_1 ABP.

In other words:

OP_1 ABQ—OPBQ = P_1 ABP which is consumer's is surplus.

Thus, the amount of demand for a firm's produce or the quantity that a businessman will be able to sell depends upon the consumer's surplus. The Business Economist must find out the consumer's surplus though indirectly. He must advice his firm accordingly. Only then the firm can maximise its profits.

Limitations of the Concept

The concept of consumer's surplus has been subjected to certain criticisms. The main weaknesses are:

1. *The concept of Cs* is psychological and as such it does not lend itself to quantitative measurement. Thus, it is not of any use.
2. *It is not uniform* to the same consumer at different stages of consumption and income. As Marshall himself has put it in the DMU Law, the MU diminishes after the want is fully satisfied. So does Cs too. Further, a consumer with very high income does not mind paying a very high price [out of prestige] though it is not an intensive want. Then, it would appear that its Cs is very high which is misleading.
3. *It is not a basis for the law of Demand* as is often made out.
4. *It is not a guide to profit maximisation* since a business firm intentionally restricts profit maximisation for many reasons. It may want to avoid *State intervention* or attention or avoid attracting new firms as *competitors* or want to retain the *goodwill* of its customers by not raising its price simply because there is Cs.
5. *It is only of historical and doctrinal interest according to Prof. Samuelson. Prof Samuelson remarks that, "The subject is of historical and doctrinal interest with a limited amount of appeal as a mathematical puzzle. The economist had best dispense with it. It is a tool which can be used only by one who can get along without its use, and not by all such."*

Thus, it has been gradually falling into disuse. Yet, it cannot be totally considered as a product of Marshall's mathematical genius and logical analysis. It is nevertheless useful in many respects. In the next section we shall assess its theoretical and practical usefulness.

Uses of the Concept Cs

Though Prof. Samuelson has remarked that 'the economist had best dispense with it' is indirectly of a great utility to the theory and practice of Economics. In this context Prof. Robertson considers it as "both intellectually respectable and useful as a guide to practical action."

The chief uses of the concept of Cs may be given as under:

1. The concept of consumer's surplus, vague as it may be, is an important '*leading lamp*' to the monopolist in his *price policy*. It suggests to the monopoly firm that it should not take away the

entire '*surplus*' because it will attract *substitutes* into the market. This may ultimately reduce the *turn-over* of the monopoly firm. It would be better to attain a large turn-over at lower profit rate is the indirect suggestion of this concept to the monopoly firm.

2. It guides the '*Policy of Indirect Taxes*' of the Government. The Finance Minister has to raise more and more resources for the various programmes of the State. However, the concept of Cs warns him against overburdening the poor with heavy indirect taxes on *goods of mass consumption* which have high Cs.
3. As a theoretical concept it guides the policy of *International Trade* of the Government. It suggests that exports with *inelastic demand* can be taxed heavily without losing international demand for its exports. At the same time it warns that the exports which have *elastic* and *relatively* elastic demand must be taxed accordingly.
4. The theory and practice of *price discrimination* under monopoly is founded on Cs.
5. 'Consumer's Surplus' is the basis of further developments in the *theory of demand* by the modern economists.

In conclusion it may be said that one of the great contributions of Dr. Marshall to the theory and practice of Business Economics in particular and to the Economic theory in general is the concept of consumer's surplus. Further, though the concept is the 'brain child' of Mr. Dupuit the credit of stating it systematically must rightly belong to this great founder of Neo-classical Economics. Marshall is at once both a great and controversial economist for all times to come in the History of Economics for this concept along with many of his other concepts.

3

Demand: Meaning

Not many of us think that 'Demand' is a highly technical term in the Economics of Business. Many of us use it in our daily conversation with our customers or consumers as if '*Demand*' is the same thing as '*Want*'—guard against it.

This is totally wrong as far as 'Business Economics' is concerned and as far as the Science of Economics is concerned.

For, '*Want*' is just a desire to consume some commodity whether the consumer has the needed resources to buy the commodity or not, and '*Demand*' is always backed by the necessary resources (*viz.* Money) to execute the desire or want into practice. Thus, there is a world of difference between 'Want' and 'Demand', as far as the producer or the businessman is concerned.

The reason is: going by the wants the seller will buy more from the producer on the basis of 'Enquiry' or demand with the fond hope of selling it; ends up with a huge '*inventory*' (unsold stocks); and going by '*demand*' the firm ends up with profit or at least ends up without losses.

This is the sum and substance of the meaning and significance of 'demand' to the business firm. A business firm must consider the 'want' and execute the 'demand' of its customer. That is the thick line between want and demand in Business Economics and elsewhere in Economics; after all that the begger 'wants' a car and the king 'demands' it is what we must distinguish between.

THE LAW OF DEMAND
[Its significance to Business Economics]

'The Law of Demand' is known as the 'First Law of Markets' (The 'Second Law of Markets' being the 'Law of Supply').

The Law of Demand was propounded by Dr. Marshall in his famous work '*Principles of Economics*' in 1890.

Dr. Marshall analysed, for the first time, the '*Cause-Effect Relationship*' between 'price' and 'demand' and arrived at the 'Law of Demand'. This law is a statement of tendency of demand of a business firm to the changes in the price of its product.

It endeavours to establish the fact that the consumers demand more at lower prices than at higher prices of the product of the firm.

That brings us to the question of '*Inverse Relationship*' between price and demand which is very crucial in the existence of the firm.

The higher you 'price' your product the lesser you will be able to 'sell' is the gist of this law.

THE LAW OF DEMAND SPEAKS TO A BUSINESS MAN

The Law: Beware the consumer lest he buys less if you over-charge your goods.

In other words, don't stretch your price beyond what the '*reasoning consumer*' thinks is the limit to the price of your product if you want to protect your own firm against the *oddities* of market.

Dr. Marshall stated the law of demand thus:

"*Other things being equal, more can be sold at lower prices than at higher prices*". In other words, the demand for a commodity will be more when its price is low and when the price is high its demand is low.

In simplest form, the law of demand states that more will be demanded when the price of a commodity falls and conversely, less will be demanded when price rises.

This is a statement of quantitative relationship between demand and price. It is a statement of tendency or responsiveness of demand to changes in the price under given *assumptions*.

The assumptions upon which the law of demand is based are:

1. Fixed and constant *income*.
2. Constant *tastes* and *preferences*.
3. Absence of *substitutes* and *complimentary* goods.
4. Absence of *speculation*.
5. The commodity is a *Normal Commodity*.
6. *Natural factors* like weather are constant.
7. Constant size of population, etc.

Given these factors that condition demand, the law establishes that the demand varies *inversely* with price; rising when price falls and falling when price rises. Symbolically:

$$P\uparrow \; — D\uparrow \text{ and}$$
$$P\downarrow \; — D\downarrow$$
$$P^{-} \; — D^{-}$$

it means that demand is a function of price *i.e.* $D = F(P_1)$

[Read as: P = price, F = functional relationship, P^{-} = constant price and D^{-} = constant demand.]

The law of demand can be presented diagramatically as in Fig. 3.1

In Fig. 3.1 the curve DD is the demand curve which slopes from left to right downwards. The slope indicates the functional relationship [*i.e.* DX = 7 (Pe)].

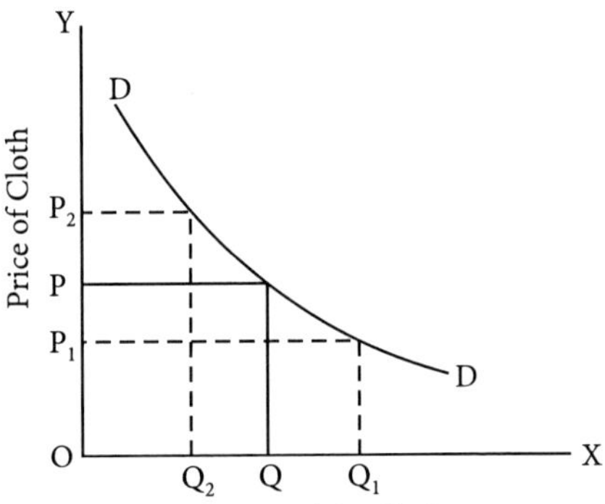

Fig. 3.1. Law of Demand

When the price of cloth is OP the total demand is OQ on the OX axis. If price rises to OP_2 (other things being constant) the demand for cloth will fall along the demand curve to OQ_2. Similarly, a fall in price from OP to OP_1 causes a rise in demand for cloth from OQ to OQ_1.

Thus, the law of demand is a basic law in Business Economics. Its awareness is very essential to a Business Firm in order to determine its price and output policy. The organisation of markets is also based on the law of demand.

EXCEPTIONS

The law of demand is based on the proverbial *'ceteris paribus'* condition: when the assumptions are relaxed the demand will respond otherwise to changes in price *i.e.*, the demand curve will rise upwards from left to right as in Fig. 3.2.

It shows that demand and price rise and fall together. Thus, when price of cloth rises from OP to OP_2 the demand also rises from OQ to OQ_2 instead of falling in terms of the law of demand. Similarly, the demand falls to OQ_1 when price of cloth falls to OP_1. However, this is unusual and occurs under very peculiar circumstances only.

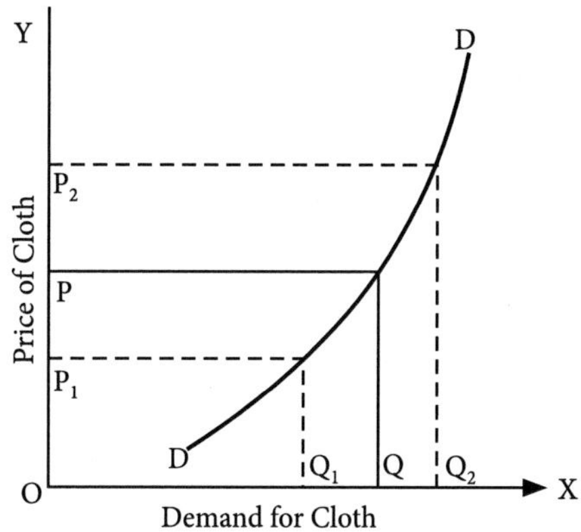

Fig. 3.2. Exceptional Demand Curve

Let us consider these exceptional conditions.

1. *Emergency:* During national emergencies like a war or civil war goods become artificially scarce. Consumers fear that the prices will rise and panic purchases take place *i.e.*, more is bought and stocked though the price has risen because the price would be higher later.

2. *Depression:* During depression prices fall continuously; goods become cheaper and cheaper each day but unemployment causes lack of purchasing power. Hence, the demand falls though the prices are falling.

3. *Giffen's paradox:* When the goods are inferior to some other commodities then less of it will be bought when its price falls and the demand for some other superior commodity increases. Similarly, if the price of wheat increases consumers will reduce consumption of less important goods and consume more of wheat though its price has increased. Sir Giffen observed this situation in Ireland in case of meat and potatoes. The price of meat and potatoes increased together. However, the demand for meat fell but that for potatoes increased as explained above. Thus, the law of demand was true in the case of meat and untrue in the case of potatoes. Hence, it is a *paradoxical* situation named after Giffen.

4. *Speculation:* The law does not operate if people anticipate a rise or Jail in price in the nearest future on the basis of comparison of *present* and *past* price trend. Suppose the price of rice has decreased from ₹ 9 to ₹ 8 today and consumers expect that it will fall further tomorrow. It would

be cheaper to buy tomorrow. Hence, the demand for rice will decrease today though its price has increased. The converse is also true *i.e.*, the price rise will cause a rise in demand if consumers expect the future price to be higher than the current price.

5. *Demonstration Effect:* In the case of *prestige symbol* articles like diamonds and gold ornaments the higher the price the higher will be the prestige of their possessors. They feel *distinct* when they buy more when the price of such goods increases. Similarly, the demand for them decreases when price falls as it has no more prestige value. They have '*snob appeal*' and no real value.

6. *Illusion Effect:* Sometimes some consumers will consider a fall in price as due to deterioration of quality and *vice-versa*. Therefore, demand and price will *vary directly* and not inversely.

7. *Necessities:* In the case of necessities like salt, matches etc. no amount of rise in price will induce the consumer to buy less nor will they buy more simply because it is now cheaper.

8. *Income Effect:* When the rise in price is compensated or more than compensated the demand will not fall with a fall in price. That is, if the income increases when price rises then the demand may not fall.

9. *Substitutes:* Suppose the price of Liril toilet soap decreases but new substitutes are put into the market with new features, then some consumers of Liril Soap will shift to the consumption of newer soaps and demand for Liril will fall though its price has fallen.

10. *Complementarity:* According to the law of demand the fall in price affects only that commodity and none else. However, in the case of complementary goods like shoes and socks or coffee and sugar the price rise of one affects the other also.

Thus, the law of demand is a hypothetical law. Yet, it is a fact that generally we buy less at higher prices and *vice versa*. It is universal and a very significant law in Business Economics.

EXTENSION AND CONTRACTION OF DEMAND

The terms '*Extension*' and '*contraction*' of demand are often confused with '*Increase*' and '*Decrease*' in demand. In this context it is needful to make a clear distinction among these technical terms as we are going to use them more frequently in further chapters,

The terms 'Extension' and 'Contraction' refer to '*variations*' in demand due to a change in the price of the commodity. In other words 'Extension' and 'Contraction' of demand directly refer to the law of demand.

Thus, demand 'extends' when price falls and 'contracts' when price rises. It is hence clear that they refer to the left to right downward slope of the demand curve. It is the inverse relation between demand and price that they speak about. It is a functional relationship expressed by them.

Thus, when we speak of Extension and Contraction, we have only one demand curve. As we move *upwards* from right to left along the demand curve the demand goes on contracting and as we slide down from left to right *downwards* it goes on *expanding* along the curve. This is clear from Fig. 3.3.

In Fig. 3.3 when price is OP the demand is stable at OQ. Above the point E extension of demand is shown. Below the point E contraction of demand is shown in Fig. 3.3.

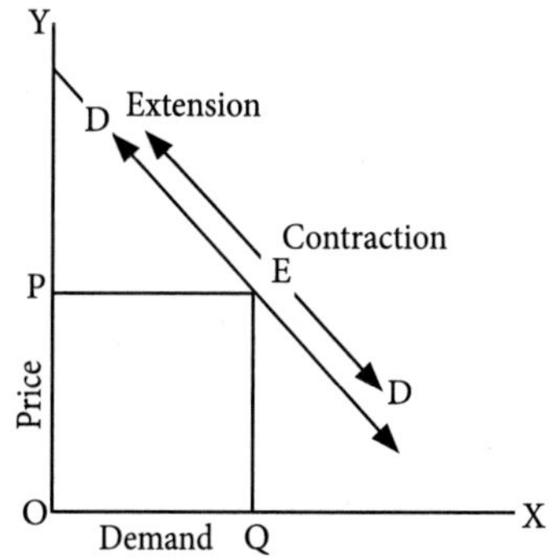

Fig. 3.3. Extension and Contraction of Demand

INCREASE AND DECREASE IN DEMAND

A change in demand refers to '*increase*' and '*decrease*' in demand (and not *variation* in demand). In other words, 'increase' and 'decrease' in demand is caused by factors other than price. It may be due to a change in the size of population, change in the size of the market, new substitutes, weather and so on.

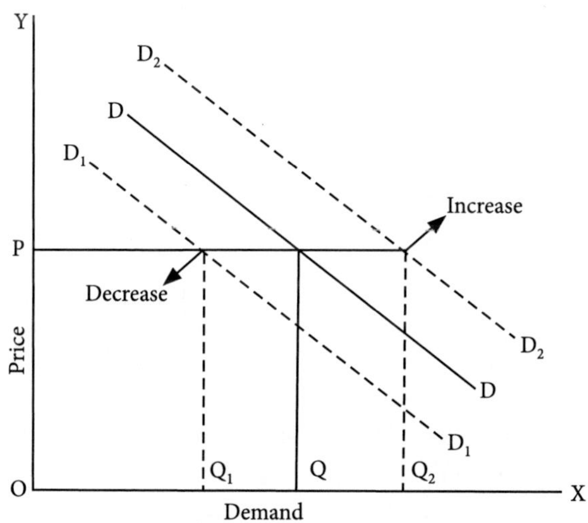

Fig. 3.4. Increase and decrease in demand

That is to say, there will be an 'increase' in demand or 'decrease' in demand even though price is *constant*. Thus, if at constant price more is demanded there is said to be an 'Increase' in demand. Then the demand curve shifts *upwards* to the right of the original demand curve as in Fig. 3.4. Thus, the demand curve shifts from DD to D_2D_2. At the constant price OP the demand increases from OQ to OQ_2.

Again, if price is constant and demand decreases then the demand curve shifts *downwards* to the left of the original demand curve from DD to D_1D_1. Then the decreased demand will be OQ_1.

In short, Increase and Decrease in demand is due to factors other than price while Extension and Contraction in demand is due to changes in price. Further, in the former case the demand curve shifts bodily to the right or left as the case may be. In the latter case the demand curve remains in its original position but demand moves along the same curve.

DETERMINANTS OF DEMAND

The quantity demanded in the market of a business firm depends on a number of factors. The Business House has some degree of control on some of these determinants while it has no hold on many others. Let us analyse the most significant determinants of demand in this section.

1. *Price:* It is now known to us that 'price' is the most potential and crucial determinant. The law of demand has clearly established that demand and price vary (*ceteris paribus*) inversely. The degree of change in demand depends on the extent by which the price has increased or decreased. This has been discussed in greater detail in Chapter 4 under 'Elasticity of Demand'. It suffices here to know that a rise in price, *ceteris paribus*, causes a fall in price and *vice versa*.

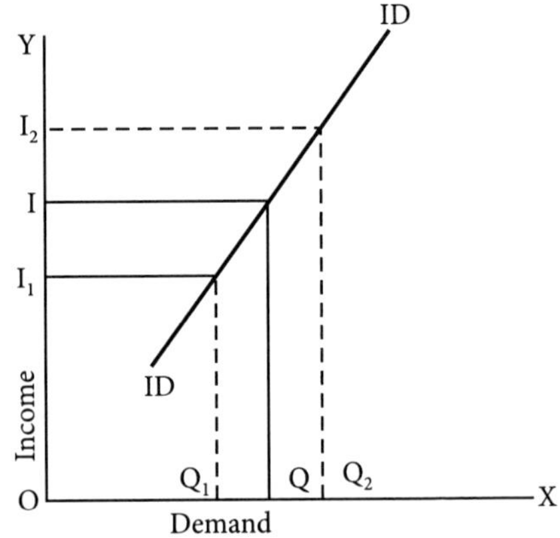

Fig. 3.5. Determinants of Demand

2. *Income:* The influence of income on demand, is well explained by the concept of 'Income-Demand'. The relation between Income and Demand is 'direct' *i.e.,* demand rises as income rises and falls as income

falls provided that the other factors remain constant. The demand for *luxuries* and *comforts* rises with a rise in income while that of necessities remain constant. Thus, in Fig. 3.5 the demand curve ID slopes from left to right upwards.

If income rises from OI to OI_2 demand rises to OQ_2. If income falls to OI_1 demand falls to OQ_1.

3. *Tastes, Fashions, Customs,* etc.: Demand also changes with every change in tastes, fashions, customs, etc. Their influence on demand is so great that they are dictatorial to the business firm. Hence, a business firm must keep its products up-to-date with current-day fashions, tastes, etc. This calls for regular and periodic research and development and survey of consumer's preferences on the part of the firm.

4. *Pattern of Income Distribution:* Modern welfare states redistribute income through various fiscal and social security measures from the rich to the poor. The *composition* of society will be changing gradually. Those who could not afford a particular product then will now be able to buy the product as their economic status has changed. For instance, a watch or a radio set which was beyond the reach of a road-maker or a house-builder has become an ordinary possession. A business firm must keenly observe such changes and enter the market.

5. *Substitutes:* Appearance of newer and newer substitutes in the market day-after-day has become the order of the market due to research. For instance, the introduction of a variety of soaps with new fragrances has reduced the demand for Life Buoy soap. Similarly, the Ball-point pens have reduced the demand for writing ink and the fountain pen, nibs, etc. A firm has to keep a close watch of such substitutes to survive in the market.

6. *Nature of the Commodity*: Demand depends on whether the commodity is a necessity or an independent commodity or a complementary (jointly demanded) commodity or is it a habitual's commodity like cigarette. While necessities like salt and rice have stable demand others face fluctuating demand. Complementary goods like pens and ink have *joint-demand.*

7. *Demonstration Effect:* This has become a great determinant recently. Prof. Duesenberry had observed it long ago. The influence of what others consume is so great that we are unconsciously changing on to new fashions and tastes. This naturally changes the pattern of demand. The best example for this is the fast disappearance of the '*Dhothi*' and take-over by pants.

8. *Cost of Production:* Though this factor is included in price as a determinant of demand it is necessary to treat it as a separate factor. Efficient firms and large-scale firms minimise cost and hence the price of their products will be competitive. Their demand will be high. The Average and inefficient firms do not have the benefit of *Internal* and '*External*' economies. Hence, their cost of production and naturally also the price of their products will be high causing low demand.

9. *Natural Factors:* They include rise in population, changes in weather, seasons, etc. and so on. (Failure of firms is often attributed to these factors of demand.) There will be seasonal variations and variations as per weather etc. in demand. For instance, cool drinks have more demand in summer than in winter, Asthmatic drugs have more demand in winter than in summer and so on.

10. *Trade Marks and Advertisements:* 'Trade marks' create '*legal monopoly*' for a firm in the market. Even today you find adament and consistent customers who have stuck to Colgate tooth paste or Lux bathing soaps in spite of new susbtitutes being available. At the same time you find long-time consumers of Colgate having changed over to newer brands due to the brain-washing effects of advertisements—both visual and audio-visual advertisements.

11. *Speculation:* The influence of speculation is explained in detail under "The Law of Demand' in the beginning of this chapter. It suffices to say that the anticipated price trends cause changes in demand specially during wars and inflation.

12. *Disposable Income:* The size of 'disposable income' means how much you are left with to dispose or spend on consumption after paying taxes and other compulsory payments are made. High taxes, heavy compulsory insurance etc. reduce disposable income and so the demand will be less and *vice versa*.

13. *Stage of Economic Development:* An economically advanced nation has a different pattern of demand than that of a developing nation like ours. Thus, while in the U.S.A. or Japan the demand for computers and electronic gadgets is high it is still to pick up in India and the rest of the developing nations.

These determinants of demand for a business firm's products or of a producer must be fully studied before releasing the product into the market. The demand for a product being a dynamic factor calls for a dynamic and vigilant business economist's advise. He has become inevitable to modern business for this reason.

THE NEED FOR DEMAND ANALYSIS

Before we venture to analyse the need for demand analysis it is worthywhile to know what is 'Demand Analysis'.

Demand analysis is a scientific method of finding out the potential quantity of demand that may be forthcoming for a product during a given period, in a given market, at a given price and degree of competition or monopoly.

A Business Firm or Producing Unit has to analyse the current and anticipated demand on the strength of facts and figures periodically. We have seen how the present day markets are dynamic. We have also noted in the preceding section how many factors influence demand and that many of them are beyond the seller's or producer's control. This is exactly the reason why demand analysis becomes necessary. It can be called the '*First Step*' in business or production. It is necessary to construct 'Market Demand Schedules'—current as well as projections.

The need for analysing demand arises due to a number of aims. The important factors or aims of demand analysis are:

1. Avoiding over-production or accumulation of stocks;
2. Avoiding unnecessary over-head costs;
3. Avoiding Risk-bearing;
4. Avoiding over-purchase or under-purchase of raw-material, machinery etc.,
5. Determination or future price-output policy;
6. Planning of advertisement and propaganda;
7. Profit maximisation;
8. Goodwill of customers or consumers through stable supply;
9. Protection of share-holder's interest; and
10. Programming for expansion of old markets and discovery of new markets at home or across the home or domestic markets.

Now a brief consideration of the above needs for demand analysis can be made.

If a scientific analysis is not made exhaustively of demand the firm is likely to over-produce or even under-produce. In either case it loses. Similarly, it may lead to unnecessary costs like transport cost, rent etc.

The degree of business risks or production risks will be high in the absence of demand projecting because of fluctuations in cost of production as related to the market price.

Further, the firm may suddenly find itself short of raw-materials or in excess of it when demand is actually more and demand is less than expected respectively—causing either dead-capital or loss of profit.

Demand analysis is also needed to avoid Risks due to possible substitutes and variation in the business prospects *i.e.*, inflation and deflation. Even the investment in '*fixed capital*' will become a burden in the absence of demand forecasting.

It is necessary for planned advertisement and propaganda in order to promote sales or output.

Demand analysis or demand forecasting or projects is necessary for framing the future price-output policy. However, the maximisation of profit is possible only if demand forecasting is accurate.

Underestimation of demand may cause scarcity of the product and some of the consumers may change over to other substitutes and it would be difficult to re-attract them to the product if not impossible. Their goodwill is essential to the firm.

The firm has a responsibility towards its share-holders if it is a joint-stock company. It has to earn enough profit to pay attractive dividend to share-holders. Otherwise, its shares will crumble in the stock exchange.

Lastly, the programme for expansion of markets in case the demand is high and discovery of new and *satellite Markets* also requires Demand Forecasting or Demand Analysis.

FORECASTING DEMAND—METHODS

Broadly speaking, there are two approaches to Demand Forecasting *viz.*, (1) *Short-term Forecasting*, and (2) *Long-term Forecasting*. While 'short-term forecasting' is meant for making *ad hoc* decisions on day-to-day working of the firm, it is generally concerned with production and sales policy. Such forecasting is limited to a maximum of *one year*. The other areas of short-term forecasting are: establishment of controls, creation of incentives to consumers, determination of financial requirements and determination of price policy.

'*Long-term forecasting*, on the other hand, is the assessment of demand and expansion of the concern. It involves strategic and crucial decisions regarding financial and man-power planning. It involves the study of technological developments, consumer's tastes and prefernces. The greatest danger of 'long-term forecasting' is that the *probability of error* may be high. Hence, competent and reliable forecasting is essential.

Thus, the two are only *approaches* to demand forecasting methods. The *Methods of Demand Forecasting* are of two broad types viz.:

1. The Survey Method, and
2. The Statistical Method.

In the former method we obtain information of consumers' tastes and desires through survey or interview of consumers and experts. It is a short-term approach to forecasting. In the latter method *past data* forms the basis for forecasting future trends in demand. It is a long-term approach to forecasting demand.

The most popularly used methods of Demand Forecasting today are:

1. Survey of Buyers' Intention Method;
2. Collective Opinion Method;
3. Trend Projection; and
4. Economic Indicators.

Let us analyse them in greater detail and see what are their merits and demerits.

1. Buyers' Intention Method

This is a method of interviewing the consumers regarding their preferences, desires and plans about the firm's product. It is a direct interview and not a questionnaire method of survey. Either all the consumers are interviewed or a *sample survey* of selected group of consumers is done. The method is also known as the most difficult method as well as *costly* method.

It is difficult because the attitudes and expectations cannot be clearly ascertained. Moreoever, these are subject to frequent changes. It is *costly* because the number of households are so many that their interview is expensive.

The buyers estimates may not be real as they may exaggerate their requirement. This may be because they fear shortage of the product in future. Further, if substitutes appear in the market they may change their pattern of purchases. Hence, this method has limited use, as a method of Demand Forecasting. Norman F. Duffy considers the method as '*passive*' and incapable of exposing the real factors. According to Joel Dean 'the consumer's plans are fragile and expensive to collect'.

Types of Buyers' Intention Survey: Buyers intention survey can be classified into three categories:

1. Exhaustive Enumeration Method;
2. Sample Survey; and
3. End-Use Method.

The 'Exhaustive' or 'Complete' enumeration Method is the interview of each and every consumer of the product. Then the *individual demand schedules* are compiled into the *Market Demand Schedule* (MDS). The MDS then gives the *Aggregate* demand for the product. The advantage of this method is that there is no chance for bias. The forecast is based on the information collected by the enumerator. The greatest demerit is that it is *cumbersome* and *time consuming*.

'*The Sample Survey Method*' reduces the cumbersomeness and simplifies the job of demand forecasting. Under this method the consumers are chosen for interview. They are taken at random or on the basis of *stratification* of consumers (*i.e.*, classifying consumers as rich, middle-class and poor or urban, semi-urban and rural). The selected consumers must be truly '*representative*' and they must give correct information. Then, this method is less costly, simple, easy and useful.

'*The End-Use Method*' is used for forecasting demand for raw materials and products used in many industries. A survey of different users of the commodity of the firm is made. Thus, the individual demands of final consumers, different sectors and industries, exporters etc. has to be made. The demand forecast by this method then becomes useful in planning product sales in future.

2. Collective Opinion Method

The 'Collective Opinion 'Method' of forecasting demand is also known as the '*Opinion Survey Method*'.

In a firm there will be expert salesman. They have close rapport with the consumers of their area of sales. They can easily and quickly estimate the expected demand with their rich expedience.

Under this method each salesman collects the data of expected demand for the product in his 'Area' or zone and passes on to the executive of the firm. All such reports are then carefully reviewed and consolidated. Care will be taken to remove optimism. If too much difference is noticed, an '*Average*' is estimated. The method is naturally based on the wiseness of salesman, executives who review the data provided by the salesmen and the heads of various departments of the firm.

Simplicity, *directness* and *low cost* are the special merits of this method. It avoids bundles of statistical work and is realistic.

At the same time it is not free from limitations. The main limitations are:

1. It is too subjective.
2. The prejudices of salesman may lead to biased information.
3. The salesmen are likely to submit data showing low demand just to get low *sales target* fixed for easy work.

Yet, if the salesmen are honest, efficient or experienced this method is very successful. It is highly useful in short-period demand forcasting.

3. Trend Projection Method

Trend projection' is a *statistical method*. It is employed and useful only in firms which have existed from a long-time in the market.

Long-standing firms have data relating to a number of years regarding sales. Based on such past data the future *trend* in sales is derived.

While doing so the past trends are arranged *chronologically i.e.*, according to period or years. This is called '*time series*'.

The time series shows how from time to time the demand has been increasing or decreasing or stable.

The data of the time series may be presented in a *tabular form* or in the form of a *graph*. If it is a graphic form the information will be in the form of a curve called '*the sales curve*'. The rise and fall or turning points and the intervals between them are studied. The demand forecasting is done ultimately on this study. If the turns of the sales curve are very frequent, it shows that the sales policy has to be changed suitably. If they are less there is no need for a change in sales policy.

The 'time series' may show different types of fluctuations in demand or sales. Generally, these fluctuations will be due to:

1. Seasonal changes in demand.
2. General changes or secular changes.
3. Cyclical changes due to inflation and deflation.
4. Irregular changes due to floods, famines, epidemics etc.

The measurement of the intensity of these four fluctuations is difficult. Their effect is *cumulative and multiple*. Therefore, when we forecast demand by this method we must eliminate all other three fluctuations and forecast on the basis of *secular changes* only.

Perhaps a table will help us to understand Trend Projection Method.

Table of Trend Projection

Year of Sales	Sales (in thousands)
1981	45
1982	52
1983	48
1984	55
1985	60

If we glance through the table we find that the sales of this imaginary firm varies between 45,000 and 60,000 units over 5 years from 1981 to 1985 and that sales is steadily rising.

Now, if we plot these data on a graph sheet we get a curve; 'sales curve' in Fig. 3.6.

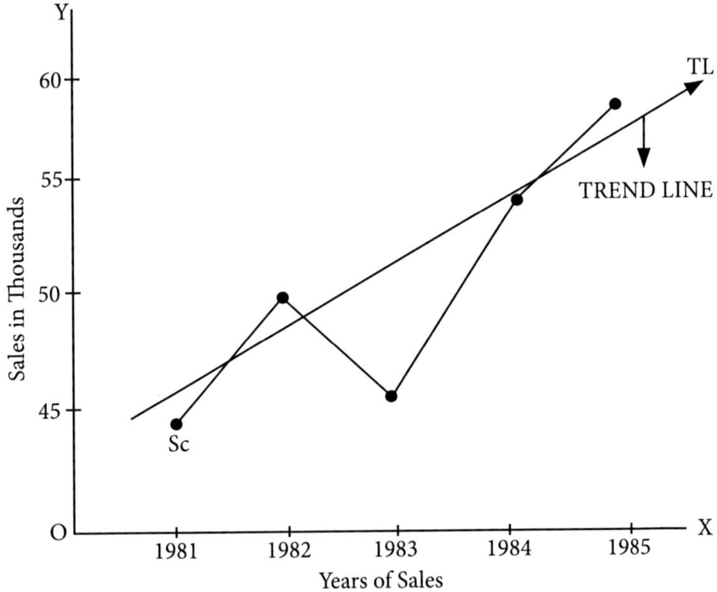

Fig. 3.6. Sales Curve

In Fig. 3.6 sales is measured on OY axis and year of sales on OX axis. The sales curve SC rises up to 50 and falls by 1983. Again it rises steadily till it reaches 60 by 1985. The line TL is the *trend line*. The sales have been obviously rising and falling. On this basis the demand is forecasted for 1986.

The trend projection method is very widely used for demand forecasting by business economists today because, it is simple and less costly.

4. Economic Indicators

The 'time series' contain two types of indicators to demand projection or forecasting *viz.*:

1. Statistical indicators, and
2. Economic Indicators.

Here, we are limiting our discussion to 'Economic Indicators' only. There are '*three*' types of series or variables in a time series.

They are:

1. Variables moving up or down faster than some other series;
2. Variables which move up or down slower than other series; and
3. Variables which move along with other series.

Further, only certain indicators have *forecasting value* to specific products only.

Below is given a list of indicators and their products for guidance.

"Indicators to Demand Forecasting"

Sl. No.	Field of output/Service	Indicator
1.	Building Materials like streel, cement, etc.	Construction Contracts.
2.	Consumer goods	Personal Income.
3.	Farm equipment	Agricultural income fertilizers, etc.
4.	Petroleum and automobile spare parts.	Registration of automobile at the R.T.O.
5.	Employment	Gross National Income.
6.	Liquors	Registration of liquor shops.

The above indicators in the table are all economic indicators. They are periodically published in the journals of the Central Statistical Organisation (C.S.O.)

Certain steps are involved in locating the 'indicator' for the required demand forecasting. They are:

1. Find out the relationship of the product and the indicator. Select that indicator which reflects the demand for the product.

2. Establish the relationship through the '*Least Squares Method*' and derive the 'Regression Equation' by assuming *Linear Relationship*.
3. After you have the Regression Equation ready, estimate the demand for the product.
4. Forget the past relationship between demand and the indicator in the past because new relationships may have appeared.

The task of finding out the right economic indicator is difficult but it is useful in short-term demand forecasting under the Statistical Method of Forecasting.

What is a Sound Forecasting Method?

Now that you know different forecasting methods you would be naturally wondering which one is the best or which one is the soundest. We have seen that some are simple but costly. Some others are less costly but less reliable and cumbersome. That brings us to the position of a child in front of a candy shop.

Broadly, there are 'four' qualities of a sound or good method of. forecasting demand. They are:

1. *Plausibility Test:* According to Joel Dean the 'plausibility test' will bring the best demand forecast. That is, the method adopted for forecasting demand should be suitable to the purpose and the executives should check and recheck whether there is any other 'plausibility' of a better method or better indicator.

2. *Simplicity Test:* The simplest and most easily interpretable method is the best. It should be easy to analyse and take less time; for instance, the diagramatic presentation of data for forecasting is one such. It gives a *birds-eye-view* at a glance. The method must avoid Mathematical and Econometric calculations (specially if the management is ignorant of such things).

3. *Economy Test:* 'Economy' refers to the 'Cost' of Demand Forecasting, the time consumed and the diversion of *personal* from *usual* work to the work of Demand Forecasting. Thus, 'Economy'should be the important qualifications of a sound method of forecasting demand.

4. *Accuracy of Data Test:* The data gathered should be accurate, reliable and should be of use to the nature of product and the period for which demand has to be forecasted. For instance, data collection relating to the short period does not help us to forecast demand for a long-period.

Thus, Demand Forecasting is an important and very significant aspect of Business Economics. Any haste at this step has a long-bearing influence on the prospects of the concern, business or firm. Any error at this stage is only a way to 'repent at leisure'. We may conclude this chapter with the following words:

The demand forecaster is like the driver of the motor car whose; steering wheel is at his command; he has to steer it safely and well. Any carelessness on his part will only swing the motor-car violently to the left land right. And the motor car is hardly on the road. He cannot afford to drive blind-folded with someone else's direction.

4

Elasticity of Demand

MEANING AND TYPES OF DEMAND ELASTICITY

Introduction

It was Dr. Marshall again who marshalled the cause of the doctrine of measurement of the magnitudes of impact of a change in price on the demand for the commodities of any sort.

Dear students, do you know that he has made the greatest contributions to Business Economics of the 19th century through his greatest work 'The Principles of Political Economy'? Do you know that Dr. Marshall was a mathematician and geometrician who became a great economist?

In short, Marshall really became the 'Marshall' of the concept of 'Elasticity of Demand' in Business Economics and lead the subject of commerce either willingly or unconsciously; the fact remains that Business Economics owes a lot to Dr. Marshall.

So much for the 'debt' of Business Economics to the 'Theory of Economic Analysis'; as its Masters propounded Economics as a systematic body of knowledge.

What is Elasticity of Demand?

In terms of 'Physics' Elasticity means the expansion and contraction of an object as force is applied and released.

Thus, Marshall as a student of science applied the concept of '*elasticity* to the Science of Economics and specially to the theory of demand forecasting elaborately.

According to Dr. Marshall, Elasticity of Demand, 'In a market (is great or small accordingly) as the amount demanded is great or small for a given commodity for a fall in price or a rise in its price as the case may be.'

Putting it in the words of Lipsey: "Elasticity of demand may be defined as the ratio of percentage change in demand to the percentage change in price" is called the 'Elasticity of Demand'.

Mrs. Jone Robinson defines it thus: "The elasticity of demand.... is the proportionate change of amount purchased in response to a small change in price, *divided* by the proportionate change in price".

All these statements are similar and can be put in the form of a formula *viz.*:

$$Ed = \frac{\text{\% change in demand}}{\text{\% change in price}}$$

or

$$Ed = \frac{\Delta D}{\Delta P}$$

Where:

A = percentage change,

D = Demand,

P = Price, and

Ed = Elasticity of Demand

In simplest terms, elasticity of demand means 'the way or degree by which demand will change when price of the product changes' (other things being constant).

'*The other things*' assumed as constant are:

(1) Income, (2) Price of other goods, and (3) The nature of the product of the firm.

Thus, we come to the question of the types of 'Elasticities of Demand'.

Broadly, there are three types of elasticities of demand which we are going to Consider presently.

Types of Elasticities of Demand

The classification of elasticities of demand is three in number *viz.*:

1. Income Elasticity (Yd);
2. Cross Elasticity (Cd); and
3. Price Elasticity (Pd).

Let us know what each one of these elasticites of demand means and how they are different from each other. Then, finally let us try to know how '*price elasticity*' has many '*degress*' of variation towards the end of this section.

1. *Income Elasticity of Demand* (*Yd*): We have already known the law of demand where the law states that if '*income*' (and many other things) remains constant demand rises if price falls and demand falls if price rises.

However, if price remains constant and income rises then the demand will rise or *vice versa*.

That is to say, other things remaining constant a rise in income will increase demand for a firm's product and a fall in consumers' income will reduce the demand for the firm's product.

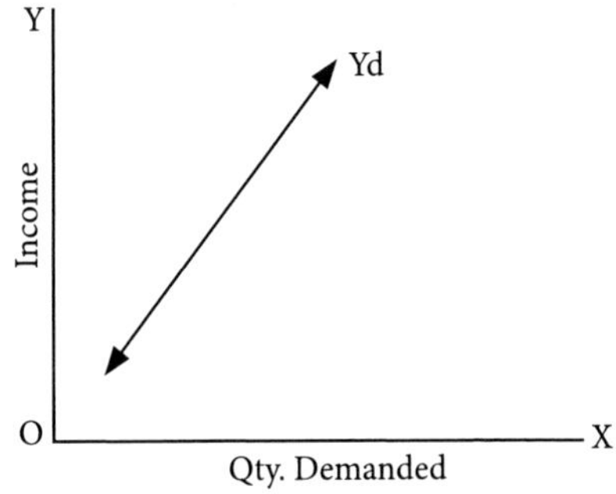

Fig. 4.1. Income Elasticity of Demand

Thus, the formula for Income Elasticity (Yd) is:

$$Yd = F \text{ (Rise or fall in Y)}$$

Where: Yd denotes income demand, F denotes the functional relationship between income and demand; and then we can say that:

$$YD = \frac{\Delta D}{\Delta Y}$$

Or

An increase in income (Y) leads to an increase in demand (D) provided that other determinants of demand remain equal. Thus, according to Marshall:

$$\text{Income Elasticity of Demand} = \frac{\text{\% Change in Demand}}{\text{\% Change in income}}$$

2. *Cross Elasticity of Demand* (*CD*): Certain goods are jointly demanded. For instance, you can't make coffee without milk or wear shoes without socks. Such goods are said to have Cross Elasticity of demand (Cd). They have "*joint demand*".

Then, if the price of coffee increases, the demand for both coffee powder and sugar will decrease or people will change over to tea which may be cheaper than coffee in which case the demand for sugar will remain constant but the demand for coffee will decrease.

Therefore:

$$\text{Ced.} = \frac{\text{Demand for Coffee}}{\text{Price of Tea}} \times \frac{\text{Demand for Tea}}{\text{Price of Tea}}$$

Where:

Ced. = Cross Elasticity of demand

Marshall's formula for cross Elasticity of demand is:

$$\text{Ced.} = \frac{\Delta \text{D of X}}{\Delta \text{P of Y}} \times \frac{\Delta \text{D of Y}}{\Delta \text{P of X}} \times \frac{\Delta \text{D of Z}}{\Delta \text{P of Y}}$$

Where:

Δ = % increase

D and P are demand and price

X, Y and Z are jointly demanded goods like coffee and sugar, tea and sugar and milk and so on.

3. *Price Elasticity of Demand* (*PED*): Price Elasticity is the most familiar form of elasticity of demand. The law of demand generally speaks of this kind of elasticity.

Price elasticity, according to Dr. Marshall, 'is the degree of responsiveness of demand to the changes in price' when *other things* are equal or constant.

Thus, the formula for Ped is:

$$\text{Ped} = \frac{\text{\% change in demand or}}{\text{\% change in price}}$$

$$\text{Ped} = \frac{\Delta \text{ d}}{\Delta \text{ p}}$$

Where:

Δ = Incremental increase

D = Demand, and

P = Price

TYPES OF PRICE ELASTICITY

It is already stated that demand generally responds to changes in price. This is in accordance with the law of demand. *Price Elasticity* is the ratio of percentage change in demand due to a percentage change in the price of the commodity.

This percentage change in demand in response to a percentage change in price is either *equal to unity* (*i.e.*, equal to one) or *greater than unity* or *less than unity* or it is infinite.

Thus, there are five types of price elasticity of demand *viz.*:

1. Perfectly elastic demand (Where Ed = infinity);
2. Perfectly inelastic demand (where Ed = zero);
3. Relatively elastic demand (where Ed > 1);
4. Relatively inelastic demand (where Ed < 1); and
5. Proportionately elastic demand (where Ed = 1).

The five types of price elasticities can be diagramatically represented as follows:

1. *Perfectly Elastic Demand:* When demand is perfectly elastic the demand will change infinitely. Thus, when a small change in price causes a very large change in demand then the demand is said to be perfectly elastic or *infinitesimal.* Then the demand curve will be horizontal to the OX axis (or the demand axis) as in Fig. 4.2.

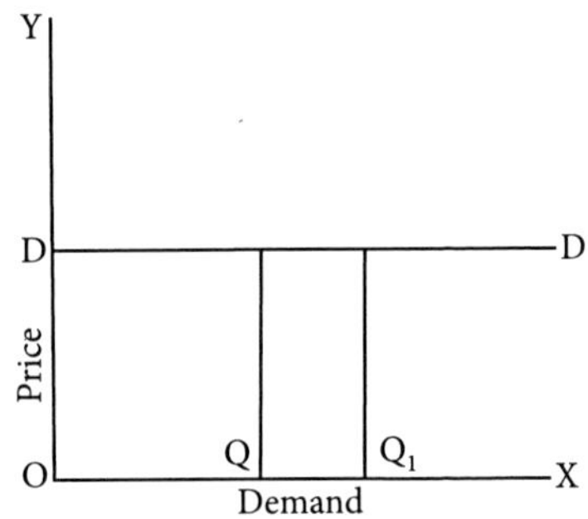

Fig. 4.2. Perfectly Elastic Demand

In Fig. 4.2 if price is OD demand will be OQ or OQ_1 and so on. If price falls slightly, the demand will increase to OX. On the contrary, if price rises slightly, demand falls to O or Zero.

2. *Perfectly Inelastic Demand*: Demand is said to be *perfectly inelastic* if any amount of change in price does not cause a change in demand. Then, Ed = O. An inelastic demand curve is always vertical to the OX axis as in Fig. 4.3.

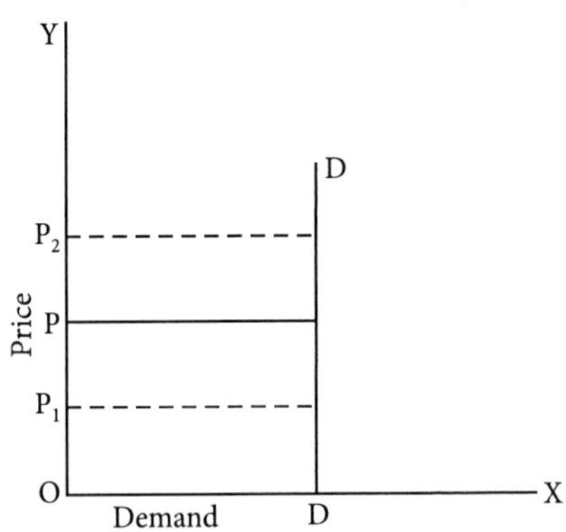

Fig. 4.3. Perfectly Inelastic Demand

In Fig. 4.3 DD is the vertical demand curve whose elasticity is zero. When price is OP demand will be OD. If price increases to OP_2 or falls to OP_1 the demand remains constant at OD.

3. *Relatively Elastic Demand:* The demand is *relatively elastic* when 1% change in price causes more than 1% change in demand. Thus, Ed > 1 (Elasticity is greater than one). In this case the rise or fall in the demand is more than proportionate to the change in price. This is represented in Fig. 4.4

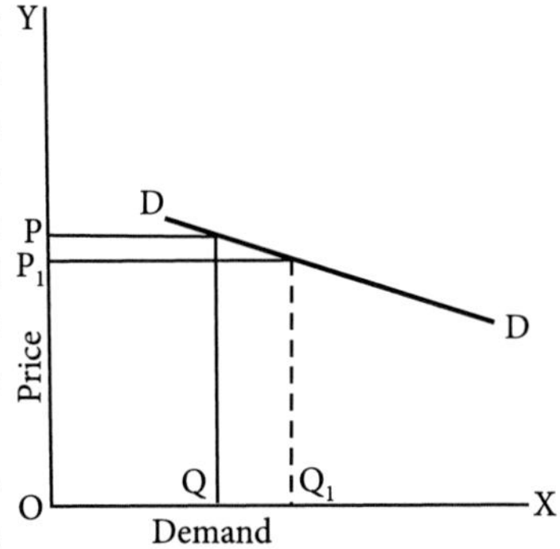

Fig. 4.4. Relatively Elastic Demand

In Fig. 4.4 the demand curve DD slopes very gradually. When price is OP the demand is OQ. When price falls from OP to OP_1 demand rises from OQ to OQ_1. Note that OQ_1 is greater than PP_1.

4. *Relatively Inelastic Demand:* When demand is *relatively inelastic* the change in demand will be less than the change in price. In other words, if price rises or falls by 1% the demand falls or rises by less than 1%. Then Ed < 1 (Elasticity is less than One) when Ed < 1 the demand curve slopes steeply like a ladder standing against the wall when it is not being open used as in Fig. 4.5.

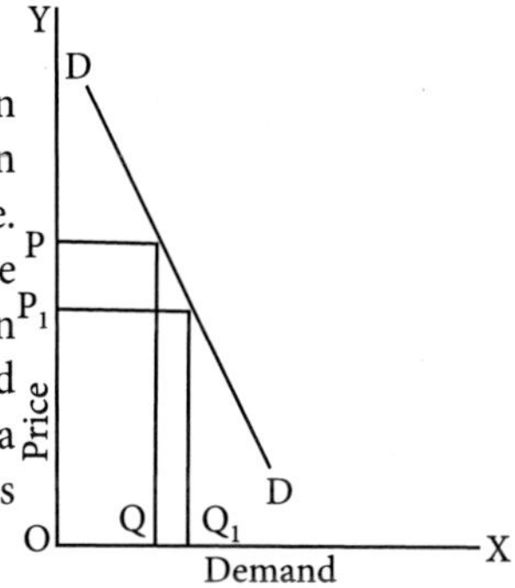

Fig. 4.5. Relatively Inelastic Demand

In Fig. 4.5 DD is the relatively inelastic demand curve. When price is OP the quantity demanded is OQ. If price rises to OP_1 the demand falls to OQ_1. Note that QQ_1 is less than PP_1. Hence, the change in demand is less than one or less than unity. Therefore the demand is '*relatively inelastic*'.

5. *Proportionately Elastic Demand:* When 1% change in price causes exactly 1% change in the demand then elasticity of demand is said to be equal to unity or *proportionate*. This is shown in Fig 4.6.

In Fig. 4.6 DD is the proportionately elastic demand curve. It slopes uniformally from left to right. When price rises from OP to OP_2 the demand falls from OQ to OQ_2. If price fells to OP_1 demand rises from OQ to OQ_1. Note that PP_2 is equal to QQ_2 and PP_1 is equal to QQ_1. Thus, the rise and fall of demand is proportionate or equal to fall and rise of price respectively.

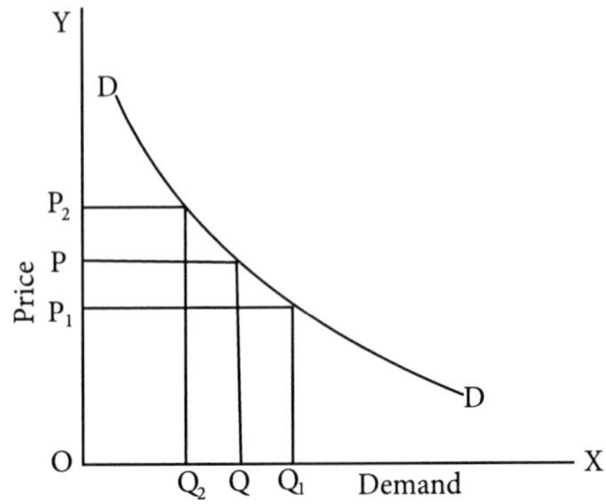

Fig. 4.6. Proportionately Elastic Demand

MEASUREMENT OF PRICE ELASTICITY

The concept of price elasticity of demand was invented by Dr. Marshall in 1890. It has a great practical and theoretical value in Economics in general, and in Business Economics in particular.

The determination or measurement of price elasticity is, therefore, important in decision-making about price and output of a firm.

There are '*three*' methods of measurement of price elasticity of demand, *viz.*:

1. Formula method or Coefficient of price;
2. Total outlay method; and
3. Point method or Geometric method.

1. *Formula Method:* The Formula method is also called as *Coefficient of price elasticity method* and *percentage method.* The formula for measuring the change in demand under this method is:

$$e = \left[\frac{\Delta Q}{Q} \times \frac{P}{\Delta P}\right]$$

Where:

ΔP = Incremental increase or decrease

Q = Original demand

P = Original price

ΔP = Incremental increase or decrease in price

(Δ means 'Delta')

We measure the ratio as under:

$$e = \left[\frac{\%\Delta Q}{\%\Delta p}\right]$$

2. *Total outlay method:* According to Dr. Marshall this is the most ideal method to measure the change in demand. In this method we compare the pattern of consumer's expenditure after a change in price with the expenditure (or outlay) before the change in price.

Thus:

1. When the total outlay remains constant if price changes, the Elasticity =1
2. If a rise in price causes a fall in total outlay or if a fall in price causes a rise in total outlay E > 1 (greater than one).

   That is, if price and demand vary in opposite directions the E > 1 or *relatively elastic.*
3. If price and outlay vary in the same direction the E < 1 (less than one) or the demand is *relatively inelastic.*

The total outlay method is illustrated in Table 1.

Table 1*

Total Outlay Method of Measurement Elasticity of Demand

Original or New Price	Price (₹)	Quantity (Units) (₹)	Total Outlay	Nature of Ed.
Original price	2	5	20	–
New price Original price	4 1	5 20	20 20	E = 1 (Prortionate) or unitary
New price Original price	4 1	4 24	16 24	E > 1 (Relatively Elastic)
New price Original price	4 1	6 16	24 16	E < 1 (Relatively inelastic)

From the above Table 1 we can say what is the *type* of price elasticity and also the *degree* of price elasticity.

Further, we can find out whether the consumer's outlay and seller's total revenue has increased or decreased. Thus, where:

1. E = 1 or is unitary — Total outlay and sellers revenue is constant.

* Modern Economic Analysis—D.M. Mithani, p. 158, Ch. 5.

2. E = 0 or Inelastic	Total outlay and seller's revenue either increases or decreases.
3. E > 1 or relatively Elasticity	(a) Increase in price causes decrease in outlay and seller's revenue; and (b) decrease in price causes increase in outlay and seller's revenue.
4. E < 1 or relatively inelastic	(a) Outlay decreases when price in inelastic creases and seller's revenue also decreases; (b) Outlay increases when price increases and seller's revenue also decreases.

Thus, the total outlay method is more direct than the other two methods. It reveals directly the *price effect* on total outlay of the consumer and the seller's revenue. It is an *indirect guide* to demand forecasting of a firm. It is a practical pointer to the price and output policy of a business firm or producer.

Defects: However, it has some limitations or defects. The chief limitations are:

1. It gives only the type of elasticity *i.e.,* whether it is unitary or relatively elastic and relatively inelastic.
2. It does not reveal the *quantitative change* in demand but gives only the value of elasticity as equal to 1, < 1 and > 1. Hence, the Formula Method is more useful than this method.
3. It is not exact or precise but vague.

3. Point Method or Geometric Method

This method was also Dr. Marshall's invention. In this method we take different '*points*' on the demand curve *i.e.,* on the lower and upper '*segments*' (or parts) to determine the elasticity of demand at various prices.

To do so, we take a '*linear*' or left to right downward sloping straight demand curve for an illustration (as in Fig. 4.7).

Let us take point D on the straight-demand curve BC in Fig. 4.7. The point D *bisects* the demand curve BC into two segments *viz.*, the upper segment BD and the lower segment CD.

Then, the ratio of CD to BD measures the point elasticity of demand or, symbolically:

$$\text{Point Ed} = \frac{L = CD}{U = BD}$$

Where:

L = Lower segment of BC (the Demand Curve); and

U = Upper segment of BC.

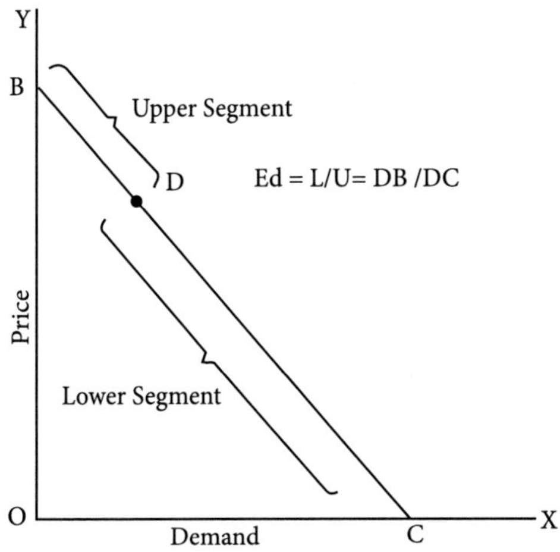

Fig. 4.7

If the diagram is drawn to scale and if BD < CD *i.e.* BD = 4 cms and CD = 6 cms then the elasticity by point method is:

In Fig. 4.8 the demand curve is *not linear* but a normal demand curve. It is DD in Fig. 4.8.

$$\frac{CD}{BD} = \frac{6}{4} = 1.5$$

In this case, to Find the elasticity by point method we have to choose a point on DD *i.e.*, point Q and then draw a '*tangent*' (a straight line touching the circumference of the circle at only one point—in this case touching the semi-circular demand curve DD) to the demand curve. It touches DD at Q.

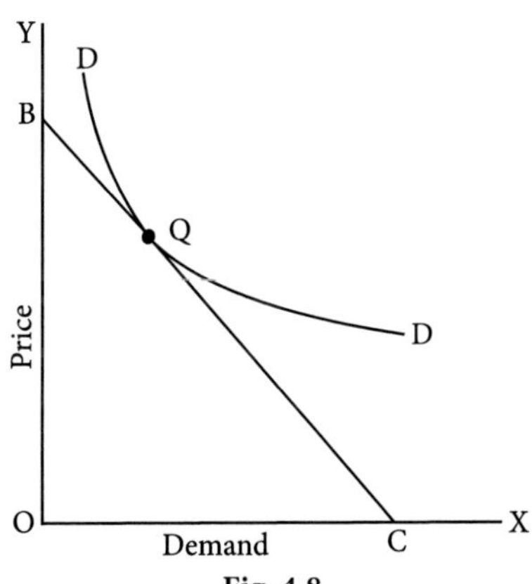

Fig. 4.8

The point elasticity at Q = $\frac{QC}{BQ}$

Let QC be 20 cms and BQ be 10 cms.

Then Ed by point method = 20/10 = 5

Ed is therefore 5 cm.

UTILITY OF ELASTICITY CONCEPT

The discovery of the concept of Elasticity of Demand by Dr. Marshall is a significant discovery. It has come to be widely used in the theory and practice of Economics; and in Business Economics in particular. It is therefore necessary to know what are the uses of this concept as students of Business Economcis. Here is a brief summary of its usefulness or utility:

1. *Guides price-output policy:* It is the final objective of every seller to attain *optimum sales*. Similarly it is the final goal of every producing firm to optimise its output. The *optimisation* of sales and output depends on the ability of the seller or the producer to arrive at a suitable price-output policy. This policy can be sound or accurate only if the firm knows or he knows the nature of elasticity of demand for the product. Hence, periodic assessment of elasticity of demand becomes indispensable to the seller and the producer. Maximisation of profit depends on their ability to price their products according to the nature of elasticity of demand.

2. *Monopolist and Elasticity*: It is well known that under monopoly '*price discrimination*' (*i.e.*, charging different prices to different consumers for a product) is possible. Here, the monopoly producer or seller calculates the degree of price elasticity in different '*sub-markets*' before fixing '*discriminatory prices*'.

3. *Aids Fiscal Policy*: The concept is fundamentally useful in '*fiscal policy*' (Income and Expenditure of the Government). The *Indirect Taxes* are levied on the basis of demand for goods. Thus, goods with inelastic demand can be highly taxed while goods with elastic demand should be moderately taxed. Otherwise, taxes will adversely affect consumption, production and investment.

4. *Guide to Tariff Policy:* Tariffs refer to *Import* and *Export* duties levied in foreign trade. The rate of tariffs is determined by the elasticity of demand for imports and exports of a country. Thus, exports which have inelastic demand can be taxed heavily while imports with elastic demand should be taxed moderately.

5. *Elasticity and Terms of Trade:* 'Terms of Trade' refer to the ratio of exchange of exports against imports. This ratio is determined on the basis of relative elasticites of imports and exports.

6. *Explains farmer's poverty in spite of plenty:* The demand for farm products is generally inelastic or relatively inelastic.

During the '*buffer crop*' (overproduction) the farmers face falling prices of their produce. The crop is already there but no *takers* for the surplus output). Thus, the farm prices fall further and further making them poorer ahd poorer though the production Is plenty. This is because of the inelastic demand or relatively inelastic demand is very clear. It explains the "*paradox of the farmer's poverty*".

It may be, therefore, concluded that the concept of Elasticity of Demand, as well as the elaborate way in which it has been classified, is a great contribution of Dr. Marshall for all times to come to Business Economics, Public Finance, International Trade and to any branch of Economics. The concept has truly made Marshall '*The Marshal*' of demand theory.

5

Production Function

(Or Isoquants and Iscorts)

The terms '*Isoquants*' and '*Isocosts*' are highly technical terms in Business Economics. They refer to the technique of selection of 'factor combination' or input-output decisions. They are applied in the *substitution* of units of one factor of production (say, capital) to another factor (say, labour) while trying to optimise output or '*Net Revenue*'.

'*Isoquants*' or '*Isoquant Curves*' are significant in the process of Marginal Rate of Substitution of one input to the other because the firm's final aim is to choose the least-cost combination of the inputs.

It is commonsense in Business Economics that as a producer I will choose that combination which is most economical or which gives me maximum profit. In technical terms we call this as the '*Equilibrium of the Firms*' (Be it the seller or producer).

The techniques used in Business Economics to determine the 'equilibrium' of a firm is called the '*Isoproduct Curves Analysis*'.

What is an Isoproduct Curve?

In simplest terms, an '*Isoproduct Curve*' is a curve indicating different combinations in a production function which yield uniform output. Such curves called 'Isoquants' or '*Equal Product Curves*'.

TABLE 1: Isoquant Factor Combination

Combination	Units of Labour	Units of Capital	Output
A	24	10	200 units
B	8	34	200 units
C	12	20	200 units

If a firm has a number of such possibilities it is '*indifferent*' among the different factor combinations.

Table 1 shows three combinations A, B and C which yield uniformally 200 units of output each.

In Table 1 though the quantum of labour and capital varies in A, B and C combinations the output of all combinations is the same or equal.

If you plot such equal production possibilities of combinations on a graph sheet you can get 'Isoquant Curves' as in Fig. 5.1.

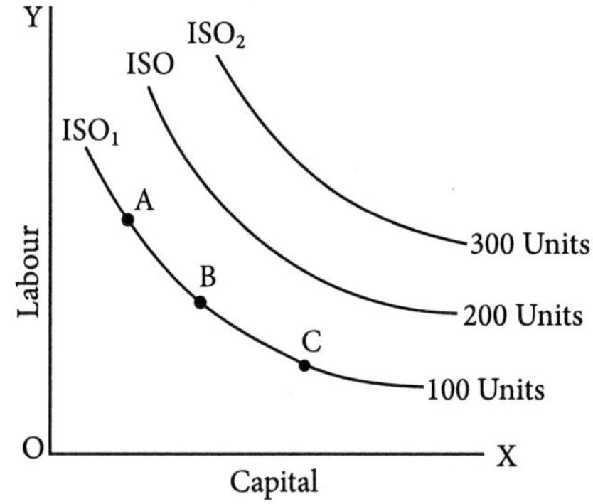

Fig. 5.1. Isoquant Curves

In Fig. 5.1 the curve ISO is the equal product curve with factor combinations A, B and C.

All of them yield 100 units of output. Though they have different quantity of labour and capital content.

The firm naturally chooses combination 'B' which has less of labour and capital than A and C. It is the '*Equilibrium point*' or the '*Optimum point*'.

Curves ISO_1 and ISO_2 show that the Isoquants may move up or down according to technology and managerial efficiency of the firm. 'The Isocost is nothing but equally costing combination sets. That is to say.

Isocost means a set of factor combinations of inputs whose cost of input is the same or equal. Then, the firm chooses that combination among them which yields relatively greater output.

PRODUCTION FUNCTION: MEANING

There is a close and expressed relationship between output and inputs. Production is the result of the combinations of various factors of production and services like banking, insurance and transport. All these transform *physical inputs* into *physical output*. Production function refers to the maximum rate of output that can be achieved with a given state of technology and management during a given period. Thus, production function is a brief "*Catalogue of output possibilities*".

Output is a *dependent variable* and input is an *independent variable.* Thus, the production function is an expression of output possibilities.

Algebraically this function can be stated thus:

$$q = f(a, b, c, d...n) \text{ where:}$$

q denotes rate of output and a, b, c, d, ...n are various inputs applied for the output of q.

G.J. Stigler defines production function thus:

> *"The production function is the name given to the relationship between the rates of input of productive services and the rate of output of product. It is the economist's summary of technological knowledge."*

TABLE 2: 'Production Function'

Input		Output per unit of time
Labour	**Capital**	
6	1	692 units
5	1	632 units
4	2	800 units
3	4	980 units
2	2	980 units

Further, a production function show the maximum output attainable by a specific set of inputs. It relates to the minimum of various inputs required to produce a certain quantity of output.

The production function differs from one firm to another. It depends on the technical know-how and managerial ability of the firm. Thus, it changes when these factors change.

Production function can be presented in a tabular form. (Table 2).

In the above table the combination of 6 units of labour and 1 unit of capital yield 692 units of output per unit of time. It can be observed in the table that the output per unit of time goes on changing as the input combination is varied. Thus, when 4 units of capital is combined with 3 units of labour the output per unit of time will be more, that is 980 units.

It should be remembered that in practice the producer will not change all inputs but only one or two of them.

It is possible that sometimes two different combinations give the same quantity of output. Then, which combination is to choose depends upon the cost of the inputs used in the two combinations. In Table 2, we find that 3L + 4C yields the same output per unit of time as 2 + 2C *i.e.* 980 units.

Thus, the production function is an *input-output relationship*. 'The least-cost' combination is the optimum combination. That is the best choice of the producer. It is the most *economical* and most *productive* choice.

However, the production function assumes the following conditions:

1. That it relates to a specific time unit.
2. That technical know-how is constant.
3. That any factor input is conveniently divisible.
4. That the technique of production is carefully chosen by the firm.

Managerial Uses of Production Function

We have seen that production function determines the *life and span* of the firm. It determines the cost of production and the net revenue (or profit) of a firm.

Therefore, the firm has to rely on the advice of the Business Economist (or the Manager) about the choice of the 'Best' combination. The Business Economist has to be conversant with the preparation of production functions. The decision-making is founded on the production functions prepared by the manager of the firm. The managerial efficiency depends on the production function.

The managerial uses of the concept can be classified as under:

1. It enables the firms to manage their affairs efficiently so that output is maximised from a given group of '*factor-combinations*'
2. It enables them to *minimise* the cost of production by choosing the comparatively Least-Cost combination and obtain the maximum output.

Thus, by varying the input combinations the firm can calculate their relative outputs. Then it can choose the '*optimum factor combination*'.

The firm can calculate the total cost of each combination and compare it with the value of its output and arrive at the best or *most profitable* combination.

The concept of production function warns the firm that it must keep varying that input whose '*Marginal Revenue*' (value added to output by the increase of a unit to total output) is more than its cost or price.

If all inputs are variable in a production function then long-term output decisions can be made.

Hence, production function is highly useful in managerial decision-making. It is the 'Rapidex' of a business firm or producer; its knowledge is immensely useful in the practice of Business Economics both in the short-run and in the long-run.

THE LAW OF VARIABLE PROPORTIONS

In the theory and practice of production the 'Law of Variable Proportions' has a unique place. It is fundamental to the practice of Business Economics. Dr. Marshall is the propounder of this concept.

The law has two stages *viz.*,

1. The Law of Increasing Returns or Decreasing Cost.
2. The Law of Decreasing Returns or Increasing Cost.

The law is related to the technological condition of the firm.

Output is a function of different inputs and their efficiency as well as cost. A firm keeps on changing the quantities of these inputs till it arrives at the 'optimum combination' of these inputs.

While varying the proportions of inputs the firm keeps the '*scarce*' and '*costly*' factor or input constant and varies the quantity of the relatively '*abundant*' and '*cheap*' factor or input. The former are called '*fixed factors*' while the latter are called '*variable factors*'.

The law of variable proportions deals with the *technicality of variation* of factor combinations.

Definitions of the Law: Dr. Marshall defined the law in the following words:

> *"An increase in the amount of a variable factor added to a fixed factor causes, in the end, a less than proportionate increase in the amount of product, given the technical conditions."*

F. Benham has this to say about the law:

> *"As the proportion of one factor in a combination of factors is increased, after a point, first the marginal and then the average product of the factor will diminish".*

Professor Stigler adds:

> *"As equal increments of one input are added, the inputs of other productive services being held constant, beyond a certain point, the resulting increments of the product will decrease, i.e., the marginal product will diminish."*

Thus, the law has universal opinion *i.e.,* output behaves according to the variation of factor or input combination.

Assumptions of the Law of Variable Proportions

Like all Economic Laws this law is based on some assumptions. They are:

1. Constancy of technology
2. It is possible to vary one input and keep the others constant.
3. Factors of production and other inputs are divisible.
4. The Marginal productivity of any factor is independent of the other inputs.
5. The different units of a substituted factor have equal efficiency or that they are homogeneous (or identical in all respects).

The Law in Operation

The law has '*three*' stages *viz.*:

1. Increasing output or decreasing cost;
2. Constant output or constant cost; and
3. Decreasing output or increasing cost.

The three stages of the law of variable proportions are graphically represented and explained in Fig. 5.2.

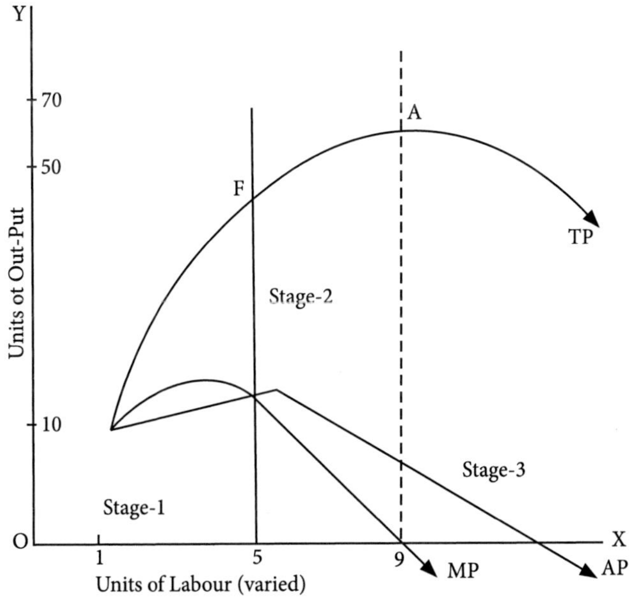

Fig. 5.2. Law of Variable Proportions

In Fig. 5.2 output is measured on OY axis and units of variable factor *i.e.* Labour is measured on OX axis. It is assumed that input of capital is constant.

As seen in the Fig. 5.2 TP is the *total product curve*, AP is the *average product curve* and MP is the *marginal product* curve. In stage 1, TP increases at an increasing rate up to the point F. At this point the marginal product MP is maximum at 5 units of Labour input. The point F is called the '*point of inflexion*'. After the point of *Inflexion* the total product curve TP becomes less steep *i.e.*, it increases at a slow rate. Thus, stage-1 is the stage of *Increasing Returns* or *decreasing cost*, where TP, MP and AP are increasing.

In stage 2 also, the total product is increasing but the increase is slow. At the point 'A' its slope is constant and the stage 2 ends then. At 'A' the Marginal and Average products are decreasing and the total output is maximum with 70 units. At the beginning of stage 3 the marginal output is *zero*. This is why the MP curve intersects the OX axis at the 9th unit of labour input. The stage is Diminishing Returns or Increasing Cost Stage.

In stage 3 TP curve begins to slope downwards. So, Total Output starts decreasing. This is known as the *Negative Returns Stage*.

The law of variable proportions shows that it is rational to stop before reaching stage 3. Moreover, the firm will not stop at the end of stage 2 because the *fixed factor* (capital) is not yet fully utilised. Further, the firm in this stage can still rise total product by adding to labour. Hence, it is, rational to choose the stage 2. It is the *Range of Rational Output*.

Why does the law of variable proprotions operate is an interesting question. According to Mrs. Joan Robinson, it operates because of *three* reasons:

1. Substitution of one input to another is not possible infinitely.
2. The proportions of fixed and variable inputs cannot be varied beyond a stage.
3. The inputs are scarce in the long run.

ECONOMIES OF SCALE

Economies of Scale of Economics or Large-scale Production refer to the method or steps that lead to economy of expenditure or cost reduction. Modern day production is on a large-scale and hence, large firms have come into existence.

Producing on a large-scale has a great cost advantage. The '*least cost advantage*' accrues due to two types of economies, *viz.*:

1. Internal Economies; and
2. External Economies.

Dr. Marshall, the exponent of this concept, has made a clear distinction between the two types of economies.

Distinction between Internal and External Economies

1. *Internal Economies:* The 'Internal Economies' are those measures which are available to a particular firm or single firm of the industry when it expands output to the optimum level. They enable the firm to increase its competitive strength in the maiket. For, its cost and price are low.

The *internal economies* arise due to:

1. The highly efficient organisational skill.
2. High grade managerial staff and talents.
3. Use of productive machinery.
4. Typical marketing strategy and technique of the firm.
5. Employment of firms, own capital for expansion.
6. Highly personalised relations with labour, etc.

2. *External Economies*: The external economies are the various measures that benefit all the firms in the industry uniformly when the '*Industry*' expands. Thus, these economies are commonly shared by the whole industry (an '*industry*' is a group of firms producing the same product). Generally, they arise out of the '*patronage of state*' *i.e.,* subsidies, bounties, tax concessions etc. and due to the '*collective efforts*' of all firms like formation of Trusts, Cartels, Joint Research Departments, etc.

Kinds of Internal Economies

The '*Internal Economies*' or economies of an individual firm are customarily classified into different types as:

1. Economies of Specialisation of Labour or Division of Labour.
2. Managerial Economies.
3. Technical Economies.
4. Financial Economies.
5. Marketing Economies.
6. Economies of Diversification.
7. Economies of buying.

It would now be useful to describe these internal economies briefly.

1. Economies of Specialisation: Specialisation of labour or *division of labour* is possible only when the firm is a large firm. Thus, a large firm can distribute the stages of production among different workers. For example, it can introduce the '*Conveyer Belt System*' in the Assembly Department so that one worker connects the wires, another fixes the screw, yet another mounts it on the plate and so on. This '*speeds up*' production and *efficiency of labour* will increase and productivity increases and costs of the firm will decrease.

2. Managerial Economies: These economics arise in a firm when it distributes responsibility of marketing, purchases, maintenance of Stock among separate but co-ordinating sections. Then '*over-head costs*' will be minimum. For instance, one engineer will suffice for a large firm just as much as for a small firm.

3. Technical Economies: The technical economies can be reaped by an individual firm through various ways. The chief of them are:

(*i*) Introduction of latest machinery which save time and enhance output.

(*ii*) Regular and cheap source of power so that '*shut-down*' is avoided.

(*iii*) Consistent efforts in research and development of new technology.

(*iv*) Utilisation of wastes and their conversion into useful byproducts (*e.g.* a large-scale textile mill can use Banian waste to produce cotton waste and supply it to the automobile shops).

4. Financial Economies: Large-scale firms have better credit facilities than small-scale firms. The financial institutions prefer to lend readily to the former on easy terms at short notice than to the latter. The former have an upper hand over the latter in this respect. Thus, a large joint-stock company of long existence can raise, additional capital through issue of additional shares but a small partnership firm cannot do so. Even '*Debentures*' can be issued or *Fixed Deposits* can be mobilised as they have a 'reputation'.

5. Marketing Economies: The 'Marketing Economies' are said to be the most significant of internal economies. They refer to cost-reduction arising out of large-scale selling of the finished product of the firm (in a wide sense, it includes economies of buying raw-materials).

These economies arise when the firm undertakes the following measures:

1. Market survey.
2. Effective and wide publicity of the product

3. Economical and cheap transport network of its own or '*standing freight contracts*' of long duration with transport firms on profitable
4. Division of markets into convenient sub-markets to separate them by distance etc., etc.

6. Economies of Diversification: This is also known as '*Risk-bearing Economies*'. A large firm can diversify or spread its '*risk of losses*' where as a small-scale firm cannot do so due to *financial constraints* or limitations. A large firm can '*stock-up*' raw-material, blocade the other firms, store its output when market conditions are bad and manipulate its stocks. In short, a large firm can both shock the rest of the (small firms) weaker part of the industry and absorb any other shocks or losses. It is, at once, and in substance, gifted with the '*Cussion-Effect*'— going down but only to come up.

7. Economies of Buying: A large firm can be compared to a *'Shark' in Business Economics. It swallows the largest chunk of raw-material and other inputs without fear and fret with the greatest ease and puts the weaker ones (small firms) in a tight Jacket.*

That is, it can 'buy up' the best inputs at the lowest cost on a large scale in quantities larger than required and block the entry of new firms or '*eliminate*' small existing firms. This, they achieve by entering into '*Hedging contracts*' with the suppliers of raw-materials. A Hedging Contract between buyers of raw-materials and suppliers of raw-materials binds both of them to stick to a pre-agreed price of the raw-material and binds both the parties as far as the supply and buying is concerned.

6

Cost of Production and Cost Concepts

The concept of cost of production is fundamental to Business Economics. So long as profit is the final goal of the business firms that long will the cost aspect remain the main concern of business firms. In brief, the manager of a business firm aims his decisions at '*Cost-profit balancing*'.

'Cost' can be defined as the sum of all money-expenses incurred by a firm in order to produce a commodity. Thus, it includes all expenses from the time the raw-material is bought till the finished product reaches the wholesaler.

Business decisions require the choice of right type of cost concept. The firm has to depend on the selection of right type of cost while determining its price and output policy. Thus, according to Joel Dean, "*...the useful decision-making concepts of costs aims at projecting what will happen under alternative course of action." Further he has classified cost concepts into the different types.* Dr. Marshall, on the other hand, has made a broad distinction between two types of costs *viz.*: (1) *Money Cost* and (2) *Real Cost.*

Money Cost and Real Cost

'*Money Cost*' is defined as the sum total of money spent to produce a given product. Thus, money cost includes wages, interest, rent, price of raw-materials, power and water cost, etc. The money cost is calculated in exact terms.

'*Real Cost*' is a subjective and vague term. It is not quantifiable or measurable. According to Dr. Marshall, real cost is in the form of sacrifice of leisure made by labour in order to work, pain and exertion of the body while working, monotony or boredom of doing the same work day-after-day, the agony of being separated from the family and so on.

Marshall introduced the concept of *real cost* into the 'Theory of Value' just to show how the wages of labour must be fixed by indirectly taking into account the nature of the job and risk involved in performing a job. Thus, the wages of a mine-worker (miner) are higher than that of a factory worker because the risk and physical exertion is more than that of the factory worker.

Further Classification of Money Cost

In the *theory of value and output determination* costs have to be clearly distinguished. This is necessary for price and output determination under different market conditions such as perfect competition, monopoly and monopolistic competition. It has managerial significance.

Broadly speaking money cost is of two types:

(1) *Fixed Cost*; and (2) *Variable Cost.*

However, it should be remembered that this distribution is not categorical in the *long-run*. According to Prof. Joel, "*Fixed and variable costs are not two distinct categories; rather, they are the two ends of a continuum.*" In other words, all costs become variable in the long-run; the distinction is necessary only to estimate their impact on total cost and total revenue of a business firm.

1. Fixed Cost: The cost of inputs that can be used over and again over a long period of time to produce more than one 'batch of goods or series' such as, plant and machinery, land and factory buildings, trucks and wagons and permanent staff may be called *Fixed Costs.*

'*Fixed Costs*' have a technical aspect and that is, they are *indivisible* and *indispensable* or inescapable irrespective of the *scale of production i.e.,* whether small or large-scale production.

For instance, you cannot *rent-out* a part of the factory building just because you have reduced production due to a fall in demand or sell away some of the machinery. May be, the fall in demand is seasonal or temporary (as in the case of cool drinks). If you does so, you have to sell away at a *depreciated value* and purchase again at *current prices* which are naturally high.

In short, '*fixed costs*' have to be incurred even if the plant or firm has to be shut-down temporarily or by a '*Standstill Firm*'. One more way of defining fixed costs is that *they do not rise or fall when output is increased or decreased.*

Therefore, fixed costs are variously named such as: constant costs, over-head expenses and supplementary costs in Business Economics. Therefore, it is well for a student of Business Economics to be equipped with the terminology of fixed costs and other costs in general.

Average Fixed Cost (AFC) and Total Fixed Cost (TFC)

Basically, a 'fixed cost' curve (FC) is horizontal to the OX axis or output axis as shown in Fig. 6.1. The reason is already explained in the preceding section of this chapter.

In Fig. 6.1 FC is the fixed cost curve. At OQ output the fixed cost is OC. If the firm increases output to OQ_1 the fixed cost remains OC or if the output is reduced fixed cost will remain at OC.

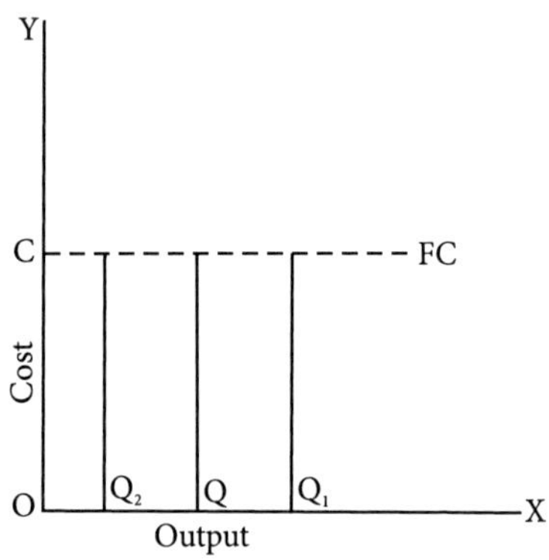

Fig. 6.1. Fixed Cost Curve

'Average Fixed Cost' is the minimum of FC incurred for producing each unit out of total output. That is, Average Fixed Cost (AFC) is obtained by dividing Total Fixed Cost from total output.

$$\text{Thus: } = \frac{TFC}{Tq}$$

Where: TFC = Total Fixed Cost, Tq = Total output and
AFC = Average Fixed Cost

The AFC curve slopes from left to right downwards resembling a demand curve as in Fig. 6.2

Similarly, Total Fixed Cost is the sum total of fixed costs incurred to produce a given quantity of output.

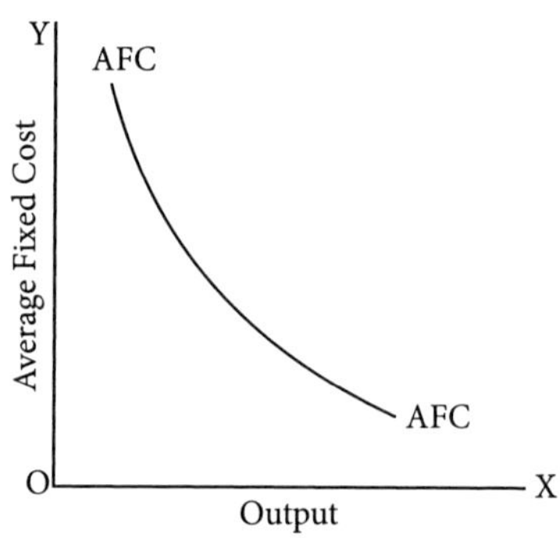

Fig. 6.2

2. Variable Cost (VC)

Such of the costs that increase or decrease with an increase or decrease in output are known as variable costs (VC). These include expenses on *'Single-use inputs'* such as raw-materials like raw-cotton, power, water, wages and so on. VC is also known as '*Prime costs*' and '*Direct costs*'.

Variable cost is further classified as *Total Variable Cost* (TVC) and *Average Variable Cost* (AVC).

The per unit variable cost is called AVC. It is found out by dividing TVC from the total quantity of output. Thus:

$$AVC = \frac{TVC}{Tq} \quad \text{or} \quad \frac{100}{10} = 10$$

Where:

TVC denotes total variable cost and Tq denotes total output.

The AVC curve is generally U-spaped. The AVC decreases as output increases upto the optimum capacity of the firm. This is because of increasing returns or decreasing total cost. After the optimum capacity is reached the AVC will begin to rise due to decreasing returns or increasing cost. Thus, the AVC curve will be U-shaped while the TVC curve rises from left to right as shown in Figs. 6.3 and 6.4.

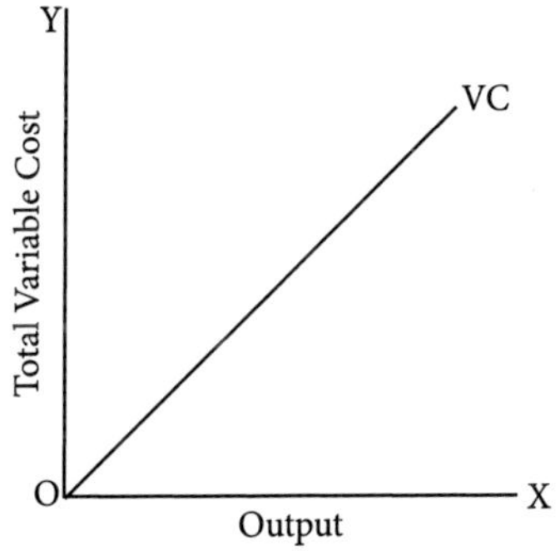

Fig. 6.3

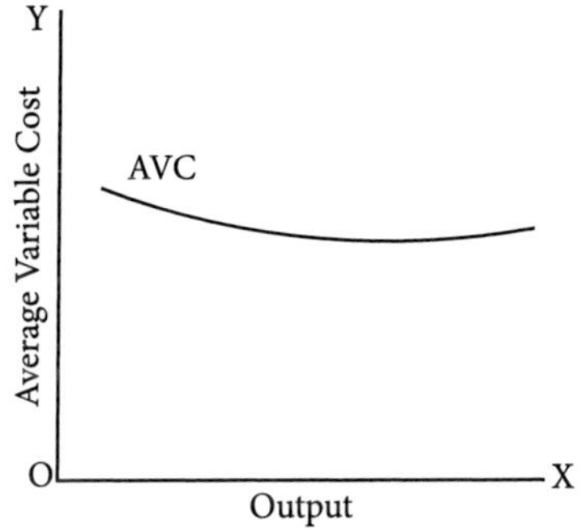

Fig. 6.4

Total variable cost curve is derived by joining the various step-points of variable cost at different quantities of output as in Fig. 6.5.

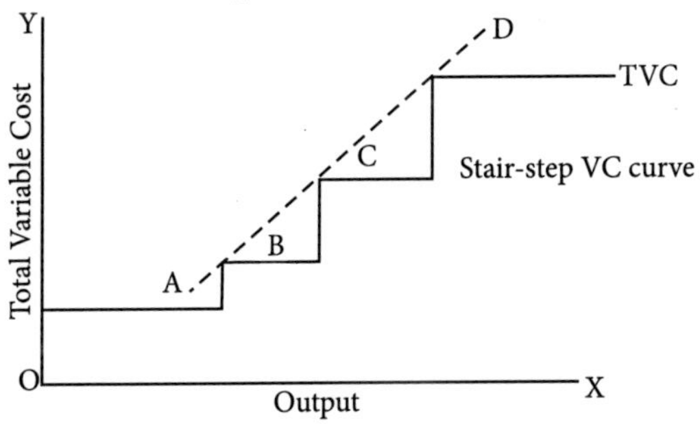

Fig. 6.5

3. Total Cost and Average Cost (TC and AC)

Total Cost (TC) of production may be defined as the sum total of money spent for purchasing the various inputs of production. It is, thus, the total of payments made by a firm to the factors of production as rent, wages and interest plus all other charges for the firms' own inputs while producing a given quantum of output.

In economic terminology TC includes '*managerial wages*' (*i.e.*, the salary that the firm would have had to pay if it had engaged a paid superviser but has been done by the proprietor himself).

A total cost curve is generally U-shaped like in the case of the AVC curve in Fig. 6.4.

'*Average Cost*' (AC) may be described as the cost incurred per unit of output. On the whole, AC is nothing but the sum of AFC and AVC. In other words, total average cost is obtained by dividing TC from the total output. Thus:

$$\text{TAC} = \frac{\text{Total Cost}}{\text{Total Output}} = \frac{\text{TC}}{q}$$

Where:

TAC = Total average cost, TC is total cost and q is the quantity of total output.

It is already said that '*total cost*' is the sum of VC and FC. It is also known that Average cost (either fixed or variable cost) is the per unit cost of production.

The nature and shape of these curves can be graphed as in Fig. 6.6. ATC can be formulised also as:

$$\text{ATC} = \text{TVC} + \text{TFC}$$

or

$$\text{ATC} = \frac{\text{TVC} + \text{TFC}}{q + q_1} \text{ or } \frac{\text{TVC} + \text{TFC}}{q + q_1}$$

Where:

ATC = Average Total Cost

TVC = Total Variable Cost

TFC = Total Fixed Cost

q = output (initial)

q_1 = output (incremental or increased output)

This can be known from Fig. 6.6

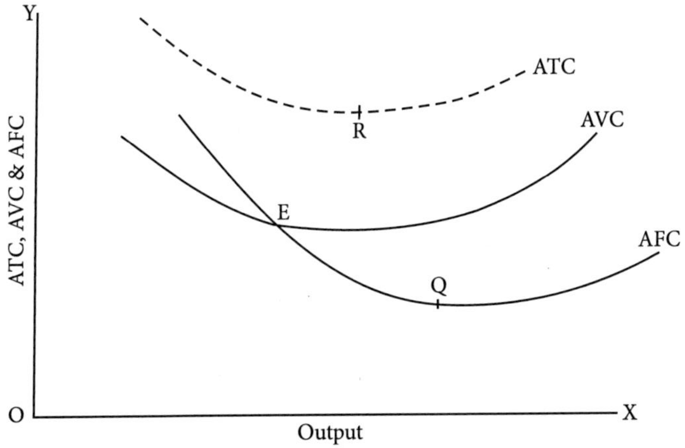

Fig. 6.6

It is evident from Fig. 6.6 that ATC curve behaves in accordance with AVC and AFC curves. AVC and AFC keep falling initially (so, they slope from left to right.) The AVC curve falls up to E but AFC falls only till Q.

If AVC rises AFC will not rise immediately. This is simple mathematics. For, if output is increased, AVC will increase faster than the decrease in AFC. Hence, AVC curve will begin to rise after the point E.

The ATC curve also falls first and begins to rise after the point R. Hence, all the three curves have the U-shape.

4. Marginal Cost (MC)

The term '*Marginal*' is Dr. Marshall's brain-child. 'Marginal' means *additional.*

Thus, '*Marginal Cost*' means the net addition made to total cost because of producing some more units.

Thus, if the firm produces 100 units the total cost is (say) ₹ 10,000. If it increases the output to 109 the total cost increases to (say) ₹ 10,100.

Then:

$$MC = ₹\ 10{,}100 - ₹\ 10{,}000 = ₹\ 100$$

In other words, when the firm increases output from 100 units to 109 units it incurs a Marginal Cost of ₹ 100. So much for the theory of MC.

Let us know tabulate the concept of Marginal cost as in Table 1.

TABLE 1: Marginal Cost

Output (q) (Units)	**Total Cost (TC) (in ₹)**	**Marginal Cost (MC) (in ₹)**
0	10,000 (FC)	Nil
1	10,500	500
2	11,000	500
3	12,000	1000
4	14,000	2000
5	16,100	2,100
6	19,000	2,900

From Table 1 it can be said that the firm incurs a fixed cost (FC) of ₹ 10,000 even if it produces *zero* units. This is because that the firm has to pay the rent for the building, wages to workers, interest on capital borrowed; etc. They are permanent commitments of the firm.

But, as output increases, it faces an increase in MC from ₹ 10,000 up to ₹ 19,000.

The Marginal Cost Curve is always U-shaped and steeper in slope than the Average Cost curve as seen in Fig. 6.7.

In Fig. 6.7 the curve MC is the marginal cost curve. It slopes like the alphabet 'U'. The slope of MC curve indicates that the firm is undergoing *three* stages of Marginal Cost and they are:

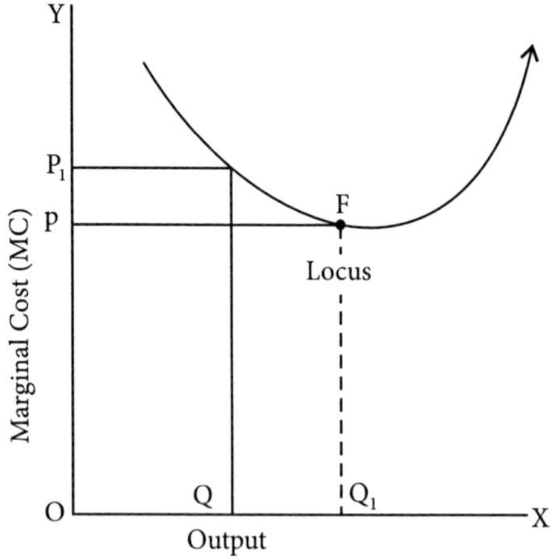

Fig. 6.7. Marginal Cost Curve

Stage-I: Where the firm can expand its output with the benefit of decreasing MC up to the point of '*Locus*' (what is 'locus' is explained under the IC analysis in Chapter II). In Fig. 6.7 the point of locus of MC Curve is F. At this point the marginal cost is at its lowest level.

Stage-II: This stage is very short. It is the point F on the MC Curve. It is the point (of constant Marginal cost. It is the point) at which the firm has attained the optimum output (*i.e.,* the firm has fully utilised its inputs).

Stage-III: Any further expansion of output requires further investment beyond OQ_1 output. Hence, MC begins to rise after the point F.

DETERMINANTS OF COSTS OF PRODUCTION

It is commonsense that cost of production determines the price. It is no easy task to say what determines the cost of production. The query brings us to the question of the various factors that influence the costs of production known as the '*cost Factors*' or '*cost-put relationship*'.

Basically, the factors that influence cost of production are:

1. Utilisation of plant capacity
2. Input markets and their price conditions
3. Technological factors
4. Managerial efficiency
5. Efficiency of capital
6. Size of Capital
7. Market organisation
8. Efficiency of Labour.

The establishment and management of 'Business' is not an easy task. It needs financial planning, budgeting and input-output management.

To be able to do so, the Business economist of a firm must equip himself with the various '*cost factors*'.

A short analysis of the determinants of costs of production is therefore necessary in this context.

1. Plant Capacity: The firm has to optimise its plant capacity. Otherwise it incurs unnecessary fixed costs. This leads to a rise in cost of production.

2. Cost of Inputs: The cost of inputs has a direct influence on the cost of output. A large firm can buy the inputs on a large-scale with large-scale economics. The quality of the raw-material and the steadiness of its supply has also a bearing on the cost of production. The greater the percentage of wastage in the raw-material the higher is the cost of production.

3. Technological Factors: The type of technology adopted in production has a great influence on the cost of production. Generally labour-saving or capital incensive technology quickens production and reduces cost. Out-dated technology increases costs and reduces profits.

4. Managerial Efficiency: The efficiency of the managerial staff increases the degree of co-ordination and quickens output. The utilisation of plant capacity and the efficiency of workers depends on the example set by the managers. The manager must be a good *task-master*, a friend, philosopher and a good guide to his employees. All these qualities reduce the cost of production.

5. Efficiency of Capital: It is not enough if the manager is a taskmaster; the machinery must also be highly productive. Frequent breakdown of machinery causes waste of labour and increases the cost of production. Thus, the choice of machinery is of great consequence.

6. Size of capital: The *per-capita* availability of capital also influences cost of production. Given enough capital the labour produces more over a shorter time. Contrarily, the poorer the capital the greater will be the cost of production.

7. Market Organisation: The organisation of markets is as important as efficient production. If the markets are well knit the product can be sold quickly and effectively. Then, the *marketing costs* will be low and the net revenue of the firm will be high. The competitive strength of a business firm is determined by its selling techniques. Effective advertisements, cheap transport etc. are included under this factor.

8. Efficiency of Labour: Labour is the ultimate determinant of cost of production. The labour selected must be efficient, well trained and skilled and healthy. Only such labour can turn out standard goods at lower cost. The firm must take care that square pegs are not put in round holes'.

These are only a few determinants of cost of production. There are many more which have an indirect influence on the cost of production like, quickness pf transport of the final product, taxes, state patronage in the form of *subsidies*, *bounties* etc. A business economist equipped with these determinants of cost is of high value to his firm. He can give '*Cost advice*' of the right type only if he is knowledgeable.

OPPORTUNITY COST

There are conceptual differences (or terminological variations) in cost concepts in Business Economics. One such concept is the concept of '*opportunity cost*'.

In the words of Joel Dean:

> "*Cost concepts differ because of differences in viewpoint. Financial records aim at describing 'what was', whereas the useful decision-making concepts of cost aim at projecting 'what will happen' under alternative course of action.*"*

Illustrating the opportunity cost Dr. S. Shankaran notes:

> "*Suppose a firm has acquired a resource by paying ₹ 10,000 .... Hence, ₹ 10,000 is the cost described by the accountant. Suppose, at present the cost of that resource has risen to ₹ 14,000. Now the economist tells the management that the cost of the resource is ₹ 14,000; but the accountant tells that the cost is ₹ 10,000. The economist argues that if the firm sells this resource, it would receive ₹ 14,000 and if it retains the resource, it would have to forego ₹ 4,000. Therefore, the cost of the resource,.... is ₹ 14,000 and this amount is the opportunity cost*".**

The concept of '*opportunity cost*' is a modern concept. It is the *off-shoot* of Dr. Marshall's Real Cost. Modern economists express '*real cost*' in terms of Opportunity Cost or '*Alternative Cost*'.

According to Prof. Benham:

> "*The opportunity cost of anything is the next best alternative that could be produced instead by the same factors.... costing the same amount of money.*"

A simple example of opportunity cost can be given for easier understanding.

Suppose a weak child has bought a *peach* and a *chocolate* and is walking slowly on the path-way. A wicked strong boy chases the weak child to snatch away the peach and the chocolate. The weak child drops the peach on the path-way and runs away so that it could at least have the chocolate to eat.

---

* Joel Dean, 'Managerial Economics', V. Edn., p. 258.

** Dr. S. Shankaran, 'Managerial Economics'. II Edn., Ch. 9, p. 154.

Thus, the cost of the chocolate is: the peach dropped away by the weak child which we may call 'Opportunity Cost'.

Similarly, the cost of land is the value of wheat that is sacrificed for growing oats, that of capital employed to produce bicycles instead of scooters and so on.

Significance of the concept

The concept of opportunity cost is highly significant in the field of Business Economics. It exercises the Business Economist's mind on matters of cost factor.

It explains the phenomena of price and input cost.

It is of greatest value to the *theory of consumption* and *public expenditure.*

The concept tells us that goods have '*value*' or price because the factors of production used in producing them have costed the *non-production* of some other goods.

Criticisms of the Concept: The concept of opportunity cost has been a subject of criticism. The chief of them are briefly listed here.

1. It has no significance in case of *fixed factor services* like that of a doctor.
2. It is of no consequence if a factor of production like *labour* is unwilling to move to another occupation. (Because of distance, weather and separation from family and friends.)
3. *Individual costs* and *Social Costs* of sacrifice cannot be estimated.
4. Opportunity cost is not measurable in exact terms.
5. It is purely imaginary as in the case of a machine already installed to produce *telephones* which cannot have an *alternative* use.
6. The concept is based on the assumption of *alternative uses* of resources under a Capitalist system, the purest form of which is an *utopia* (or imaginary).

Yet, the concept is fundamental to Business Economics. It is fundamental since every producer psychologically aims at the best use of his resources and at maximisation of revenue or net profit.

COST-OUTPUT RELATIONSHIP
(*Long and short-period Relationships*)

It was already stated in this chapter that the behaviour of cost of production is closely related to the scale of production (large & small scale). It is also said already that there can be no distinction between Fixed Costs (FC) and Variable Costs (VC) in the long-run because all factors are variable in the long period.

However, it is a fact that there exists a close relationship between cost of production and quantity of output. This is our present concern in this section.

Dr. Marshall was the first economist to introduce the concept of '*time element*' into the theory of value and distribution. Dr. Marshall classified the '*Product Markets*' on the basis of time allowed for the adjustment of supply to demand under different time periods (such as *Very short period, Short period, Long period and Very Long or Secular Period markets*).

Relationship of Cost to Output (Short Period)

As noted earlier, Dr. Marshall distinguished among different kinds of markets and analysed cost conditions accordingly.

The *short-period* is a period during which only the *variable factors* of production can be increased or decreased and *fixed factors* cannot be. During the short-period the firm can increase the output or supply by making fuller use of its existing plant and machinery and by working in extra shifts.

In this period, an increase in total output increases the Marginal Cost (MC). Thus, in the short period costs are distinguished as Fixed Cost (FC) and Variable Cost (VC). FC is independent of volume of output. They have to be incurred even at lesser or zero output. Total Variable Cost (TVC) rises and falls with a rise and fall of output. Thus, short-run Total Cost is the total of FC and VC. Short-run cost-output relationship is shown by the slope of the AC curve. It is the sum of AFC and AVC curves. As the output rises, AVC falls and increases as output increases. As soon as the output reaches optimum level AVC will begin to rise sharply as in Fig. 6.8.

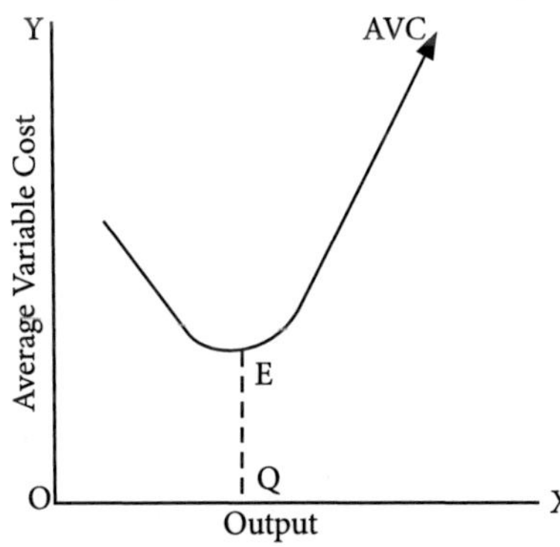

Fig. 6.8. Cost-Output relationship in the short period

In Fig. 6.8 AVC is the Average Variable Cost curve. It rises from left to right upwards. Upto E it is falling and beyond E it is rising because total output is maximum at OQ in the short-run.

The extent of the rise and fall of AC depends on the ratio of FC to total cost. In other words, TC = FC + VC in the short-period market. The cost-output relationship in the short period is represented in Fig. 6.8.

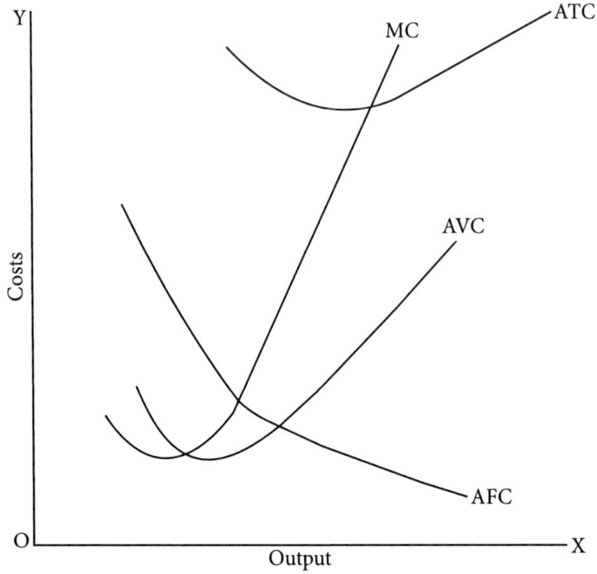

Fig. 6.9

In Fig. 6.9 the AC curve is U-shaped in the short-run. The rise as well as fall is steep as can be seen. The cost-output relationship in the short period can be summarised thus:

1. AVC falls in the initial stages and then rises sharply along with ATC.
2. AFC decreases as output increases upto a stage
3. AVC incrases even before ATC begins to increase
4. The cost is least at Q (Fig. 6.9) when MC curve intersects ATC curve.
5. The Marginal Cost Curve intersects AVC and ATC curves at their lowest level.

Cost-Output Relationship (Long-Period)

The long-run or long-period is a sufficiently long period. It is such that the firm can vary all factors of production. Thus, there is no distinction between FC and VC in the long period.

The output can be increased or decreased as per demand conditions. If the demand has increased it can add another building to the factory, install more machinery and increase the staff also. It can reduce all these, if demand falls, and reduce output and costs.

All factors are divisible in the long-period. The *divisibility* leads to economy in the use of factors of production. The scale of output can be changed easily. Thus, the cost curves in the long run are drawn on the basis of the *laws of returns* (In the short-run they are drawn on the basis of the law of variable proportions.)

The long-period is a collection of a number of short-periods. The long run cost is the minimum cost incurred for any given level of output.

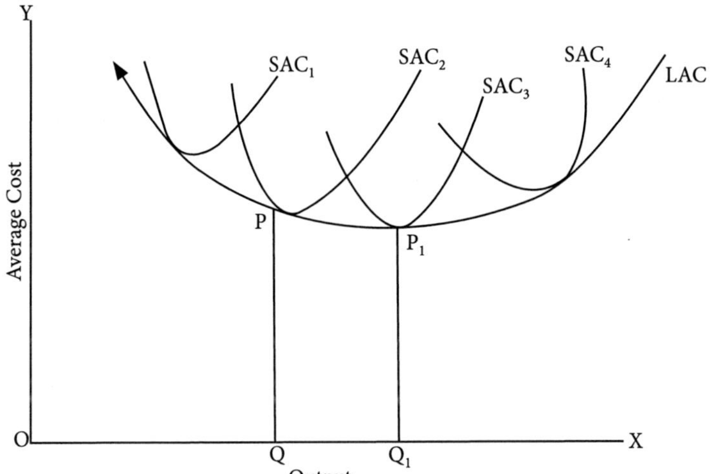

Fig. 6.10. Cost-Output relationship (Long Period)

The Long-run Average Cost (LAC) is obtained by dividing Long-run Total Cost (LTC) from total output. It represents the short-run average costs at different quantities of output (also called *plant curves*) as shown in Fig. 6.10.

In Fig. 6.10 LAC is the Least Average Cost of the firm in the long run. It is the sum of Short-run Average Cost Curves SAC_1, SAC_2, SAC_3 and SAC_4. The LAC curve is therefore a flat U-shaped curve. It shows that in the long run AC rises and falls slowly.

7

Supply

Meaning of supply: The term 'supply' is a highly technical term in Economic Theory and in Business Economies it has a significant meaning; such as '*stock*'. However, *supply* and *stock* are two different entities in our terminology.

To a business economist 'stock' is what the seller is able to hold in his *godown* or *store-room*. The entire quantity of the stock may not be supplied if the price is not profitable. For instance, a wholesaler has 10,000 bags of sugar in his '*stock*' but he knows that the price of sugar is not remunerative. He would like to wait till the price of sugar rises to a profitable level. Hence, he '*supplies*' only 1,000 bags of sugar at the '*market price*'.

Thus, his '*supply*' is 1,000 bags of sugar while his '*stock*' is 10,000 bags of sugar. Hence, *stock* may be more than *supply*, but supply cannot be more than stock.

On the other hand, there is unanimity of opinion among economists that '*supply*' *is the actual quantity offered for sale in a given market at a given price over a given period of time* by wholesalers and retailers or the producer himself.

Harvey gives the following simple definitions of supply:

Supply is defined as "*How much of a good will be offered for sale at a given time*".*

Harvey's definition is not complete, as it does not speak of the market and price. The higher the price the greater will be the supply and wider the market larger will be the total supply.

On the other hand, McConnel offers a more exhaustive definition of supply when he says that, "*Supply may be defined as a schedule which*

* Harvey: 'Intermediate Economies', p. 18

*shows the various amounts of a product which a producer is willing to and able to produce and make available for sale in the market at each specific price in a set of possible prices during some given period."**

THE LAW OF SUPPLY

The law of supply is known as the '*Second Law of Markets*'. It is the twin brother of the law of demand. The law of supply as stated by Dr. Marshall thus: "*Other things being constant, more is offered for sale at higher prices than at lower prices.*"

The law of supply is a statement of tendency of supply to changes in price under a set of assumptions.

The law establishes a "direct relationship" between price and supply per unit of time. It states that the quantity of supply is a function of price. The supply rises or falls as price rises or falls respectively.

The law of supply can be represented in a tabular form for easy understanding as in Table 1.

TABLE 1: Law of Supply

Price (in ₹) per unit	Quantity supplied (in units)
10	1000
15	1500
25	2500
30	35000
50	50,000

In Table 1 as you go in the *descending order* the supply rises as price rises. In the ascending order it falls as the price falls.

The schedule of supply can be plotted on a Graph sheet which gives us the supply curve. It slopes from right to left downwards as in Fig. 7.1.

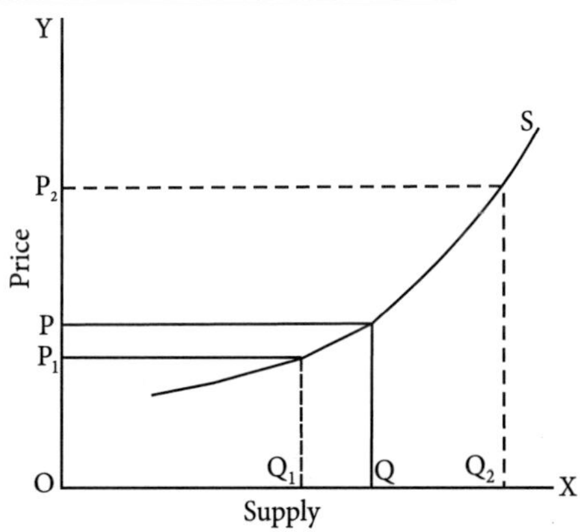

Fig. 7.1. Supply Curve

The Supply Curve SS has a negative slope. It

* McConnel: 'Economic Principles, Problems and Policies', p. 55.

expresses the direct relationship between price and supply. Thus, when price rises from OP to OP_2 supply increases from OQ to OQ_2 along the supply curve. Conversely, if price falls to OP_1 the margin of profit declines. Hence, less is offered for sale *i.e.*, OQ_1.

Exceptions to the Law: The law of supply is a hypothetical statement of tendency. It is based on the assumption that *'other things remain constant'*. The basic assumptions of the law are:

1. There are no expectations on the part of suppliers.
2. It assumes that services do not come under it.
3. It is also assumed that tastes, fashions, weather, etc. remain constant.
4. It assumes that factor supply is highly elestic.
5. It assumes constant cost.

However, these conditions may not remain constant always. Thus, if sellers expect a fall in the price in the near future they may offer more for sale in order to avoid losses. Similarly, changes in fashions and tastes, weather conditions, etc. affect supply. The cost of production may change with changes in technology. Further, in the case of services like labour a rise in wages may cause workers to prefer leisure to work and the supply of labour falls when its price (wages) rises. In this case, the supply curve of labour slopes backwards as in Fig. 7.2.

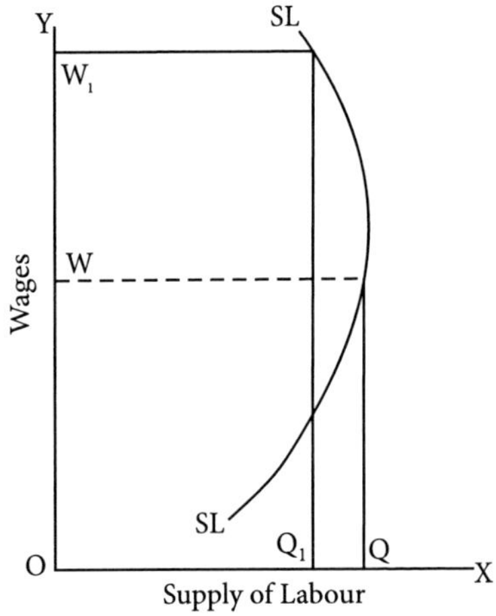

Fig. 7.2

In Fig. 7.2 SL is the Supply Curve of labour, and it slopes backwards. When wages increase from OW to OW_1 the supply of labour falls from OQ to OQ_1.

ELASTICITY OF SUPPLY

The concept of elasticity of supply is a major concept. 'Elasticity' is the capacity to expand and contract. Thus, Elasticity of supply may be defined as the increase and decrease in supply due to a given change in price while other things remain constant.

Thus:

$$E = \frac{\text{Change in Quantity of Supply}}{\text{Change in Supply}} \div \frac{\text{Change in Price}}{\text{Price}}$$

The co-efficient of elasticity of supply is always positive. In the above formula of co-efficient of elasticity q = quantity of supply P = Price per unit and Δ (delta) = % change.

Types of Elasticity of Supply

Elasticity of supply can be classified into different types as:

1. Perfectly elastic
2. Perfectly inelastic
3. Relatively elastic
4. Relatively inelastic
5. Elasticity equal to unity.

1. Perfectly Elastic Supply: Supply is said to be perfectly elastic when a small change in price causes an infinitely large change in supply. Thus:

$$\text{Perfect elastic supply} = \frac{\text{Infinite rise in supply}}{1\% \text{ rise in price}}$$

Fig. 7.3 depicts perfectly elastic supply curve (SS). If price rises infinitely (*i.e.* very negligibly) the supply expands to infinity *i.e.* to OQ_1. Conversely if price falls infinitesimally supply falls to 0 (zero). Hence, a perfectly elastic supply curve is *horizontal* to the supply axis.

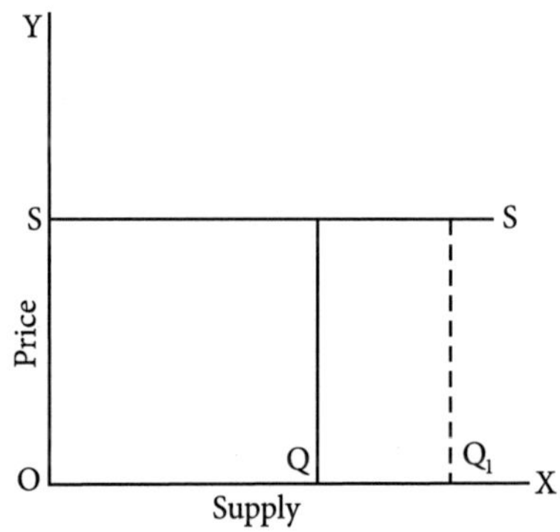

Fig. 7.3. Perfectly Elastic Supply

2. Perfectly Inelastic Supply: When a change (rise or fall) in price leaves supply *constant* the supply is said to be *perfectly inelastic.*

In that case the supply curve will be *vertical* in nature or slopes as in Fig. 7.4.

In Fig. 7.4 the supply curve SS is vertically sloped. At all prices (OP, OP_1 and OP_2) the quantity supplied remains OS. Thus, elasticity (Es) is equal to zero.

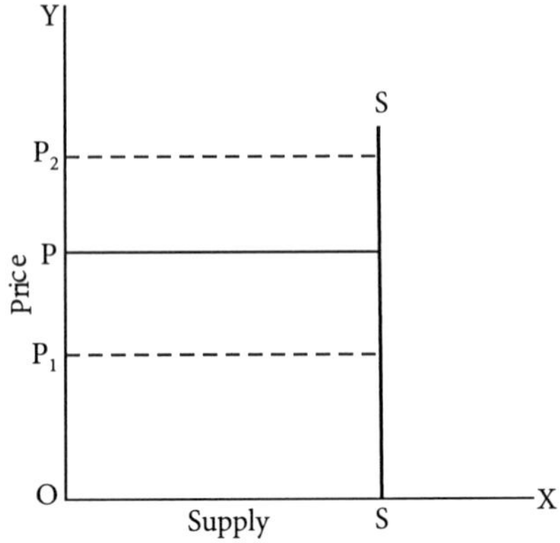

Fig. 7.4. Perfectly inelastic supply

3. Relatively Elastic Supply: When supply is relatively elastic a given change in price causes a more than proportionate change in supply.

$$\text{Thus: Relatively elastic supply} = \frac{\text{More than 1\% change in S}}{\text{1\% change in Price}}$$

i.e. Es > 1

Where: Es is elasticity of supply and S is quantity supplied.

When supply is *relatively elastic*, the supply curve will rise or fall slowly as in Fig. 7.5.

In Fig. 7.5 SS is the relatively elastic supply curve. If price rises by 1% (*i.e.* from OP to OP_1) Supply increases by more than 1% (*i.e.*, from OQ to OQ_1). Since QQ_1 is more than PP_1 the supply is *relatively elastic* and Elasticity of supply (Es) is greater than one (Es > 1).

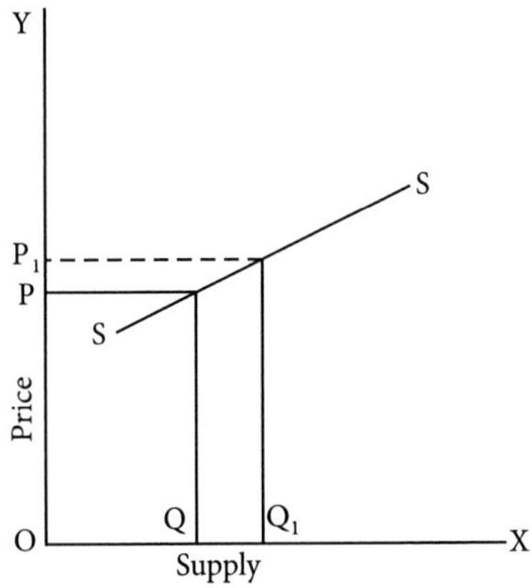

Fig. 7.5. Relatively Elastic Supply

4. Relatively Inelastic supply: When a given change in price causes a less than proportionate change in supply we say that supply is relatively inelastic or less than elastic. Thus:

$$\text{Relatively Inelastic Supply} = \frac{\text{Less than 1\% Change in Supply}}{\text{1\% Change in Price}}$$

That is: ES < 1

The supply curve in Fig. 7.6 represents relatively inelastic supply. If price rises from OP to OP_2 supply rises slightly from OQ to OQ_2 and if price falls from OP to OP_1 supply falls from OQ to OO_1. If you compare PP_2 to QQ_2 and PP_1 to OQ_1 you find that the change in the quantity of supply is less than the change in price. Hence, supply is relatively inelastic or Es < 1.

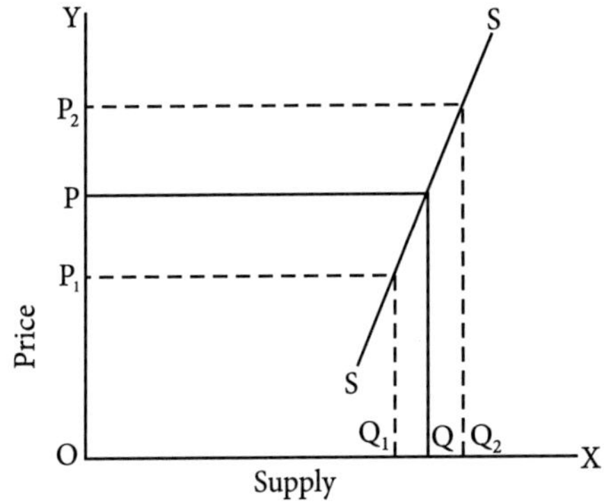

Fig. 7.6. Relatively Inelastic Supply

5. Unit Elasticity of Supply: The elasticity of supply is equal to unity when a given change in price causes a proportionate change in supply.

That is:

$$\frac{1\% \text{ change in Supply}}{1\% \text{ change in Price}} \quad \textit{i.e.}, \text{Es} = 1$$

Fig. 7.7 depicts unit elasticity of supply. The curve SS in it slopes at 45° to show proportionate change in price and supply. If price rises from OP to OP_1 the supply rises from OQ to OQ_1. Note that $PP_1 = QQ_1$. Hence, the change in price and the resultant change in supply are equal. Hence, the elasticity of supply is equal to unity or *proportionate.*

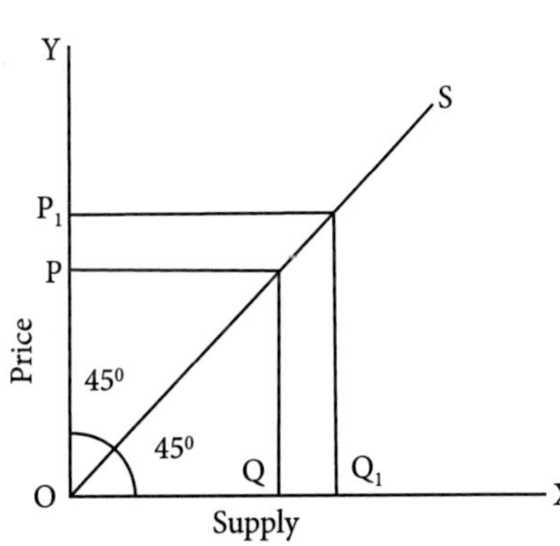

Fig. 7.7. Unit Elasticity of Supply

Measurement of Elasticity of Supply

Like it is important to measure elasticity of demand it is significant to measure the elasticity of supply in Business Economics.

Prof. M.L. Jhingan has demonstrated the measurement of elasticity of supply in the following words:

> *".....at any point on a curved supply curve, a tangent has to be drawn at that point on the curve. If the tangent touches the vertical axis, (OY) supply is elastic at that point.....When the tangent touches the X axis (Horizontal supply axis i.e. OX axis) ....supply is less elastic. If it passes (the tangetial line) through the origin, (i.e. O) the elasticity of supply is unity...."**

Thus, in Fig. 7.8 the measurement of elasticity of supply is simplified for easy analysis and understanding.

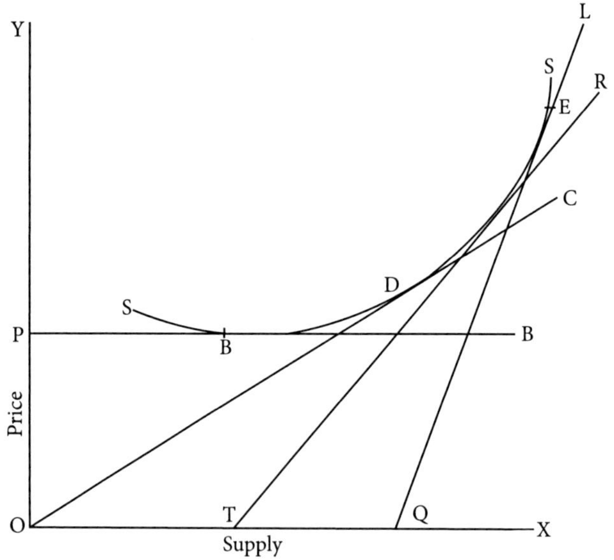

Fig. 7.8. Measurement of Elasticity of Supply

In Fig. 7.8 supply is elastic at 'B' (where Tanget PB touches Q and add SS axis). The supply is less than elastic at E where the tangential line touches the supply curve SS at that point when the tangent is drawn from the OY axis or *supply axis.*

* Jhingan: 'Advanced Economic Theory'., Sixth Edn: 1984., Ch. 17; p. 152 (Words or Symbols in brackets are my own).

If the tangential line is drawn from the origin 'O' it touches the supply curve SS at D. At D supply has *Unit elasticity*.

After knowing the nature of elasticity of supply it is necessary for a student of Business Economics to be aware of the '*influence of elasticity of supply on the costs of production also*.' The reason is very simple: any firm, marketing firm or producing firm makes its decisions on the basis of the condition of elasticity of its output or supply. That is; whether it will be able to adjust its supply to the changes in price and (or) demand. This brings us to the analysis of the relation between elasticity of supply and costs of production which we are presently going to consider.

INFLUENCE OF SUPPLY ELASTICITY ON COSTS OF PRODUCTION

Supply is influenced by a number of factors just as cost is influenced by many factors. In other words, the prices of factors of production and their elasticity of supply have a great influence on the cost of production. For the sake of easy analysis let us assume that the firm is operating under perfect competition. Then, the ability of the firm to increase or decrease its output or supply causes its cost of production to change.

The nature of influence of supply on the cost of production depends on the time available to the firm *i.e.*, short-run or long-run.

Supply-Cost Relationship in the Short-run

The short-run is a period during which a competitive firm cannot alter its output capacity; it can only increase or decrease the variable costs by changing the input of labour, raw-materials, etc.

In the short-period the firm will produce and supply a quantity at which the Marginal Cost (MC) equals its price (or Average Revenue: AR). The price therefore covers its variable cost (VC). If it is unable to recover the Average Variable Cost, it will not produce and supply at all.

In other words the short-period supply cost curve of a firm will slope upwards from left to right since the Marginal Cost curve has a positive slope.

Further, the entire *Industry's* supply curve depends upon the elasticity of MC curves of all firms in the industry. The supply curve of the competitive industry is elastic at lower cost and less elastic at higher costs.

The supply curve in the short-run may also shift up or shift down when variable cost increases or decreases.

Supply-Cost Relationship in the Long-run

The long-run supply of a competitive firm represents the different quantities supplied at different costs of production.

The long-period is such that supply or output can be changed by altering the plant capacity. Thus, a firm can install additional machinery and start a new unit and reduce the costs of production. Thus, in the long-period supply is more elastic than in the short-period.

The long-run supply curve of a competitive firm may be *upward sloping, horizontal* or *downward sloping.* It depends on whether the firm is working at decreasing cost or constant cost or increasing cost.

Supply Under Increasing Cost: In the long-run under increasing cost, new firms enter the industry. Hence, the demand for factors of production increases. This rises their cost. Hence, the long-run supply curve of the industry slopes upwards to the right.

Supply Under Constant Cost: When the industry is working at constant cost it obtains *economies* and *diseconomies* equally. The supply of factors of production will be elastic. New firms also obtain them at the same price as existing firms. Costs remain constant. The average cost also remains constant. Therefore, the long run supply curve, at constant cost, will be *horizontal.*

Supply Under Decreasing Cost: When the industry is operating at decreasing cost the supply curve slopes downwards. The profit being high due to decrease in cost of production causes new firms to enter the industry. The supply curve slopes from left to right downwards.

8

Revenue Analysis

In Chapter Six we have discussed at length the various cost concepts. We have seen how costs of production have a great bearing on the production of a business firm. In the present chapter let us consider the revenue aspect of production.

The '*Revenue*' of a firm and its '*Costs*' together determine the Volume of output and profit. 'Revenue' may be defined as the sale proceeds of a firm of a given output at a particular price. Thus, if a firm produces 10 scooters and sells them at ₹ 6,000 each, its revenue is ₹ 60,000. It should be noted that revenue is not *profit*. In this case, ₹ 60,000 is the *Gross income* of the firm. It contains only a certain amount of *Net profit*.

Total Revenue (TR)

Total revenue is the total sale proceeds got by selling a product at a given price. Thus, if a firm sells a total output of 10 units at ₹ 100 each Total Revenue (TR) = 10 × 100 = ₹ 1000. Hence, TR is price per unit multiplied by the total sales *i.e.*, TR = P × q

where P is price per unit q is the total number of units sold.

Average Revenue (AR)

Average Revenue is the average receipts of a firm on selling a certain number of units of a commodity. It is arrived at by dividing the TR from the number of units sold.

If we go back to the previous example Q

AR = 1000: 10

i.e., AR = ₹ 100

Average revenue is nothing but the price per unit sold. The average revenue curve (AR) of a firm therefore represents the quantity demanded at each level of price. Thus, the AR curve is also the demand curve of a firm.

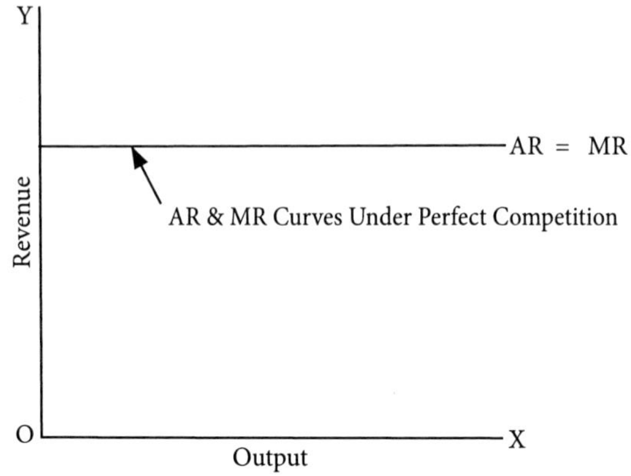

Fig. 8.1. AR and MR Curves under Perfect Competition

The AR curve under *perfect competition* will be a *horizontal straight line*. The Marginal Revenue curve (MR) coincides into AR curve as in Fig. 8.1.

This is due to the fact that the demand for the product of a competitive firm is perfectly elastic. It is perfectly elastic because the products of all firms are identical. Each firm has to charge a uniform price. (Refer to Table 1.)

Table 1: Under Perfect Competition

Units sold/price	AR ₹	TR ₹	MR ₹
1	10	10	10
2	10	20	10
3	10	30	10
4	10	40	10
5	10	50	10

Table 2

Units sold/price	AR ₹	TR ₹	MR ₹
1	10	10	10
2	9	19	8
3	8	27	8
4	7	34	7
5	6	40	6

Under *Monopoly* or *imperfect competition* the AR will be more than Marginal Revenue (MR). The monopolist can increase his revenue by reducing the price. Since AR and MR differ under such a market condition the AR and MR curves will lie one above the other. Since, AR is greater than MR the AR curve will be above the MR curve as shown in Fig. 8.2 The nature of AR and MR is indicated in Table 2.

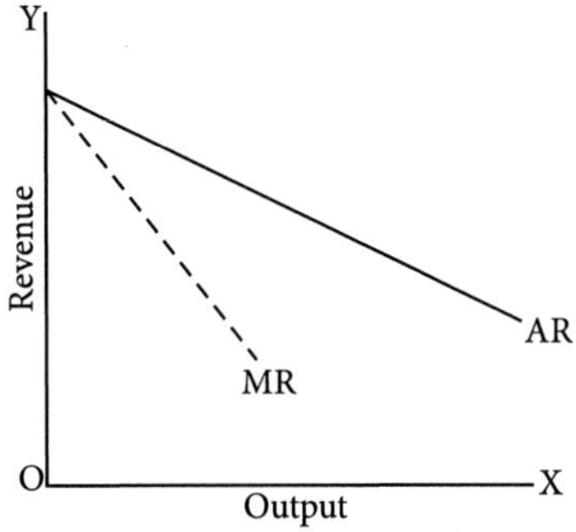

Fig. 8.2

Marginal Revenue

Marginal Revenue can be defined as the net addition made to total revenue as a result of selling one more unit or as a result of addition to total sales.

In other words, if the firm gets a total Revenue of ₹ 1000 by selling 10 units and if it sells 11 units instead then the total revenue may increase to ₹ 1080. Then, the net addition to total revenue (TR)

= ₹ 1080 – ₹ 1000 = ₹ 80

Thus, algebraically:

$$MR = TR_2 - TR_1$$

or $\Delta TR - TR$

Where: MR is Marginal Revenue, TR_1 is Total Revenue before the addition to sales, TR_2 is Total Revenue after increasing sales and is the increase in Total Revenue. This is clearly indicated in Tables 1 and 2.

The Relation between AR and MR

The relationship between AR and MR depends on the nature of the market condition. That is, whether the market is perfectly competitive or monopoly or monopolistic competition.

The relationship is described in Tables 1 and 2 in the preceding section of this chapter. It is also diagramatically illustrated in Figs. 8.1 and 8.2 in this chapter. The same explanation is sufficient in this context also.

9

Market Structures

It is customary to classify the markets into different types according to the degree of competition or its absence. Such a classification is highly necessary to Business Economics.

The Market Structures broadly fall into five groups, *viz.*:

1. Perfectly competitive markets;
2. Monopolistic competition;
3. Monopoly Markets;
4. Duopoly Markets; and
5. Oligopoly Markets.

Economists for a longtime (specially classical economists) believed that there are only two types of markets *i.e.* perfectly Competitive and pure monopoly markets. Prof. Chamberlein came out with the proof that these two types of markets are simply imaginary and proved that what exists in the real world of business is imperfect competition and that pure competition and pure monopoly are a myth (or non-existant).

In this chapter, we shall analyse the features of different market structures and then try to know how price and output are determined under different market conditions.

While preparing this chapter I assume, that the reader is already well versed with the Cost and Revenue concepts, their differences under different market conditions and also their relationships (discussed in chapters VI and X).

PERFECT COMPETITION

Perfect competition is the fertile imagination of the classical economists like Adam Smith and his contemporaries. Indeed, the whole of classical economists' doctrines are based on this market condition.

Features of Perfect Competition

A perfectly competitive or purely competitive market exists if certain conditions are fulfilled (which are seldom fulfilled, which is why it is a myth).

The conditions that must exist or obtain in a perfectly competitive market are summarised below for easy memory and the same are described later in greater detail,

1. Existence of large number of buyers and sellers;
2. Homogeneous (or identical) products with uniform price.
3. Absence of Transport cost and cost of advertisement.
4. Perfect knowledge of the markets on the part of buyers and sellers.
5. Freedom of '*Entry*' to new firms and freedom of 'Exit' to existing firms.
6. Perfect '*mobility*' of factors of production (so that factor prices are the same in all firms).

Implications of the Conditions

There must be a large number of buyers in the market so that if a single customer buys a little less or a little more it does not influence the aggregate market demand. Similarly, there should be a large number of sellers or producers so that if any one of them decides to sell or produce a little more or less in the market it will not affect the aggregate supply. Hence, the price will remain stable. Similarly, the individual firm's decision to expand or contract output does not depend on the prices of factors of production in the factor market so that cost of production remains unaffected.

The products must be *homogeneous* or identical in quality, model, packing, etc. Then, if any one firm charges a price higher than the others, it loses all the customers and it has to close down and leave the industry. This condition ensures uniform price policy.

The absence of transport cost is necessary, otherwise firms far away from the market will add to total cost through transport cost, in which case they have to charge a higher price. To do so is impossible as products are homogeneous.

Both buyers and sellers must be perfectly aware of prices. Other firms and specially, the producers, must be aware of factor prices also so that they buy from the cheapest seller.

Free entry and *Exit* is necessary so that when there is super-normal profit new firms can enter the industry and the aggregate supply rises and price comes down to remove super-normal profits. Conversely, firms incurring losses (sub-normal firms) can shut down and leave so that aggregate supply decreases and price rises so that profits reappear. Thus, there should be no blocading of entry or exit.

Lastly, perfect mobility of factors of production keeps the factor *prices* uniform and their supply steady. That is, if (say) the wages in one firm is slightly higher than in another firm then the *marginal productivity* must be high in that firm. Then, labour from other firms leave their firms and seek employment in the other firm where wages are high. Large supply of labour brings down wages of the firm to the level of other firms. So, also in the case of all other factors of production.

Is Perfect Competition a Myth?

Without a second thought the answer to this query or question is 'Yes'. The conditions or features of perfect competition are seldom found in the real business world. It is a fine imagination in the Jargon of the economist (the classical economist in particular).

It is a myth because the products are not homogeneous but heterogeneous (or differentiated by brand names, trade marks, etc.). Further, markets have a number of restrictions (both artificial and natural) to the entry and exit of firms like blocking the entry under *duopoly*. The number of firms are never large enough to keep supply unaffected. Nor are the buyers large enough for each firm has a limited number of customers for its own differentiated product.

Moreover, the existence of advertisements influence the customers and each firm can have an independent price policy in reality. The existence of transport cost makes it more than a myth. Otherwise, why will textiles be cheap in Bombay and costly elsewhere in India?

The factors of production are not perfectly mobile. As an example we may quote Dr. Marshall who said, "*The most cumbersome of all commodities to transport is that of labour.*" Thus, the mobility of factors of production is limited by the degree of risk, linguistic differences, seasonal variations in weather, food habits, etc.

It is a fact that what exists in the real Business world is imperfect 'competition or monopolistic competition (*i.e.* the real market contains a certain degree of competition and some degree of monopoly; not the whole of either of them). The very Existence of '*selling costs*' and '*product differentiation*' prove the mythical nature of the idea of perfect competition. The credit for proving this goes to Prof. Chamberlein and Mrs. Joan Robinson. They have launched a stem-and-branch attack on the concept.

Price and Output Determination

The problem of pricing and determination of output forms the core of Business Economics. Price-output decision-making is a scientific task of the business economist. These decisions have their ultimate influence on profitability because they affect costs of production while price depends on *Cost, Revenue* depends on price per unit and total sales. Costs of production depend on total output and prices of factors of production.

In all our discussions we should remember in this chapter that demand and supply are as influential as cost, price and output in any market condition.

We can now consider the question and mode of price and output determination under Perfect Competition (and this in spite of the non-existence of perfect competition).

I have kept in mind the students of commerce only while preparing this chapter. Hence, I have simplified this chapter by theoretising wherever possible because 'Business Economics' is fundamentally based on 'Economic Theory' and the knowledge of the latter is limited in the case of commerce students in general. Now, I proceed to analyse price and output determination under perfect competition on the assumption (that you have already understood the features of perfect competition and their implications (explained in the first section of this chapter).

Under perfect competition, price is determined by the interplay of aggregate demand and aggregate supply. Buyers and sellers have no individual control over price. But, their collective decisions will influence the aggregate demand and supply which in turn influence price.

The demand for a product depends on its Marginal Utility (MU) but its supply depends on the cost of production and profit.

As already said, the interaction of aggregate demand and supply determines the price of commodities under perfect competition. This price is called the '*Equilibrium price*'. At that price, Aggregate supply and demand will be equal as shown in Fig. 9.1.

If the price is more than OP or less than OP the equilibrium between aggregate supply and demand will be disturbed and demand-supply decision will change to push back price to equilibrium level E.

As in Fig. 9.1 the market demand is shown by DD and market supply by SS. At E the price is stable because market demand curve and market supply curve intersect each other. At E the two are equal. At OP price the competitive firm is producing an optimum output of OM quantity.

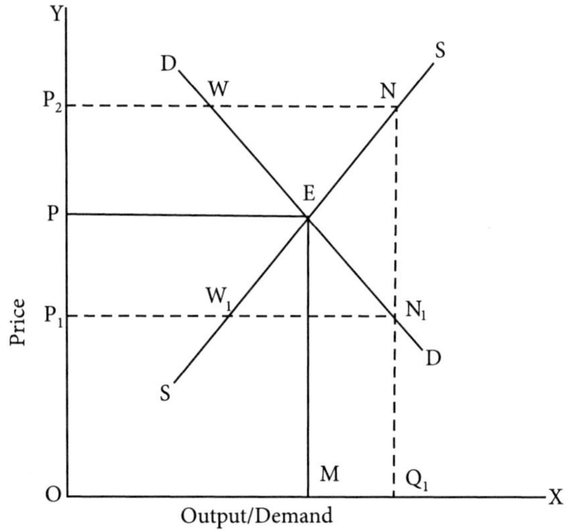

Fig. 9.1. Price-Output Determination under Perfect Competition

At E equilibrium price is OP and equilibrium output is OM. The entire industry produces only OM output at OP price. There is no accumulation of stocks or losses at that price and output.

If the price increases to OP_2 output rises to OM_2 because of high profits but aggregate demand falls to OM_1. This causes excess supply equal to WN. Since supply exceeds demand the output falls to OM and price falls back to *normal price* or *equilibrium price i.e.*, OP.

Conversely, a fall in price to OP_1 causes excess Demand equal to MQ_1 and shortage of supply equal to W_1N_1 and this pushes the price up to OP (where DD = SS). The output will be reduced to OM again.

Thus, when price rises to OP_2 the seller's competition increases output and reduces prices to the *Normal level.* When price falls the competition among buyers to buy more pushes the price upwards to the equilibrium level and bring down output to equilibrium level.

We have already noted that demand and supply, in the entire market, decide *price-output decisions* under perfect competition. We have seen by now, what happens to the price and output determination when only the price changes; and now, let us find out what happens to price when only demand or supply changes.

Price-Output Decision [Demand being constant]

Since demand and supply determine price under perfect competition a change in either of them must cause a change in price.

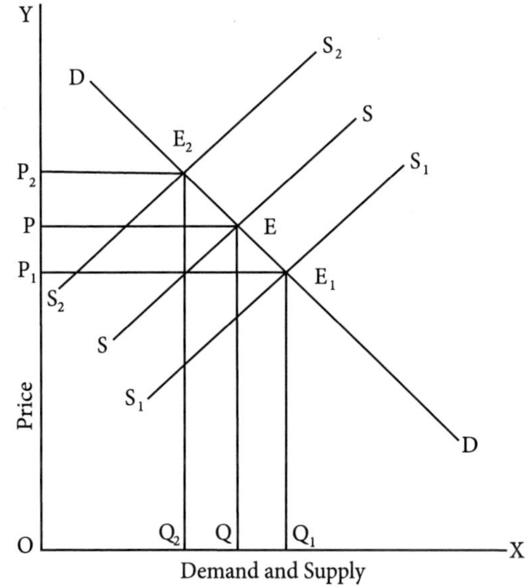

Fig. 9.2

Thus, if demand is constant and the supply rises price will decrease and vice versa. In Fig. 9.2 DD, the demand curve is constant. The supply curve SS shifts upwards to S_2 which means that supply has decreased. Then, the price rises from OP to OP_2. Conversely, if supply increase from OQ to OQ_1 the supply curve will shift downwards to S_1S_1. Then, the price falls to OP_1.

Price-Output Decision [Supply being constant]

On the other hand, if demand changes when supply is constant the equilibrium price will move either up or down. Thus, if demand increases while supply is constant, the price will increase. Conversely, if demand decreases when supply is constant, the price will decrease. This can be observed in Fig. 9.3.

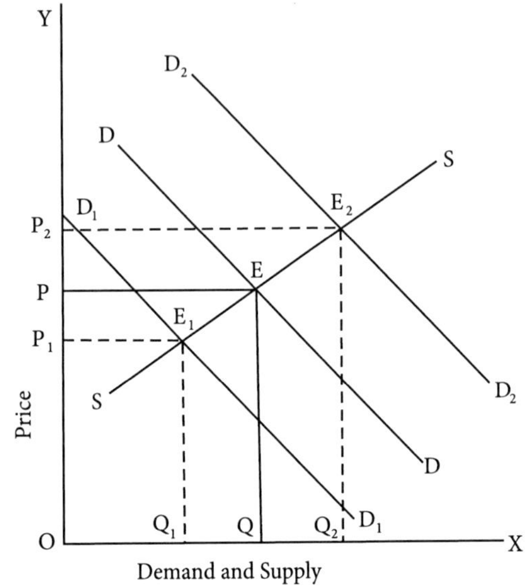

Fig. 9.3.

In Fig. 9.3 SS is the Constant Supply curve and DD is the Original Demand curve. The two curves intersect each other at E. The point E is the original equilibrium with OP price and the output is OQ. Suppose, the demand increases. Then the demarid curve shifts from DD to D_2D_2. The demand will exceed supply and hence price rises from OP to OP_2 where a higher equilibrium is attained with OQ_2 output at the point E_2.

If the demand decreases, the price falls from OP to OP_1 at a lower equilibrium point *viz.*, E_1 where output will decrease to OQ_1 by a similar process.

The Time Element & Cost, Output and Price Determination

We have noted elsewhere that the '*time element*' was introduced into the '*Theory of Value*' by Dr. Alfred Marshall. It is a very significant contribution of Dr. Marshall to the '*Theory of Pricing*'.

Dr. Marshall rightly felt that the time or period available for adjustment of supply to changes in demand has a great influence on the price, output and cost of production of a commodity.

Thus, he classified markets into four types as:

1. Very Short Period Market;
2. Short Period Market;

3. Long Period Market; and
4. Very Long Period Market or Secular Market.

1. Very Short Period Market: The very short period is also called the '*market period*'. It varies from a few days to a few weeks. The supply is perfectly inelastic and price depends upon demand. If demand increases supply can be increased only out of the available stock in the case of durable consumer's goods. However, the supply of perishables like meat, milk and flowers have a single day market. Their supply is equal to stock and output. The price determined in the short period is called the Market Price'. The market price is temporary and subject to changes as and when demand changes.

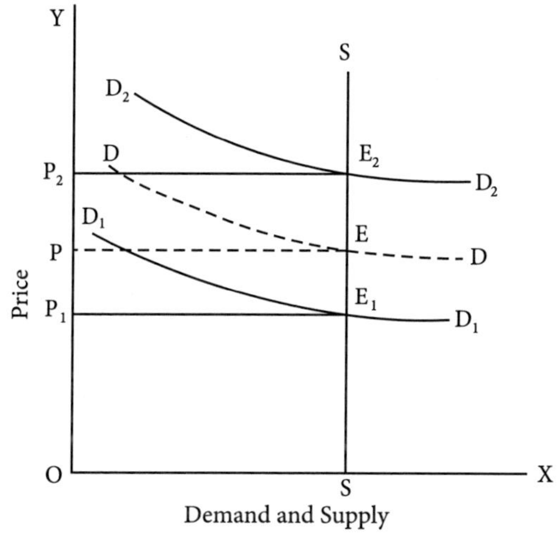

Fig. 9.4. Determination of Price under very short period

The determination of price under the very short period is depicted in Fig. 9.4.

In Fig. 9.4 SS is an inelastic very short period supply curve. DD is the original demand curve. DD and SS intersect at E. Thus, the *Market Price* is OP. If demand rises, the demand curve shifts upwards to D_2D_2 and the price goes up to OP_2 but supply remains OS. Conversely, if demand decreases the demand curve shifts to D_1D_1 and market price falls to OP_1.

Thus, demand is the prime factor that determines price in very short period markets. Supply depends on storage facility, cost of production and the expected prices.

2. Short Period Market: In the short period time is available to the firm to increase supply or decrease supply as per demand conditions by reducing output. However, it cannot change the installed capacity. That is, it cannot alter the fixed factors but only the variable factors. Thus, if demand increases supply can be increased by working in more shifts by utilising the idle capacity and through better organisation.

In the short period, the sellers may hold back a part of their stocks if the price is not sufficiently profitable. Thus, *stock* and *supply* will be different in the short period. There is a minimum *expected price* below which goods will not be offered for sale. The *minimum price* depends on many factors. It generally depends on: (1) *Existing stock of goods*; (2) *Expected future demand*; and (3) *Sellers' expectation of future price.*

Thus, the short period market applies to durable use goods and reproduceable goods. Further, the supply determines price and to some extent also determines demand. *Distress sales* or *panic sales* does not occur as in the *very short period market.*

Therefore, the supply curve in the short period will be *relatively elastic* as in Fig. 9.5. The Fig. 9.5 illustrates short period price and output determination.

In Fig. 9.5 SS is the short period supply curve. It is relatively elastic and therefore rises from left to right upwards. The curve becomes vertical after output reaches OQ_2 which is the maximum produceable in the short period. It is the optimum capacity. D_1D_1 is the original or initial demand curve. It intersects SS at E_1 where OQ_1 quantity is the output.

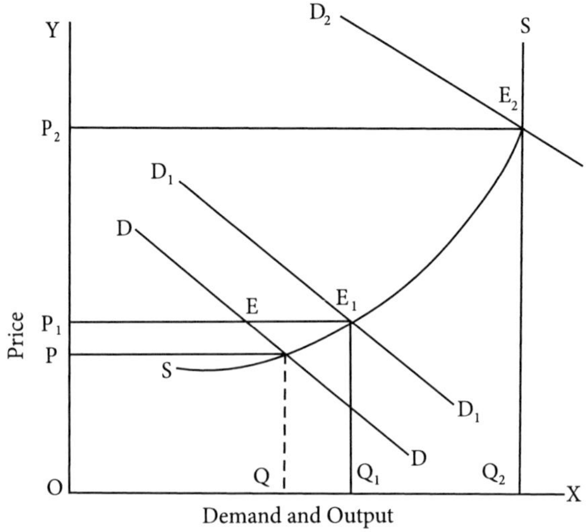

Fig. 9.5. Short-Period Supply

If demand increases to D_2D_2 supply increases to OQ_2 and the price will be OP_2. OP_2 is the maximum price that producers or sellers can expect in the short period. It is the '*Optimum Price*'.

If demand decreases to DD, supply will be reduced to OQ. It is sold at OP price. OP is the minimum price below which nothing is offered for sale, as costs cannot be recovered. OP price covers variable cost fully and a part of fixed cost. It should be noted that at OP_2 price and OQ_2 output, supply curve becomes vertical to OY axis. From S to Q on SS curve, the price is minimum; from S to Q_2 is the '*maximum price phase*'.

Thus, market supply in the short period depends upon demand. Further, the role of demand is very significant. It is the demand that makes supply to increase above minimum price OP in the short period.

3. Long period: The long period market is a market for durable commodities. It is a period over which supply and output can be increased or decreased by changing the size of the firm. Thus, in the long period all factors of production are *variable*. The distinction between '*Fixed*' and '*Variable*' costs disappears. Both demand and supply determine the price and output. However, the ultimate determinant is cost of production in the long-period.

The long period price is called the long period '*Normal price*'. In the long period, the '*Market price*' (*i.e.* the price on any particular day, or from time-to-time) oscilates around the '*Normal Price*'. On the whole, the price is '*stable*' over the long period.

In the long run, if the price is below the cost of production, the profits will decrease and production and supply will decrease. '*Old firms*' which have such a situation will leave the industry and aggregate supply decreases. Then, the price rises to Normal Level.

If the price is more than the cost of production, the profits will be '*Super-Normal*'. This attracts '*New Firms*' into the industry. Market supply rises and price comes down to the normal level. In between this there will be a temporary fluctuation in the price. Ultimately price and cost of production become equal and equilibrium output will be restored.

The long-run price and output determination is illustrated in Fig. 9.6.

SS is the original supply curve intersecting the original demand curve DD at M. This yields the normal price OP. At this price OQ quantity is produced and demanded. If the demand increases to D_1D_1 (when the supply remains constant) price will rise to OP_1 or Q_1M_1. Then there will be super-normal profits equal to M_1R. This induces firms to increase output. Then the supply curve will shift to S_1S_1. It will intersect D_1D_1 at

M_2. The price will fall to Q_2M_2 and super-normal profits will disappear and Normal Price is re-established.

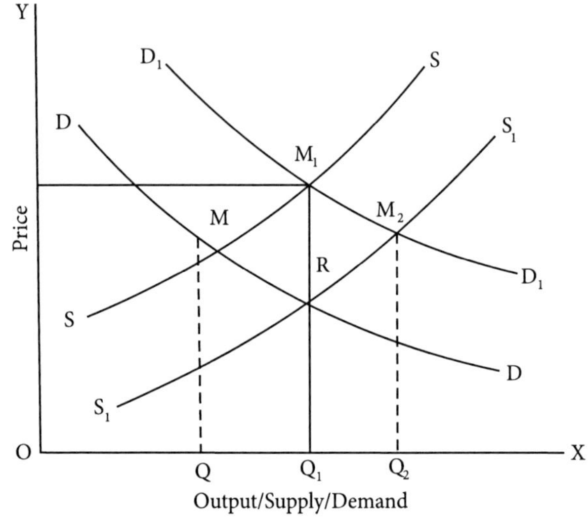

Fig. 9.6. Long-run price and output determination

For a more detailed analysis of short and long period cost and output determination the students are advised to go through Chapter Seven.

4. Very long period or Secular period: Very long period is a period more than 20 years. Under this market the changes take place in the *supply of factors of production and their prices.* In this period the cost of production depends on changes in factor prices and not on demand.

A number of '*secular changes*' occur in the very long period markets. The changes are *inter-related* and are *far-reaching.*

However, the secular period has no practical use in business-decisions regarding price and output. The changes are cumulative and difficult to separate and analyse. Therefore, business decisions are seldom (never) based on such possible changes.

Therefore, for practical reasons, Business Economics can conveniently neglect the *very long period.*

MONOPOLY

The name 'Monopoly' is a grouping of two Greek words *Mono* (single) and *poly* (seller). Together they become 'Monopoly' meaning '*single seller*'.

Thus, a market in which there is a single seller or single firm producing or selling in the market is called 'Monopoly market'.

Therefore, the '*firm*' is also the '*industry*' in a monopoly market.

There is a misunderstanding that a monopolist can charge any price for his product. In reality, it is not so. If the monopolist does so, he will lose sales. His demand curve is *relatively elastic* and not really *inelastic*. If the monopolist produces more to sell at higher prices he will reduce his Average Revenue or price.

This means, that if he charges a higher price he has to leave the demand to be determined by the price; if he decides to sell more he has to reduce the price and then supply depends on demand.

In short, a monopolist can either fix a high price but sell less or produce more and sell at a low price. He cannot control both price and volume of sales or demand.

Main Features of Monopoly: Then it is clear that in a monopoly market the main features are as under:

1. A single individual or a group of individuals (A single joint-stock company) controls the entire market.
2. There are a large number of consumers who have no choice regarding consumption of that firm's product, *i.e. no consumers' sovereignty.*
3. There are no substitutes to the product of the monopoly firm.
4. There is no distinction between '*the firm*' and '*the industry*'.

Price and Output Determination

We have already noted that a monopoly firm cannot control both price and output. It has to choose such a price at which it can maximise Total Sales and Total Revenue.

The *Marginal Cost curve* under monopoly is also U-shaped like in perfect competition. So is also the Average Cost curve (like in perfect competition the former is steeper than in the latter) as in Fig. 9.7.

However, the Average Revenue (AR) will be higher than Marginal Revenue (MR) under monopoly whereas AR = MR in perfect competition. Hence, the AR curve will be above MR curve under monopoly.

Technically, it means that the AR and MR curves will *slope downwards from left to right* as in Fig. 9.7.

The reason is that when AR is decreasing, extra units sold will bring lesser and lesser revenue.

A Monopoly Firm's Profit Maximisation Condition

A monopoly firm's profit maximisation condition is vertically the same as that of a competitive firm *i.e.,* it maximises profit when MR = MC. Such a position is called the '*Equilibrium position*' of the monopoly firm.

As long as additional production brings additional revenue the firm will go on expanding output. If addition to output causes addition to Marginal Cost (MC) production stops expanding further.

Fig. 9.7 depicts the cost and output relation of a monopoly firm at different prices. It also shows how a monopolist fixes his price.

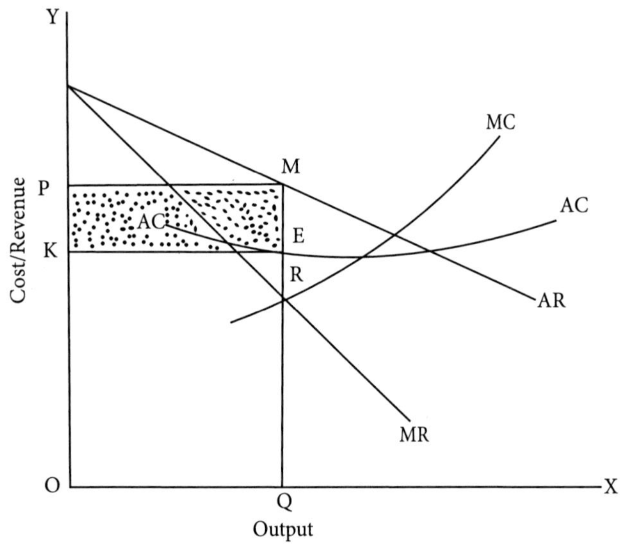

Fig. 9.7. Price, Output and Profit Maximisation (Monopoly)

In Fig. 9.7 MC and AC are Marginal and Average Cost curves respectively. MR and AR represent Marginal and Average Costs respectively. R is the point where, MR = MC (the point of equilibrium) and MPKE is the area showing net revenue or net profit of the monopolist.

MC curve intersects MR curve at R where MR = MC and the monopolist produces OQ quantity of output. The firm sells the entire output at OP price (and not at OK price). Below that AC is higher than MC. Hence, it incurs a *loss* if it sells at OK price.

Since the demand is more than supply it can conveniently sell at OP price and maximise profit equal to MPKE. *i.e.* the area of the rectangle which is *dotted* in Fig. 9.7.

At OM output the monopolist gains a profit equal to ME on every unit sold our of OQ of output. So, AR = ME.

This is, therefore, the condition of Monopoly profit-output maximisation and price maximisation.

You must remember that this condition is applicable to the long as well as short period under monopoly. The question of distinction arises only if there is competition; and monopoly is the total absence of competition.

PRICE DISCRIMINATION OR DISCRIMINATING MONOPOLY

Price Discrimination is a special possibility of the monopoly market; you can never practice it in any other market condition.

In very simple terms price discrimination is: '*The practice of the monopolist where he charges different prices to different consumers of his product*'.

The act of charging different prices on the basis of income of consumers, separation of markets by distance and the nature of uses of the product may be technically called *price discrimination* or *discriminating monopoly*. It is a rare case of *simple* and *pure monopoly*.

Types of Price Discrimination

Assuming that 'price discrimination' is possible we can distinguish among three types of price discrimination *viz.*:

1. *Personal Price Discrimination*;
2. *Place Discrimination*; and
3. *Use Discrimination*.

Let us, briefly know what each type of discrimination means, for a better understanding of the practice of price discrimination.

1. *Personal Price Discrimination* is the practice of collecting low charges for the poor and low income earners while higher charges (price) are collected from the rich consumers. For instance, a doctor has the monopoly in a small town. The patients have nobody else to go except to the only doctor of the town. The doctor of the small town knows this fact. So, he charges the lesser fee to the poor patients than to the rich patients. The doctor is practising *personal price discrimination*.

2. *Place Discrimination* is the practice of charging different prices to customers (collectively) in markets separated by a cost distance (*i.e.* where it would cost more to buy in another place). For instance, as a,

rational customer you will not go all the way from Commercial Street by car or taxi to buy a shirt at Gandhi Bazaar just to save a rupee (because the difference in price is less than the cost of your going there). You would go to Gandhi Bazaar to buy the shirt only if the cost of your transport is sufficiently less than the difference in price between the two markets.

The monopolist, therefore, discriminates when markets are separated by a good distance ('*good distance*' means '*cost of transport*').

3. '*Use Discrimination*', on the other hand, depends upon the 'purposes' for which the buyer wants the product of the monopolist.

The '*End-use Principle*' is applied by the monopolist in this type of discrimination. Thus, the monopoly of electricity by the state charges high price for commercial uses of electricity than for domestic uses of electricity.

The way in which price and output are determined under *discriminating monopoly* are different from price and output determination under '*pure monopoly*'.

It is enough if we know that:

1. It is possible to divide a monopoly market into '*sub-markets*'.
2. That the *elasticities of demand* are different in all the sub-markets.
3. That the monopolist is able to practise '*Mail selling*' of his product (where he sells by 'pamphletted information' with markets widely separated).

Price Determination Under Price-Discrimination

We have seen that a monopoly firm sells at a price where its MR = MC. However, there is a possibility that it can sell at different prices also, which is called the practice of '*price discrimination*'.

It could be *First Degree* Price Discrimination or *Second Degree* Price Discrimination or *Third Degree* Price Discrimination.

In order to charge different prices a monopoly firm has to have the following conditions fulfilled:

1. The market has to be divided into smaller sub-markets.
2. The elasticity of demand in different sub-markets must be different.
3. The different markets must be sufficiently separated by distance.
4. The cost of production must be constant.

To simplyfy the whole thing, it can be said that the monopolist decides about the output for each sub-market on the basis of total cost

(TC) and Average Revenue (AR), Marginal Revenue (MR) and Marginal Cost (MC).

Let us suppose that there are two sub-markets 'A' and 'B'. (The Average Revenue is different in 'A' and 'B'). The demand in sub-market 'A' is *inelastic* and in sub-market 'B' it is *elastic*.

In such a case price-output decision will be as shown in Fig. 9.8.

In Fig. 9.8 'A' and 'B' are two markets under the total monopoly of the firm.

In sub-market 'A' AR_a is the Average Revenue curve-cum-the demand curve and in sub-market 'B' AR_b is the Average Revenue Curve-cum-demand curve.

Still, the slope of AR_a is steeper than that of ARb which means that the elasticity of demand in sub-markets 'A' and 'B' are different. That is to say, in sub-market 'A' the demand is *inelastic* and in sub-market 'B' the demand is *relatively elastic*.

In the diagram the MR curves are located below the AR curves meaning to say that the average revenue (AR) is always more than the Marginal revenue in the two markets.

The *Aggregate Market Revenue* of the discriminating monopolist is shown on the extreme right of the same diagram. AR_3 is the total Revenue (TR) of the discriminating monopolist from sub-markets 'A' and 'B'.

Of 'A' and 'B' similarly, the total of Marginal Revenues are shown by MR_3.

As seen in Fig. 9.8 $AR_a + AR_b = AR_3$ and $MR_a + MR_b = MR_3$. This is the sum total of Average and Marginal revenues at different quantities of output of the monoploy firm.

The MC curve shows the marginal cost (which is constant) for the total output sold in sub-markets 'A' and 'B'.

The total output, in this example, is determined at the point where $MC = MR_3$ at E_3 in the diagram. The total output or supply, is therefore, equal to OM_3 (*i.e.* $OM_1 + OM_2 = OM_3$).

The quantity of total sales in the two sub-markets is shown by the straight line from E to AR_3 which cuts the MR curves of the two sub-markets at E_1 and E_2.

This means that in sub-market 'A' the supply is equal to OM_1 and that in the sub-market 'B' it is equal to OM_2. At both these points MC = MR as shown by the line E_1 to Q in Fig. 9.8.

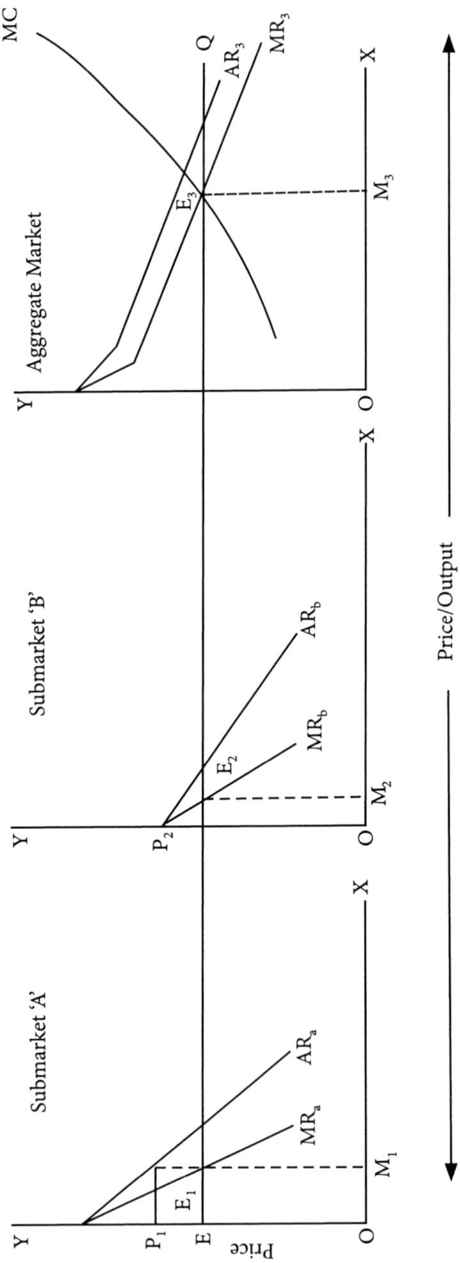

Fig. 9.8. Price Output Determination under Price Discrimination

Equilibrium of the Monopolistic Firm (Short-run)

A monopolistic firm attains equilibrium output and equilibrium price when its Marginal Cost (MC) equals its Marginal Revenue (MR). At that point of equilibrium the firm is said to be an *optimum firm*. An optimum firm is one which earns maximum (or normal) profit.

Fig. 9.9 illustrates this situation.

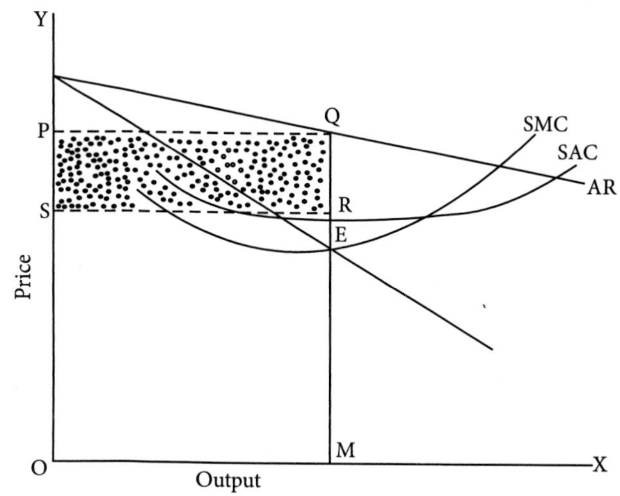

Fig. 9.9. Short-run equilibrium of a firm

In Fig. 9.9 SMC is the short-run Marginal Cost Curve and SAC is ne short-run Average Cost Curve. MR and AR are Marginal Revenue nd Average Revenue curves of the individual firm under monopolistic ompetition.

The point E is the point of equilibrium price and output where SMC urve intersects the MR curve from below. Thus, at 'E' SMC = MR. That oint yields OM quantity of output.

However, the SAC curve lies above the SMC curve at the point of quilibrium. Therefore, the average cost is less than average revenue hen output is OM and price is OP. The firm sells OM output at OP rice.

Then, there is a difference between SAC and AR which is equal to Q. Logically, it means that the monopolistic firm in the short-run is rning a profit equal to SP per unit sold. Therefore, the total profit is ual to the area of the *dotted rectangle* PQRS. It is the maximum profit rned by the firm in the short-run.

The corresponding, quantity of output is OM_2 in the sub-market-B.

The point to be noted is, that the monopolist produces OM quantity (as shown on the extreme left of the diagram) and sells OM_1 quantity in sub-market 'A' at the price OP_1 and OM_2 quantity in sub-market 'B' at the price OP_2.

Thus, the price in sub-market 'B' is higher than in sub-market 'A'. Thus, the monopoly firm has been selling the same product at different prices though the marginal cost is constant.

Control Over Monopoly Practices

The growth of monopoly power is certainly detrimental to the society in general and to the economy in particular. Therefore, it is necessary to regulate the growth of monopoly power. Gone are the days of the monopolist; the governments all over the world have awaken to the disadvantage of the monopoly.

Why Control the Monopoly?

The need for the control of monopoly power arises due to its evil effects. Let us know some important evils of monopoly practices now.

The major evil effects of monopoly practices are summed up below:

1. Monopoly leads to reckless use of scarce resources and the absence of competition makes it worse.
2. Monopoly exploits customers as the monopoly price is generally high.
3. The monopolist discriminates against the customers; while doing so he may consider the rich customer as poor customer and *vice versa*. Then, the wrong is very costly.
4. Monopoly in essential products is *socially* and *economically* unforgivable.
5. Monopoly is politically corruptive because the monopolist brings pressure on the *policy of taxation* of the Government.
6. Monopoly exploits the worker by paying them low wages and blocks collective bargaining of workers through *Trade Unions*.
7. Monopoly power increases the inequalities of income, power and wealth in the society.

Therefore, there is an urgent need for the restriction of monopolies and Trade practices. Such a step is justifyable both socially and socioeconomically. Monopoly is a social sin and an economic offence which warrants control. Therefore, many steps have been taken to restrict the growth of monopolies (Both national and international monopolies) all over the globe.

MONOPOLISTIC COMPETITION

'Monopolistic Competition' is a recent concept. It was brought into limelight by Prof. Chamberlein and popularised by Mrs. Joan Robinson in her famous work '*The Economics of Imperfect Competition*'.

A cursory look at the term shows that imperfect competition is a market condition in which there is neither pure competition nor pure monopoly.

However, it would do well to analyse the features of monopolistic competition. That would help in not only comparing price and output determination under different market conditions but also in knowing what kind of a market condition really exists in the real world.

Hence, let us take a quick look at the features of monopolistic competition before we venture to analyse price and output determination under this market condition.

Features of Monopolistic Competition

Monopolistic Competition is one of the forms of imperfect competition. It is a situation where there is a combination of competition and monopoly. Therefore, it is interesting to study the peculiar features of monopolist competition. The basic features may be classified thus:

1. Large Number of Firms: Under monopolistic competition the number of firms is so large that there can be no *collusion*. Each firm has an independent price policy because it enjoys the benefit of product differentiation. Thus, what each firm produces and how much of it is produced is not influenced by the other firms in the industry. However, the products of other firms are *close substitutes* to the product of any other firm. Hence, there is a certain degree of competition also.

2. Heterogeneous products: The basic feature of monopolistic competition is the existence of heterogeneous products or *dissimilar products*. Though many firms produce the same product they are different in brand names, trade marks, packing and model. Each firm offers its consumers attractive schemes like door-delivery, gifts, discounts, hire-purchase schemes, etc. to attract them. The degree of monopoly varies with heteorogeneity of the product.

3. Selling Costs: The existence of *selling costs* is yet another major feature of monopolistic competition. The selling costs are incurred in the form of advertisement, salesmanship, complementaries, etc. They are meant

to influence the consumers. A large part of the price under thi situation consists of selling costs.

4. Downward Sloping Revenue Curve: The AR and MR cur this market condition are neither horizontal (as in perfect con nor are they very steeply sloping straight lines (as in monop slope less steeply as in Fig. 9.9.

5. Freedom of Entry and Exit: There is complete freedom fo firm to enter the industry and to go out of the industry. Thus, be no artificial barriers or blocades as in monopoly.

6. Non-price Competition: Though there is a degree of comp only by way of product differentiation and not by way of price. to branding, patent rights and trade marks.

7. Relatively Elastic Demand: The firms face a relatively elas for their products whereas it is *perfectly elastic* under perfect c and *perfectly inelastic* under monopoly. Again the reason i being close substitutes to each other. For instance, the con either buy Colgate tooth paste or Promise tooth paste or C paste since all of them serve the same purpose. Thus, each fi *setter* and not a *price-taker* under monopolistic competition.

8. Short-run Super-normal Profits: Super-normal or win can exist in the short-run (as well as some firms may incur is because the AR may be more than AC even though MR = incur losses if AC is more than AR though MC = MR.

Thus, we find a combination or intermixture of com monopoly which is why it is called Monopolistic Comp greatest distinction being the existence of product differ selling costs.

Price and Output Determination Under Monopolistic C

The determination of price and output Under monopolisti is based on costs and revenue of the firms. As already notec curves are (also the demand curves) neither too steep nor are slightly inclined from left to right downwards as in Fig

Further, there is a limit to the sales or output of each fi close substitutes produced by other firms.

We are now well equipped to analyse the det price and output under this real world market situati output determination is technically known in Business '*Equilibrium Condition*' of the firm.

Long-run Equilibrium or Group Equilibrium

Only established old firms earn super-normal profits in the long-run. Some of them may have an advantage of latest technology over the other firms in the industry or goodwill of customers or preference of consumers due to the psychological attachment.

The '*new firms*' have to adopt a *low price policy* till they get established in the trade or industry. Hence, their profits will be lower. They may even incur losses. They try to recover only the average variable cost and keep down the losses. They are unable to recover the average fixed costs in the short-run.

According to Prof. Chamberlein, 'as different firms under monopolistic competition produce the same product with a difference, the equilibrium of a firm must be regarded as the group equilibrium in the long-run'.

The Group Equilibrium is represented in Fig. 9.10.

In Fig. 9.10 LMC = MR at the point 'E' and AC = AR at the point 'R'. In the long-run, the *super-normal profits* or abnormal losses will be removed by either *entry* of *new firms* or exit of old firms respectively. If new firms charge a lower price, the old firms will be forced to follow suit. Hence, price will fall and *windfall profits* will disappear. Hence, the long-run AR curve shifts down, AR and LAC curves will get closer. *Normal profits* will be restored.

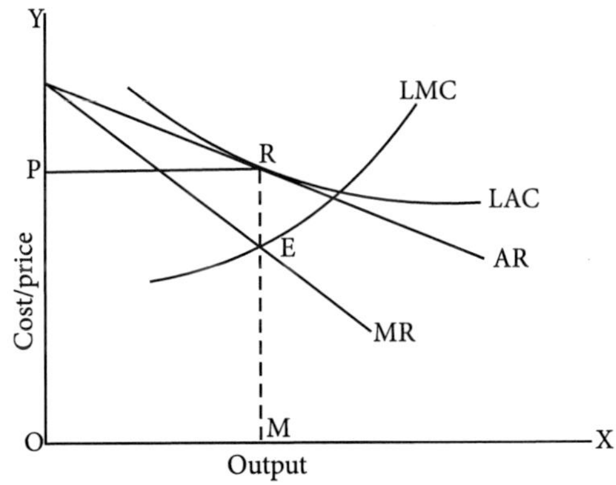

Fig. 9.10. Group Equilibrium (Monopolistic Competition)

A Note on Product Differentiation Methods

Modern business practice is based on the practice of product differentiation, price discounts and other methods of sales promotion have become *necessary* in monopolistic markets through advertisements of various sorts.

According to Prof. Joel Dean price differences in a monopolistic market depend upon the following factors:

1. The status of the buyer;
2. Quantity of purchase by the buyer;
3. The distance between the buyer and the market;
4. The credit worthiness of the buyer; and
5. The season of purchase by the buyer.

These factors are significant in discriminating among the consumers in the '*Business World*' according to him. They help in capturing the best customers, to dig into new markets and face the competition with a stiff neck.

Accordingly, the seller or producer may offer the following incentives to his customers or consumers:

1. Distributors' Discounts
2. Quantity-wise Discounts
3. Cash-purchase Discounts
4. Market-wise Discounts
5. Seasonal Discounts or clock and calender time discounts (as in the case of Trunk-calls and Cooling agents in Winter).

A Note on the Wastes of Monopolistic Competition

Basically, Monopolistic Competition is wasteful. The most common wastes under this market condition are of two types, *viz.*: (1) Economic Wastes; and (2) Social Wastes.

Economic Wastes:

1. It leads to underutilisation of production capacities.
2. Too many varieties of the same product will be produced with the scarce resources which can be put to better uses.
3. The cost of advertisement is the greatest waste.
4. Selling costs are unnecessarily incurred.

Social Costs or Wastes:

1. Its economic costs are a burden to the weaker sections of the society.
2. It forces consumers to buy in far away markets at a tremendous labour when the price is too high.

Thus, it is necessary to direct monopolistic competition in the right direction to make it socially and economically useful.

DUOPOLY AND OLIGOPOLY—THEIR FEATURES

Duopoly: Meaning and Features

Duopoly is simply a special kind of oligopoly. In '*Duopoly*' the seller or producer either takes into consideration the price and output policy of the competitor or ignores it. Thus, the duopolist is both dependent and independent at the same time (whereas, the oligopolist is in competition with a few more producers or sellers).

That means, Duopoly is a market situation in which there are only two-producers or sellers who face close competition from each other but yet each is able to retain an independent price and output policy.

Suppose, there are two firms X and Y. Then, X-firm determines carefully what should be its price because, it is sure that Y-firm will also adopt the same price policy. Firm-X is as sure as firm-Y that the reaction of the other is going to have an effect on its own profits.

Then in the case of X and Y firms there is mutual dependence.

If X-firm considers that its price does not affect Y-firm then firm-X will act independently. In this case, firm-X assumes *that the supply of the firm-Y is constant*. This is known as 'The *Cournot Solution*' to the problem of duopoly. It was offered by the French economist A.A. Cournot in 1838.

Though there are a number of versions of Duopoly we may note the following features of duopoly in general.

Features

Duopoly has the following features:

1. Existence of two sellers or producers who sell or produce *homogeneous products*.
2. Independent price and output policy.
3. Production is either perishable or not storable.
4. Large number of buyers for the product.
5. The cost of production is zero.
6. Each of the two firms is ignorant about the output capacity of the other rival firm.
7. Each of the two producers considers the supply of the rival firm as constant.

8. The market demand is taken as accepted by both the firms.
9. The utlimate objective of both the rival firms is maximisation of *Net revenue*.

The above features were pointed out by the French economist Cournot. The same were criticised by the French mathematician Joseph Bertrand saying that the assumption of *rival's constant price and supply* is unreal and said that the reality is that the rival firm bases its price on the price of the competitor's product. On the other hand, Prof. Edgeworth tried to bring about a compromise between the two opinions but left the *duopoly problem* as and where it was. Then, the German economist Heinrich Von Stackelberg came out with a new solution called the '*Stackelberg solution*' where he agrees with the *interdependence* of the duopolists on price decisions. According to him the output and price of firm-X is a function of output and function of firm-Y and vice-versa. Prof. Chamberlein has fully agreed with the *Stackelberg Solution.**

Chamberlein sums up his solution to Duopoly problem thus:

"Let each seller, in seeking to maximise his profit....and look to the total consequences of his move. He must consider not merely what his competitor is doing now, but also what he will be forced to do....which he himself is contemplating."

Oligopoly: Meaning and Features

Oligopoly is one of the types of imperfect competition. It is a market condition in which there are only a few sellers whose products are either homogeneous or close substitutes. It is 'competitions among the few'.

According to Prof. Stigher, oligopoly is "*a situation in which a firm bases its market policy, in part, on the expected behaviour of a few close rivals.*"

Kinds of Oligopoly: There are different kinds of oligopoly. The main types are as under:

1. Perfect oligopoly
2. Imperfect oligopoly
3. Open oligopoly
4. Close oligopoly
5. Partial oligopoly
6. Full oligopoly
7. Collusive oligopoly

* Quarterly Journal of Economics, November 1929.

8. Competitive oligopoly
9. Syndicated oligopoly.

If the products are *homogeneous* the situation is *perfect oligopoloy*. It products are differentiated it is called *imperfect oligopoly*. The cement industry is an example of the former type and that of soap for the latter type.

In open *oligopoly* the entry of new firms is allowed and in *closed oligopoly* entry of new firms is not possible.

On the other hand, oligopoly is *partial* when the industry is dominated by one large firm called the *price leader*. In *full oligopoly*, price leadership is absent.

Collusive oligopoly is one in which the few firms have an understanding or act in collusion with each other regarding price and output. In *competitive oligopoly* there is no such collusion but there is competition. Lastly, *syndicated oligopoly* exists when the few firms sell their output through a *Central Syndicate*.

Features of oligopoly

The main features of oligopoly are as follows:

1. A Few sellers: In oligopoly there will be a few sellers. They may produce homogeneous products or differentiate their products. The share of each firm is quite large in market supply. Hence, the output and price policy of an individual firm can affect market conditions.

2. Interdependence: Since the individual firms have a bearing on the market conditions, each firm depends on the price and output decisions of other firms while determining its own policy. Moreover, interdependence is also due to substitutability of products.

3. Advertisements: The policy and fortune of one firm dependes on that of the other firms. Hence, advertisement costs are incurred. Advertisement becomes an unavoidable necessity under oligopoly.

4. Competition: There is close competition among the few firms because their products are close substitutes to one another.

5. Lack of Uniformity: There is no uniformity in the size of the oligopoly firms. Some firms may be small and others may be large. Uniformity of size is very rare.

6. Indeterminate Demand: Interdependence is responsible for this feature. No single firm can forecast its demand. An estimation of sales cannot be made by reducing the price. Thus, it is difficult to construct a demand curve. The price-output changes of one firm will have *backward* and *forward effects* on that of the other firms. At best, the demand estimation is only a guess work.

7. Price Rigidity: The prices are not easily changed due to fear of retaliation by the other firms. Thus, prices remain rigid and sticky. If one firm cuts its price it leads to a *price-war* which finally benefits none of the firms.

8. Monopoly Power: When products are differentiated each firm enjoys a certain degree of monopoly in sales and price. Each firm can have its own customers as they have been attached to that product. Thus, there is *monopoly within oligopoly.*

Thus, oligopoly is a characteristic market condition which combines monopoly, competition, homogeneity and product differentiation. It is at once all of these and also none of these.

10

Pricing Policy

1. General consideration of price policy

Formulating a sound price policy and selection of the *right method of pricing* is a keystone to a business firm. In other words, fixing the '*most workable price*' is a very careful and difficult task of the business economist. It has a tremendous influence on the success or failure of a business organisation. The management of a firm has to adopt a carefully worked out price policy to suit its goals.

Pricing has always been one of the central problems, especially, in a competitive economy and in a mixed economy, price affects profits through cost of production and revenue of the business firms. The total revenue of a firm is dependent upon the price at which each unit of the product is sold.

Pricing is a key element in both the *factor market* and *product market*; both the prices have their impact on the profits of a firm. In short, price policy has a pivotal role to play in profit maximisation.

A discussion on price policy is never complete or total if it has no reference to the objectives of the firm. Thus, the price policy is framed according to the basic objectives of a firm.

The objectives of the firm form the framework for price policy. The objectives may be:

1. Achievement of targeted returns on investment.
2. Achievement of targeted growth of the firm.
3. Maintenance and further improvement of its share in the market supply.
4. Maintaining its status and goodwill
5. Stability of the price of its product.

Thus, the basic considerations involved in formulating a price policy must include these five objectives of the firm. Most of the considerations are of *long-term* nature but some of them are also *short-term* in nature.

The other factors involved in formulating a sound price policy are:

1. The nature of demand for a product;
2. The Cost of production;
3. Competition and its extent; and
4. Government's influence (*i.e.,* taxes, subsidies, price controls, etc.)

The relationship of *demand* to *supply* are important in determining the price of a commodity. A product will have no price if it has no demand or utility. It was Dr. Marshall who gave a definiteness to the theory of price determination. According to him both demand and supply are equally significant in formulating a price policy. He likens, the process of price determination to the act of cutting something with a pair of scissors. It is just like both the blades of a scissors operating together; when one blade maybe held still, the other moves up and down and only then something can be cut. Similarly, the supply and the demand must operate with lesser or higher influence in order to arrive at a price.

The cost of production is no doubt another important consideration in price policy. It is not the only consideration but yet it is a major consideration. A price policy should be such that the cost of production is recovered. Again, it depends on the size of the firm and the period of the market (*i.e.* short or long period).

Thus, *competition* comes into its own at this stage of price policy. If the competition is very keen, the price policy will be such that the price does not lead to loss of sales and revenue. Moreover, whether the products are *homogeneous* or *differentiated* (as in, imperfect competition) also has to be taken into consideration. If there is perfect competition the demand is distributed among many firms and the price is more uniform than different. There will be no independence in price policy.

The Government's policy towards pricing also has to be given due consideration while deciding the price policy of a firm. For instance if the government is granting *subsidies* (*i.e.,* the Govt, bears a part of cost of production) the *non-subsidised* firms must make note of it and fix their prices. Similarly, *taxes* affect pricing decisions. Heavy taxes raise prices. The firm has to find out if the tax is *shiftable* or not; if it is shiftable then it should find out to what extent it can be shifted *i.e.* fully or only partly.

Thus, a price policy must include all the objectives in its fold. Then only it can maximise profits without sacrificing the long-term objective of survival and flexibility to adopt to cyclical fluctuations in business. The policy must be *basic* as well as *tactical* and *competitive* as well as *monopolistic* in structure.

2. Objectives of Price Policy

A broadly conceived price policy of a business firm must have certain objectives. The broadest objective of any price policy is *survival* of the firm in the long-run. Since the price policy has both *short-term* and *long-term* telling effects, its objectives must be clearly laid-down.

The total revenue of the firm is a function of its price per unit. Thus, profit is dependent upon pricing. Therefore, extraordinary caution has to be exercised while the pricing decision is taken.

The chief objectives of price policy can be listed as:

1. Fulfilling the *target of revenue* on investment;
2. Fulfilling the *target of growth* of the firm;
3. Improving the firm's share in *aggregate supply*;
4. Improving the *firm's image*;
5. Better *good-will* of the customers;
6. *Stable Prices*;
7. *Adaptation* to changes in the tactics of rival firms;
8. Better *ability to withstand* cyclical variations in business activity; and
9. *Limiting the competition* from rival firms.

Now, a brief explanation of each of the above objectives.

Each firms fixes a *target of revenue* for the year which it has to fulfil by the year end. The price fixed must be such that it enables the firm to attain the target without sacrificing its own growth-rate, share in the market supply, good-will of customers etc.

Attainment of revenue target is not the only objective of a price policy; but it must also do so by ensuring *steady growth* of the firm. The growth should be alround.

Especially under oligopoly and monopolistic competition, the objective of *achievement of better share* in the total supply of the market is important. This is due to the existence of close substitutes. To achieve this objective, the firm has to note the rivals' prices and *selling tactics* such as *price discounts, gift schemes,* etc.

Further, the price policy should be such that it does not spoil the *image of the firm* in the opinion of the consumers. Frequent revival of prices may lead to the firm losing its image in a competitive market.

Price policy and *Customers' good-will* go hand-in-hand. A longstanding goodwill will help the firm to have permanent customers for its product. Hence, initially, a new firm must pay more importance to this objective. It can rise the price of its product to cover the *lost ground* some time later (Caution is necessary to cover at least the costs in the beginning).

Stability of prices is an objective of a sufficiently established firm. The price policy of successive years must not vary widely so that the rise in price covers the rise in costs and allows the firm to have a marginal rise in profit, in which case both the good-will and growth are achieved.

Adoptation to changes in *cyclical fluctuations* and to changes in the *tactics of competitors* in capturing the market are important objectives in a monopolistic market and oligopolistic market. This is because of the independent price-output policies and interdependent price-output policies respectively in the two types of markets.

The last, but not the least, objective of price policy is to limit the possibility of *competition from rivals*. This objective can be achieved by keeping the profits *normal* in an organised way.

3. Factors of Pricing Policy: Costs, Demand and Consumer Psychology

A number of factors are involved in taking a *price-decision* and the chief of which are; (1) The Objectives of the firm; (2) The objectives of pricing in the long and short-run; and (3) The factors involved in taking a pricing decision.

The first and the second aspects of price-decision have been discussed in the preceding sections of this chapter. Therefore, let us limit ourselves in this section to the factors that guide the business economist in determining the price policy.

In the modern set up of the markets, firms produce multiple kinds of products either with product differentiation or without it.

Some firms may be engaged in more than one kind of production. A firm may be engaged in many or any one of the following lines of business:

1. Production of joint-products or complementary products.
2. Production of a totally new product.
3. Production of an unimitated product.

4. Production of a group of products which satisfy similar needs (self-manufactured substitutes).
5. Products for the sale of which the firm itself has sales outlets.

The pricing policy of a firm depends, therefore, on the nature of the product. It is, therefore, well to analyse specific or particular cases of price policy in this last section.

1. Pricing of Jointly Demanded Products: There are some firms which produce not one commodity but more than one. The products may be jointly demanded products or *complementary* products like shoes and socks, tables and chairs and so on.

In the case of complementary products, the demand functions are different but cost functions are common. Therefore, price determination is of the pattern of price discrimination.

In other words, the prices of jointly demanded products produced by the same firm depends on the relationship between Marginal Cost and Marginal Revenue. The price of such goods will be equal to each other's marginal costs and marginal revenues.

Fig. 10.1 illustrates the pricing of complementary commodities.

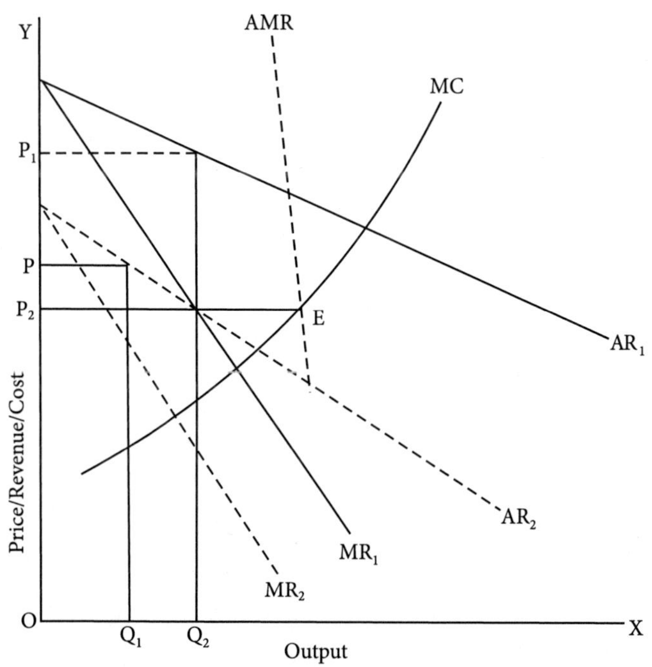

Fig. 10.1. Pricing of Complementary Commodities

In Fig.10.1 AMR is the aggregate marginal revenue from product 1 and product 2 as combined vertically. AR_1 and AR_2 are the average revenue curves of products 1 and 2. The aggregate Marginal Revenue AMR = Marginal Cost at 'E'. The marginal curve MC intersects AMR at E. The equilibrium price is OP_2. The prices of product 1 and product 2 are OP_1 and OP_2. They are sold at OQ_1 and OQ_2.

2. Pricing of New Products: Selling a new product by a new firm in a new industry is a challenging task. Readily available market information is absent and hence *trend projection* and assessment of consumer's reaction is difficult. However, the price policy for a new product is similar to that of an old product. The price of a new product should recover *full costs* in the long-run and *variable cost* in the short-run.

Broadly speaking, there are two *price strategies* for a new product, *viz.*:

1. Skimming-price strategy; and
2. Penetration-price strategy.

Under the former method, the firm fixes a high price and '*skims the cream of demand*' in the beginning. This is possible if the demand is less elastic in relation to the prices in the initial stage of a new product. It is also possible to employ this method when the market is small but profitable and market is in the area of ignorant buyers. It is most useful when the firm has patent rights and no competition.

The latter strategy is that of fixing a low initial price to penetrate into the market or capture the market. It is risky and may result in losses in a small market.

3. Life cycle pricing: After a new product is put into the market it gradually loses its *distinctiveness* and becomes a '*common product*'. Joel Dean calls it as "*the cycle of competitive degeneration*" of a new product. That is, sooner or later competition begins in the market. The time taken for 'degeneration' may be either long or short.

Prof. Joel points out five *stages in degeneration*, *viz.*:

(A) *Introductory Stage:* When consumers' awareness is less and selling costs are high.

(B) *Growth Stage:* When sales grow quickly.

(C) *Maturity Stage:* When sales growth slows down and profit slides down gradually.

(D) *Saturation Stage:* When consumers change over to substitutes or another new product.

(E) *The Decline:* When competition is very keen and sales decrease absolutely and the original *distictiveness* totally disappears as in the case of a new toilet soap or shampoo.

The price policy keeps changing according to the stages of degeneration but covers full costs in the long-run and variable costs in the short-run.

4. Pricing a Mature Product: The brand of the product may begin to lose its popularity and then it is said to have become mature. Yet another symptom of maturity is the *appearance of substitutes*. Then price discounts have to be shown to keep the market going. It may or may not be a '*price-war*'.

5. Product-line pricing: A firm producing a number of products which maybe complementary to each other or substitutes to each other must fix their prices after finding out their relative costs, demand elasticities and the psychology of the consumer or their reaction to the product and preferences.

If prices cover the *full costs*, the percentage of profit will be the same for all *products in the line*. If the prices cover just the *variable cost*, then the, *marginal revenue* (MR) will be the same for the entire '*productline*'. The pricing of some of them in the *product-line* also depends on the nature of elasticity of demand in various markets (according to the psychology of the consumers).

6. Manufacturers' price and Retailers' price policy: The price policy of a manufacturer (or a producer) is different from that of a retailer.

The manufacturer fixes his price on the basis of a vague calculation or '*hindsight costs*'. They sell their products to the wholesalers who do not consume them but pass them on to the retailers. Some manufacturers may even fix the retailers price inclusive of local taxes, packing and freight charges in order to preserve good-will of the consumers.

In the case of retailers '*Invoice Cost*' or the cost of procuring the commodity from the manufacturer or wholesaler is the guide to pricing policy. Then, the price includes retailers' profit. The retailer can influence the consumer by selling many other goods (complementary or otherwise) whereas a manufacturer cannot. In case there is keen retail competition, they may cut down their profit margin and sell at a lower price also. The retailer varies his price (be it high or low) more often according to the consumer's psychology and according to the terms of sale.

11

Pricing Methods

The success or failure of a business organisation solely depends upon the *pricing method* adopted for its product. The method of pricing that a firm adopts depends upon a number of *considerations* that we have analysed in the previous chapter. The method of pricing is always commensurate with the *objectives* of the firm.

A decision on the price policy is a crucial factor. The problems of pricing may be the same for all firms but the way in which each firm optimises the factors involved in pricing varies from firm-to-firm (depending on the nature of the product discussed in the previous chapter-last section). It is the primary duty of a business economist to suggest the most suitable method of pricing to the firm for which he is working. The Business Economist, therefore, holds the key to the success of his firm. Here, he has to take into account a variety of considerations into account.

Generally least assumptive and easy to implement price-policy and pricing method is preferably to any business firm.

However, it is wise to analyse a few important pricing methods in this context. They are:

1. Cost-plus (or Full Cost) Pricing Method;
2. Going-rate Pricing Method;
3. Target Pricing (or pricing for a Rate of Return); and
4. Administered Price Method (of the government).

Let us now discuss each of these methods of pricing in brief.

1. Cost-plus or Full-Cost Pricing Method

This is the simplest and easiest method of pricing. This method is also known as '*Margin Pricing* and 'Mark-up Pricing'.

This is a method under which the price of the product recovers both *Fixed Costs and Variable Costs.* The price also includes the profit margin. Thus, the average total cost of the firm and a certain per cent of profit equals the price under this method. The '*margin*' and '*mark-up*' are the profits of the firm.

In this method of pricing, the price covers:

1. Variable as well as Fixed Costs,
2. Selling Costs,
3. Administrative Costs.

Advantages and Disadvantages of Cost-plus Method

The Cost-plus or full-cost pricing method has mixed benefits and limitations. Let us presently consider these merits and demerits.

Advantages of Cost Plus Method:

1. The Cost-plus method of pricing is the best pricing method in the case of a new product - where the consumer is ignorant of the new product's quality and cost of production.
2. It helps the firm to become a '*price leader*' *or price-setter* for the whole industry.
3. Both *Single-product* and *Multi-product* firms can adopt it easily.
4. It safeguards a firm against the changes in elasticity of demand in the long-run.
5. Costs the least in price-decision.
6. It protects a '*new firm*' with a 'new product' against '*price-war*'.
7. It is also *flexible.*

Disadvantages of Cost-plus Method: The cost-plus method of pricing has some demerits. The main demerits are:

1. This method neglects the influence of demand on price and takes only supply and cost of production into account.
2. It does not fully explain the influence of competition
3. The allocation of costs is over-emphasised.
4. It is based on circular relationship between price and demand, price and cost of production, demand and cost and so on.
5. It employs average cost as the leading guide to pricing and ignores marginal cost.

Yet, these demerits do not completely reduce the utility of the method. Especially, its utility is great in pricing commodities made to consumer's choice and taste, monopoly market pricing and pricing of public utilities.

2. Going-rate Method

This method of pricing has particular reference to oligopoly markets. Under oligopoly one of the few firms fixes a certain price as the *price-leader* and other firms follow this price. Oligopoly firms adjust their prices to the general price structure prevailing in the market or the industry or the going-rate. The industry price is called the '*Going-rate*'. Since, oligopoly firms accept the leading firm's price it is also called the *Acceptance Rate* and the method is called '*Acceptance-Pricing*'. Another reason for calling it as Acceptance Pricing is that the price is always such that it is low enough for the buyers to readily accept the price.

Textiles, motor vehicles, L.P. Records, etc. are priced as per the going-rate method. It is generally useful in pricing '*Matured Products*'. The going rate method gives uniqueness to selling costs when products of different firms are homogeneous. On the other hand, the products are heterogeneous, the prices will have a series and they are set at separate intervals.

Merits of Going-rate Method

The Going-rate Method of pricing has certain basic advantages These accrue especially in an oligopoly market. They are:

1. It avoids *cut-throat competition* through such practices as *dumping* or under-selling of products to destroy competing firms.
2. This method is most *rational* when the product cost cannot be estimated accurately.
3. It is *simple* and costs the least, as no expenditure is necessary to calculate cost of production or to forecast demand.
4. *Price-obstacles* can be easily overcome through the going-rate method under oligopoly.
5. It gives incentive to pricing by firms, which is safer instead of taking the risk of pricing differently and face the consequences. It is *risk-proof* for a new firm to follow or *imitate* the price pattern of others than risk a higher or lower price. Hence, the going-rate pricing is also known as '*Imitative Pricing*'.

3. Pricing for a Rate of Return or Target-Pricing

By the very name and definition of this method, the producer or seller sets his price in such a way that he gets a pre-determined average revenue on his investment. The *average mark-up* on the cost of production is determined for a particular target of returns or revenue.

While doing so, the firm prepares *estimates* of future sales, costs, etc. Prof. Davies and Hughes have developed a formula for calculating the '*Anticipated Rate of Return*' on capital invested with mark-up on cost. That is:

$$\%\ \text{mark-up on cost} = \frac{\text{Total Capital put-in}}{\text{Total Annual Cost}} \times \frac{\text{Planned or Targ etted}}{\text{return}}$$

Example: A firm has invested ₹ 3 crores whose total cost is ₹ 6 crores per annum. The firm expects a rate of return equal to 10%.

To find out the percentage of mark-up on cost let us use Davies and Hughes' formula,* *i.e.*:

$$\frac{\text{Total capital put-in}}{\text{Total annual cost}} \times \text{Planned or Targeted Return}$$

Thus: (in ₹ Crores)

$$\text{Mark-up on cost} = \frac{3\,(\text{Investment})}{6\,(\text{Investment})} \times 10\ (\text{Target of return})$$

$$= 5\%\ (\text{which is the mark-up on cost})$$

(*Note:* If the cost per unit is ₹ 10 with 5% mark-up on cost then the selling price will be fixed at ₹ 11 per unit)

The price policy cannot be rigid in any firm because the market forces, costs, the size of the competitive firms, etc. are subject to changes. These changes compel firms to change their prices to suit new circumstances.

There are at least '*Three*' methods to cope up with such changes. They are:

1. A Firm can push-up or push-down the price to maintain the constant mark-up variable costs;
2. Push-up or push-down the sale-price and maintain the margin of existing profit; and
3. Change the perunit price to hit the targeted rate of return on investment.

There is a great demerit in doing so *i.e.*, it overlooks the influence that demand may have on price-revival (specially upward revival on consumers).

4. Administered Prices

The modern business work is no more the 'Smithian Utopia' where Adam Smith and many of his followers *day-dreamt of non-interference* by the

* 'Management Economics'—I.R. Davies and S. Hughes, p. 157.

government in any kind of business activity. The days of the '*Natural Order*' and '*Individual Liberty*' are long gone. So also the utopian sovereign consumers of capitalism and by the passage of time, the consumer has become an object of *slavery* in the hands of the monopolistic firms. In short, *the buyers is at the other end of* the producers' stick and: it is the *dirty end* of the stick.

Therefore, the governments all over the world, have imposed certain '*Legal Constraints*' as to the price at which some goods must be sold by the private sector.

The governments have *regulated*, fixed and controlled certain prices of commodities of common consumption, of basic necessities etc.

The principle of pricing is that of No-profit-No-loss in these sectors.

As this is done, the pricing method is really the 'Cost-plus Method' as in the case of *new-products*. The price covers taxes, revenues and dividend on company shares.

The most productive unit is studied before administering the prices of such commodities. Sometimes even the 'Marginal Unit' (the unit which is just able to exist) and the '*most productive unit*' are juxtaposed to arrive at the *administered price*.

The 'Depreciation Costs' (cost of replacement of worn-out capital or replacement of it) are calculated on the basis of '*cost history*' of the selected firm or firms.

The rate of returns on capital is generally on the basis of 'fixed capital or fixed assets' of the chosen firm.

12

Collective Bargaining and Wages

There was a time when the exploitation of labour was unlimited and very low wages were paid to labour for very long hours of labour. In the modern system of production labour has organised itself into unions all over the world. The collective bargaining strength of labour is certainly better today.

The most important function of collective bargaining (or trade unionism) is that it secures uniform wages to all workers of the category in the whole industry.

Collective bargaining has come into its own specially since the 'Great Depression' and the World War II. Collective bargaining has become a force now. Adam Smith and David Ricardo believed that wages cannot rise above the *subsistence level.* If it does, the profits will decline and reduce investment and employment. This was the essence of the 'Subsistence Theory of Wages'.

'The Marginal Productivity Theory of wages also ruled out the possibility of collective bargaining's success in raising wages. This they maintained that '*Wages tend to be equal to the marginal revenue product of labour*'. Further, it maintained that trade unions can raise wages only by reducing employment. In that case a rise wages above marginal revenue product will reduce the demand, real wages and the purchasing power.

The Subsistence Theory as well as the Marginal Productivity Theory of wages have been found to be defective and invalid. The trade union have been able to secure better wages for at least three reasons, *viz.*,

1. Labour monopoly in the Labour market
2. Monopoly in labour market (*i.e.*, a single buyer) while labour is unorganised; and
3. A strong trade union challenging the Association of Employers.

In these situations workers can collectively bargain from the employers.

In a perfectly competitive labour market, wages depend on the supply of and demand for labour in the long-run. However, in the short-run, the supply of labour can be decreased and wages can be increased.

In that case the Unions have to take the following steps to reduce the supply of labour:

1. Motivate unemployed workers to seek jobs in other industries.
2. Rise the membership fee for newly recruited workers.
3. Force the employers to rise the term of apprenticeship.
4. Influence the authorities to impose restrictions on immigration of labour.

However, the possibility of reducing the supply of labour finally depends upon the *elasticity of demand for labour*. If it is relatively inelastic then supply of labour cannot be reduced considerably.

If the labour union can increase the Marginal Revenue Product of Labour, wages can be increased significantly. Then employment can also increase. However, it is only a long-run possibility. In the long-run, the demand for the product of the industry may rise and the demand for labour may increase. Then the Unions can demand a higher wage rate and negotiate collectively.

According to Dr. Marshall, wages can be raised by the Unions of Workers under the following conditions:

1. When the demand for certain group of workers is inelastic.
2. When the demand for the product of labour is inelastic.
3. When the wages of that group of workers is only a negligible part of the total Wage-bill.
4. When the reward of other factors can be reduced.
5. When prices of raw-materials could be brought down.

All this is possible only in the short-run.

Under monopolistic market conditions wages are likely to be below the Marginal Revenue product. The trade unions can succeed in rising wages to the level of Marginal Revenue product.

Trade unions can also improve the productivity of workers through various measures. This would increase the productive capacity of the firm. At that stage the union can demand a rise in wages.

REAL AND NOMINAL WAGES

It is a custom in Economic Theory to distinguish between two types of Wages *viz.*, Real Wages and Money Wages or Nominal Wages.

Wages paid in terms of money for the work done by labour is called '*Money Wages*' or nominal wages. On the other hand, the quantity of goods and services that can be bought with the Money Wages is called '*Real Wages*'. Hence, real wages represent the purchasing power of money wages at a given price level.

The real wages can be measured with the aid of a formula *viz.*,

$$R = \frac{W}{P}$$

Where R = Real Wage, W = Money Wage and P = Price Level.

If the Money Wage is constant and the price level rises then the Real Wages will fall. Similarly, if the Money Wages rise and the price level is constant then the Real Wages will rise. With a rise in real wages the standard of living of workers rises and *vice-versa.*

The real wages are therefore relative. They are related to the *Cost of living index number.* If the index number increases, the real wages fall. Thus, real wages can also be measured through the formula:

$$\text{Real Wages} = \frac{\text{Money Wages}}{\text{Cost of Living Index Number}}$$

In the words of Adam Smith, "*Labour is rich or poor, is well or ill-rewarded, in proportion to the real, not to the nominal value of his wages.*"

Thus, the real remuneration of labour is measured in terms of advantages and disadvantages associated with the work.

Determinants of Real Wages

The real wages at any point of time depend on certain important factors. The price determinants of real wages can be summed up as under:

1. The General Price Level: Real wages rise or fall inversely with the price level. This is why the real wages fall when there is inflation.

2. Fringe Benefits: Additional benefits provided by the employer such as rent-free accommodation, transport, subsidised food, etc. should naturally increase real wages.

3. Working Conditions: Real wages are affected by the hours of work, regularity or irregularity of work, "agreeableness of work", etc.

4. Opportunity to Earn Extra Income: If an employee can earn extra income in addition to the regular wage the real wages will be high. For instance, a worker may earn *over-time wages*, a teacher may write a book during his spare time and so on.

5. Risk or Ease of Job: Risky and dangerous jobs have high money wages but low real wages. (*e.g.* Mining workers' wages).

6. Promotional opportunities: Workers who have chances of quick promotion and success earn more and real wages rise after some time.

7. Expenses of Profession: A profession which needs more training or involves more professional expenses gives less real wages. For instance a lawyer has to maintain an office and staff. So his real wage is less though his money income is high.

LIQUIDITY PREFERENCE THEORY OF INTEREST

The Liquidity Preference Theory of Interest was propounded by Lord Keynes. According to him '*interest is the reward for parting with liquidity*'. In simple terms, interest is determined by the supply of money and the demand for money. Hence, Keynes' liquidity preference theory is also known as the '*Monetary Theory of Interest*'.

Supply of Money: The supply of money at any time consists of total currency and coins in circulation. The supply of money over a *point of time* is fixed or constant or inelastic. It is determined by the central bank. As it is constant, the supply curve of money will be horizontal to OX axis.

Demand for Money: In Keynesian terminology the demand for money is called as '*Liquidity Preference*'. Keynes defines Liquidity Preference (LP) as 'the desire of the community to hold cash during a given point of time'. It may also be called that part of the income of the community which is *hoarded*. Hoarding of income, according to Keynes "*lulls our disquietude*". The rate of interest that people demand to dishoard income or savings measures the '*degree of their disquietude*' according to Keynes.

Keynes defines the rate of interest as "*The premium which has to be offered to induce people to hold the wealth in some form other than hoarded money.*"

In other words, if the liquidity preference is very strong a high rate of interest must be offered to induce them to *part with liquidity*. Thus, according to the liquidity preference theory, there is a direct functional relationship between the rate of interest and LP. They rise and fall together.

Lord Keynes has pointed out *three* reasons for holding liquid cash or *cash balances*. He calls them '*Motives for liquidity preference*'. These motives hold the stage in the theory. Hence, it is useful to analyse the motives in some detail.

Motives for Liquidity Preference

Keynes distinguishes among three kinds of motives. They are:

1. Transactionary Motive;
2. Precautionary Motive; and
3. Speculative Motive.

Let us analyse each one of them in some detail.

1. Transactionary Motive: Keynes defines the Transactionary Motive as the savings held by the community over a point of time to meet the "*needs of cash for the current transactions of personal and business transactions*".

As far as individuals are concerned this motive means that they hold cash balances to meet day-to-day expenditure.

The firms and the government hold cash balances to meet administrative expenses of the miscellaneous kind that arise from day-to day.

Thus, the transactionary motive is further sub-divided into two types *viz.*,

(a) Personal Transactionary Motive; and

(b) Business Transactionary Motive.

Keynes defines the former as the "*need to bridge the interval between the receipt of income and its disbursement*' by house-bolds. The latter is called by him as the "*interval between the time of incurring business costs and that of the receipt of the sale proceeds*" by business firms.

Thus, persons or house-holds and firms which earn income daily or weekly hold less cash than those who earn income monthly or annually (as the case may be).

There are many determinants of transactionary motive. They are:

(a) Expectations of income recievers;

(b) The level of per-period income;

(c) Nature of Employment *i.e.,* regular or seasonal or part-time employment;

(d) The nature of price level *i.e.,* whether there is inflation or deflation etc.

(e) The volume of turnover of the firm; and

(f) The easiness of getting credit facility.

2. Speculative Motive: While house-holds hold a part of each balances to stock-up consumers' goods when they fear a rise in their prices in the nearest future, the firms, on the other hand do so to buy and stock raw-materials or stocks and shares for the same reasons.

As Keynes puts it: Money held for this purpose is for "*securing profit from knowing better, than the market, what the future will bring forth.*"[1]

The amount of cash held for this purpose depends basically on:

1. The Rate of Interest (short-term rate); and
2. Bond values and share values.

Thus, the speculative demand for money is *inversely related* to the rate of interest. In other words, higher rates of interest reduce the speculative demand and *vice-versa*.

3. Precautionary Motive: The precautionary motive refers to according to Keynes, '*Money kept (is) like water kept in reserve in a water tank' which is to be used up soon.*[*]

Keynes defines precautionary motive thus: It relates to "*The desire to provide for contingencies requiring sudden expenditures and for unforeseen opportunities of advantageous purchases*".

The precautionary motive is regulated by the following factors:

1. The *level of income of the house*-hold or firm.
2. The level or nature of business activity.
3. The degree of chances of availability of liquid assets.
4. The cost of holding cash relative to its investment.
5. The rate of interest offered by commercial banks on Bank Deposits, etc.

Rate of Interest Under the LP Theory

Now that you have known the various fundamentals of the LP theory I think that you are prepared to know or understand the way in which the rate of interest is determined under the Keynesian Theory of Interest.

It was Dr. Marshall who compared price determination to the '*pair of scissors*' and Keynes rightly vowed it to him in his '*General Theory*' when he called him "The greatest of the economist for another hundred years to come" (or so).

The determination of interest rate has been theoretically analysed till now. This is diagramatically illustrated in Fig. 12.1.

---

* The wording in brackets and outside the quote are mine.

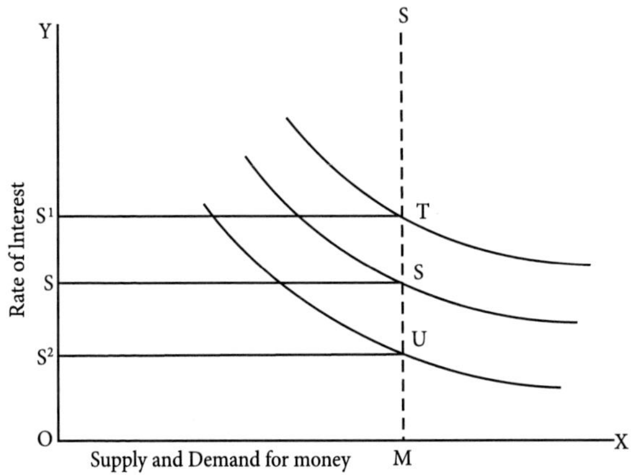

Fig. 12.1. Determination of Interest Rate

In Fig.12.1 the equilibrium rate of interest is OS where the supply of money is equal to the demand for money (*i.e.* LP and supply of money are equal to each other). If LP falls to OS^2 the rate of interest falls to OS^2.

Criticisms

Keynes' theory of interest is subject to the following criticisms in brief:

1. It ignores other factors than monetary factors such as the share prices and bond prices.
2. It is inadequate and misleading because it deals with the rate of interest in the short period only.
3. It suffers from methodological fallacy, as there are so many other things than money to part which the hoarders have to be induced.
4. The theory regards money only as a store of wealth and disregards it as other kinds of functionary agent.
5. Liquidity preference as such is not essential to explain the causation of interest, because a man investing in bonds or shares would still be having liquidity according to Vener.
6. It ignores the real factors of the rate of interest according to Prof. Knut Wicksell and Hazlit.

It is apt to conclude with the following words about the LP theory: That the theory is indeterminate as well as adequate, both too broad and too narrow at the same time.

Which of these is used, will depend upon the nature of the economy (*i.e.,* industrial economy or monetised economy or agrarian economy or dual economy). It also depends on the purpose of calculation of National Income.

Uses of National Income Estimates

The estimation of National Income provides a fund of information when carefully analysed. It is of national importance. It can be rightly called '*National Accounting*'.

The aggregate picture is presented by such estimates as about the performance of the economy. The following are the major uses of National Income Estimates:

1. The estimates give a *Cinematographic picture* of the performance of the economy over a period of time.
2. They throw light on the *sectoral contribution* to National Income.
3. The estimates form the *infrastructure of Economic policies.*
4. They form the basis of *planning for growth.*
5. The different constituent data enable producers and investors to undertake *forecasting* and *decision-making.*
6. They provide useful data to economic theoreiticians to propound Economic Theories.
7. They also enable us to find out the *per capita* income and compare the; same with that of the preceding year or years.
8. They help *comparative economic analysis* of economic variables of different periods.
9. They are useful in comparing international standards of living.
10. Lastly, they serve as a useful guide to the *policy of taxation* to be adopted in future by the Government.

Thus, National Income Statistics have varied uses. They are useful both theoretically and practically. They have become indispensable in the modern world. Hence, regular National Income estimates are made annually in all countries and published by the respective Central Banks.

The success of any business is usually judged by its profits. It is the standard test of any firm's strength. It is generally agreed that profit maximisation is the primary objective of a business firm. It is also true that it is not the only objective. However, the study of a firm under Business Economics hovers around the concept of profit.

Thus, Profit maximisation as a concept is very useful in choosing the right decision. However, there are *non-profit* business objectives also. Often, a firm may aim at *Industry* leadership instead of profit maximisation. It may do so by maximising total sales or by producing maximum *product lines.*

Many firms may aim at maximum *consumer welfare* through goodwill. Very often dominant firms may wilfully avoid profit maximisation for fear of attracting competition state intervention by way of taxes, nationalisation, regulation of prices etc.

Profit maximisation is also avoided to evade the demand for higher *wages* and *bonus.* Some firms may consider *solvency* as more important than profit maximisation.

This does not mean that such firms do not earn profit at all. Nevertheless, they do earn adequate profit and cover the risk of losses. According to Peter Drucker, "It is the first duty of business to survive. The guiding principle of Business Economics..... is not the maximisation of profits; it is the avoidance of loss."

There are a number of alternative profit policies. There are at least *six alternatives* to profit maximisation policy. They are:

1. Long-run Survival: Rothschild has put forward the objective of long-run survival of the firm as a primary motive. According to him securing profits should come next to security of the firm in the long-run.

2. Safety Margin: According to William Fellner, a business organisation must aim at a policy to ensure *safety margin* as an alternative to profit maximisation.

3. Leisure: According to Scitovsky, leisure is an alternative to profit maximisation. He argues that a business man can either choose leisure or profit. If the choice is leisure, he has to sacrifice profit and if the choice is maximum profit, he has to forego leisure. If he wants both then he has to compromise between them.

4. Liquidity: Adequate liquidity is proposed by W.W. Cooper as an alternative to profit maximisation policy. According to him, *solvency* or liquidity can be ensured through a sound financial position and control. According to Reader, a businessman cannot have both maximum profit and financial control but has to choose between the two. Often, he is in the position of *an as paralysed between two equally attractive bundles of hay as in the parable.*

5. Sales Maximisation: According to Prof. Baumol of Princeton University, a modern business firm must maximise sales with constraint of profit. He argues that sales have become an 'end-all' and 'be-all' of business firms. This does not imply maximisation of physical volume of sales; it simply means maximisation of total revenue. It does not mean that the firm does not earn profit. The firm should earn minimum rate of profit after which sales become the prime concern.

Prof. Baumol defines minimum sales as "*the funds (required) to pay some satisfactory rate of dividends, to re-invest for growth and ensure financial safety.*"

6. Satisfactory Return: Lastly, H.A. Simon suggests that a firm must try to earn a Satisfactory rate of return on investment instead of maximising profit. For instance, the Indian Tariff Commission has suggested a minimum of 15% on investment. After taxes and allowance on average net fixed assets and working capital the minimum final rate of return works out to about 7.5%.

Therefore, the selection of an appropriate *profit policy* is an arduous task. The market conditions and *managerial decision* regarding the basic objective of the firm ultimately becomes the guide to profit policy.

Basic Objectives of Profit Policy

A Business Entrepreneur may have umpteen goals in view but all of which cannot be fulfilled. A firm with low profits is surely under poor management is even a common man's conclusion.

Consciously, any firm works towards a '*targeted rate of return*'. Then, the immediate question is 'are there any guidelines or aims to profit policy?' Certainly, the answer is *Yes*.

There are *Four* popularly practised guidelines to profit policy decision and they are:

1. *Attraction of sufficient equity capital* - without harming the interests of the existing share-holders;
2. Equality between profit rate and *Normal Rate of Profit*;
3. *Comparably equal rate of profit* of the firm in question with that of competing firms; and
4. *Profit rate commensurate with projected growth* rate of the firm.

PROFIT PLANNING

(A) Meaning and Definition

Risk-bearing and *uncertainly bearing* are two aspects of a business organisation. Prof. Clark and Prof. Knight have clearly demonstrated this long ago in their *'Dynamic Theory of Profit'* and the *'Risk-bearing Theory of Profit'* respectively. Hence, a business firm has to insulate itself against the dynamic changes in tastes, fashions, technology etc. which generate risk and uncertainty. This requires profit planning.

Profit planning can be called as all those precautions that a firm takes in order to ensure a more or less stable rate of profit against the most unforeseeable risks or uninsurable risks of the market changes.

Profit planning, therefore, involves demand forecasting according to the nature of the product of the firm (whether the product is *new* or *matured* and so on).

Profit planning has to be done very carefully during inflation to overcome the uncertainty of inflation.

In short, profit planning refers to a wide number of factors affecting profitability ranging from price, cost and size of the firm to the whims and fancies of the consumers and technology.

(B) Some Leading Definitions of Profit Planning

A number of managerial economists have defined profit planning variously but all of them boil down to the basic fact that profit planning is fundamental to profit-making in the long-run.

Let us presently see what these men of Managerial or Business Economics have to say about profit planning.

(a) *Alfred and Beatty:* Profit "*Planning is the thinking process, the organised foresight, the vision based on facts and experience that is required for intelligent action.*"

Thus, the Alfred-Beatty definition stresses the logicity and scientific nature as well as the practical experience required in preparing a profit policy.

(b) *Koontz-O'Donnell: "Profit planning is planning in advance (as to) what to do, how to do it, when to do it and who is to do it...."*

(c) *Profs. Fanner-Richman: "Profit planning is essentially decision making as it involves choosing alternatives"* of profit-making.

(d) *George Terry: "planning is .... selecting and relating of facts ... making and using of assumptions ... necessary to achieve the desired results."*

Thus, profit planning requires foresight, analysis of the market situation and information, selling of objectives, choice of aims, results of the past and so on.

Major Considerations in Profit Planning or Main Characteristics of a Sound Profit Plan

Any healthy business firm makes profit consistent with the soundness of its profit planning; or more reasonably, consistent with its risk planning. Profiteering cannot be left to chance and has to be scientifically planned on the basis of calculated risks.

A business firm often drifts away in the absence of profit planning. It is therefore useful to know what makes profit planning sound or effective. More precisely, a sound profit plan possesses certain basic characteristics. The chief of them are briefly noted below.

1. An Intelligent Process: Profit planning involves a high degree of intelligence and alertness. It is a kind of *mental gymnastics* regarding demand forecasting, risk calculation, economy, profit policy-making and so on. Thus, according to Profs. Koontz and O' Donnell, "*It is the intellectual process of detennination of the best course of action under a given market situation.*"

2. Focusing Objectives: Profit planning is essentially objective. It involves policies, procedures, strategies and targeting.

3. Selective: There may be a number of alternative courses of action. A firm has to *select* the best course of action based on the nature of its product, demand elasticity, degree of competition, etc. It is basically concerned with the *what, when* and *how* of production.

4. All-pervasive: Profit planning is all-pervasive. That is, it covers all stages of organisation *viz. Strategy, administration* and *Operation* of the business organisation. Thus, it calls for top brass, middle and lower level administration or management.

5. Integration: Profit planning is an integrated process. It covers setting down objectives, policy-making, programming and laying down procedures and strategies.

6. Productivity: The ultimate goal of profit planning is to increase the efficiency or productivity of the firm. Maximum output at minimum cost with maximum profit should be the final goal.

7. Flexibility: Profit planning must incorporate *adjustability* or *flexibility*. A profit plan must continually assess and reasses, ascertain and re-ascertain, adopt and re-adopt itself to the dynamic changes in demand, competition, substitutes, etc.

In short, a good profit plan must have clear objectives, be simple and rational. It must be comprehensive, flexible and balanced, all at once. It should be unbiased and must coordinate long and short-term objectives.

Why to Plan Profits?

Then a fundamental question arises namely, why does a firm plan profits? Or is it necessary to plan profits? Or is it all that important? And, are there no limitations to profit planning? These queries lead us to a discussion on the importance and limitations of planning.

It is needless to emphasise the important part played by profit planning in the life and survival of a business firm.

The following is a summary of the significance of profit planning.

1. Insures against Risk and Uncertainty: Profit planning is an insurance against the vagaries of business conditions. It helps the management to prepare for the uncertainties of the market forces and lends a certain degree of *orderliness* and certainty to the conduct of business and to profit.

2. Simplifies complexity: Modern business is complicated. It needs an army of specialised personnel and special machines; unplanned business cannot cope with all these. Planning helps a firm to decide what to do, when, where and how to do a job; all of which influence profit.

3. Lends Co-ordination: Planned programmes, policies, objectives and procedures enables better co-ordination of various aspects business management and group-action.

4. Lends effective control: Planning costs, fixing responsibilities duties, work and time adds effectiveness to control over business. Planning helps in judging performance and profit. We can easily discover the causes for any deviation from the predetermined objectives or decisions. It would be foolish to expect effective control over business without planning.

5. Leads to fuller and better utilisation of resources: The resources of the firm can be utilised fully without wastage of time or money or men and material through proper planning. *Optimisation of capacity utilisation* and economy are a great benefit of planning and results in good profit.

6. Removes confusion and duplication of work: Planning is the '*sine-qua-non*' of unity in action at different levels of decisions. The whole set of *predetermined policies* from production to pricing and marketing gain *decisiveness* and *exactness* and there will be no room for confusion and duplication of work or consequent *wastes* when everything is preplanned. All this is essential for profit maximisation.

Thus, H.G. Hicks rightly concludes that, "*Planning is clearly a prerequisite..... It is utterly foolish to think that controlling could be accomplished without planning; without planning there is no pre-*

determined understanding of the desired performance." Further, according to Koontz and O'Donnell, "Planning bridges the gap between from where we are to where we want to go." In short, planning is relating of facts with the furture with a thread of well founded assumptions to fulfil the desired objects. Hence, planning is the essence of successful business.

Limits of Planning

In the preceding section, we found that planning is primary to business management. We saw how it gives orderliness, effectiveness and stability to business: continuity and coordination in operating.

It is wise to be aware of some of the limitations of planning also. In other words, planning is beset with certain obstacles. It is thus hindered in its scope.

The basic and most familiar limitations maybe classified as follows:

A. Forecasting Limitation: The whole of planning is based on forecasting. The forecasting itself is based on the availability of reliable and *adequate* data. Very often a certain forecast such as '*Demand Forecast*' may fail due to inadequate and ureliable data supplied by the consumers or *manufactured by* the salesmen and sales representatives. Then, the firm would have to face *rough-weather conditions*.

B. Limitation of Time: Planning consumes a lot of time since the whole set of forces to be analysed are dynamic and the whole market is the *laboratory of the planner*. More often than not, planning may be done in a hurry in which case the firm may incur losses or uncertainty. Then, it has to *repent the hurry in planning at leisure*.

C. Money-Cost Limitation: The cost of planning may be high in certain types of planning. The process of collection of data, etc. involves huge expenses. Hence, the method of forecasting of planning selected should be simple and economical. Lest, the firm's costs increase and bloat up the price. This could be dangerous in an oligopoly market with homogeneous products.

D. Limitation of Rigidity: Sticking to schedules of supply, price, profit, etc. becomes compulsory under planning of business. It makes decisions least flexible. It makes a firm feel that it is in a *tight Jacket* when actuals go in the wrong direction (as in the case of a sudden *Depression* or *Recession* in the level of business in general). A *sudden dip* in the market will make room for a hoast of uncertainties and risks thereby reducing profit.

E. Exogenous Limitations: Planning need not become a disadvantage due to indigenous or internal shortcomings of the firm. There are many exogenous or external forces at work also. A number of natural factors, like the break-down of law and order, a war, etc. can upset business. The political environment may also change to the disadvantage of the firm's planned decisions.

Essential Questions Involved in Profit Planning

The limitations of profit planning can be overcome by bearing some basic questions or considerations in mind to a certain extent. The profit planning personnel must ask themselves the following questions before settling down to actual planning of profits:

1. What are the likely business opportunities or new problems that may arise?
2. Which are the alternative objectives open to the firm to maximise profit?
3. What are the possibilities of competition?
4. Whether it should prepare a new plan or will it be sufficient to modify the old plan?
5. What were the reasons for higher or lower profits in the preceding year or years?
6. Which of the methods of profit planning is most suitable to its product and market situation?
7. Are the other competing firms efficient?
8. Which is the best course of action to work out a workable plan?
9. Are there any peculiar problems facing competing firms in profit maximisation? and so on.

BREAK-EVEN CHART OR ANALYSIS

Meaning: The concept of break-even analysis or a break-even chart reveals the relationship between cost and output. It has a great relevance to the practice of costing in Business Economics. Profit forecasting is founded on this concept.

It also serves profit planners, trade union leaders (in demanding better wages and bonus) stock-market agents (in dealing with shares of companies) and the government in levying corporate taxes on business firms.

A Break-even Chart' (BEC) depicts the various alternatives of cost and output possibilities in a tabular form (The same can also be diagramatised as we will soon illustrate in Fig. 12.2).

The Break-even Chart contains a particular 'Break-even Point.' *The Break-even Point (BEP) is the point at which the firm neither earns a profit nor incurs losses.* Thus, at the BEP the firm's '*net income is zero*'.

That is, any further expansion of sales or output will bring *decreasing minimum profits.* After the BEP the firm will incur losses.

The BEC can also be defined as under: *It is a graphic representation indicating the short-term relation of TC (Total Cost) to TR (Total Revenue) per increase in input.*

A break-even chart is a quick look at the beginning of profits, beginning of losses and the 'safety area' in between.

Finding the Break-Even Point

The break-even point can be found out by two methods, *viz*:

A. Physical Method; and

B. Money-value of Output Method.

Dr. S. Shankaran has demonstrated the physical method of finding out BEP with the help of the following Table.

TABLE 1*

Out-put in units	Total Revenue (TR) at ₹ 4 per unit	Total Fixed Cost (TFC) (₹)	Total Variable Cost (TVC) (₹)	Total Cost (TC)
0	0	300	0	300
100	400	300	300	600
200	800	300	600	900
300	1,200	300	900	1,200
400	1,600	300	1,200	1,500
500	2,000	300	1,500	1,800
600	2,400	300	1,800	2,100

Note: Selling [price is ₹ 4 per unit]

Break-even point by physical Method: A single-product firm generally uses the *physical method* to discover the break-even point (BEP). The BEP is the point at which the total sales earn revenue equal to *fixed* and *variable costs.* It is the point of intersection between Total Cost curve and Total Revenue curve.

* Prof. Shankaran—Page 188: 'Management Economics', Ch. 11.

To find the BEP we must assume the price per unit as constant (*i.e.*, ₹ 4/- per unit) in our table. Thus, the market is assumed as perfect competition.

It can be observed that Total Revenue (TR) is increasing proportionately in column 2 of the table. All the units are sold out at ₹ 4 per unit. The Total Fixed Cost (TFC) is kept constant at ₹ 300 throughout while the Total Variable Cost (TVC) is increasing throughout column 4.

As per the table, when output is zero TR and TVC are also *zero* but the firm incurs a TFC of ₹ 300. At 100 units of output TR is ₹ 400 and TC is ₹ 600 (*i.e.* TVC + TFC = 300 + 300). The net loss is equal to ₹ 200 (*i.e.*, TC – TR = Total loss of 600 – 400 = 200).

Similarly, the loss at 200 units of output is ₹ 100. When output reaches 300 units TR (₹ 1200) = TC (₹ 1200) and hence there is neither losses nor profits. Thus, *the firm reaches BEP at 300 units of output.* Beyond that level of output the firm earns profits (The profit being ₹ 100 at 400 units, ₹ 200 at 500 units and ₹ 300 at 600 units).

Break-Even Chart

The break-even point can also be located diagramatically or in a chart as in Fig. 12.2. The diagram is prepared on the basis of the same assumptions as in the foregoing Table.

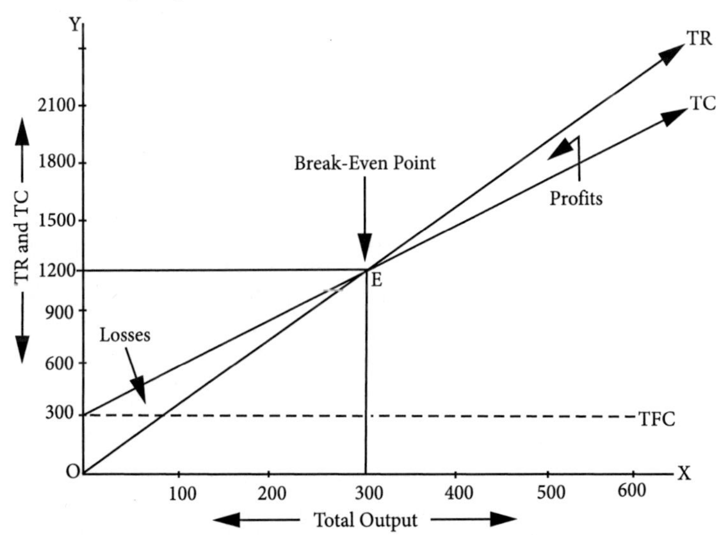

Fig. 12.2. Break-even Chart (at ₹ 4 unit)

In Fig. 12.2 the Revenue and Costs are measured on OY axis while total output is measured on OX axis. TR and TC are Total Revenue curve and Total Cost curve respectively. TFC is the dotted Total Fixed Cost curve which is horizontal to OX axis because Total Fixed Cost is constant.

TR and TC curves intersect at the point 'E' when output is 300 units and Total Cost is ₹ 1200. At E, the TR =TC. As per the definition of BEP the point E is the *Break-even Point*. Above E the firm earns profits and below E it incurs losses. Hence, E is the only point at which the firm reaches the break-even point.

Some More Methods to Find out BEP

There are two more methods of finding out the BEP for a firm.

They are:

1. Physical Units Method; and
2. Sales Value Method.

1. Physical Units Method: In this method the BEP is determined in terms of Average Revenue and Average Cost (AR and AC). Under this method the firm reaches BEP at the output level where AR or price per Unit = AC. Then, the AR or price covers both Full Average Variable cost (AVC) and a *part of the Average Fixed Cost* (AFC). *That part of the price or AR which covers a part of AFC is technically called the 'Contribution Margin'* (because it contributes to the recovery of part of AFC).

Hence, the BEP by this method is the point or stage where the Total Contribution Margin (TCM) = Total Fixed Costs (TFC).

The following 'formula' can be used to find out BEP by *Physical Units Method.*

$$\text{BEP (by physical Units Method)} = \frac{\text{TFC}}{\text{TCM Per Unit}}$$

(To find out the Contribution Margin the formula is: AR—AVC)

$$\text{BEP} = \frac{\text{TFC}}{\text{AR or price} - \text{AVC}}$$

Numerical Example: Let TFC = ₹ 600,

AR = ₹ 8 and AVC = ₹ 6. Then:

$$\text{BEP} = \frac{₹\,600}{₹\,8 - ₹\,6} = \frac{₹\,600}{₹\,2} = ₹\,300$$

2. Sales Value Method: BEP by Physical Units Method is suitable only to *single-product firms.*

In the case of a *Product Line firm* the BEP should be found out only through '*Sales Value Method*' or by Money value of sales or Total Revenue.

In this method also we use the concept of *Total Contribution Margin*. However, TCM is expressed as *a ratio to sales* and not as contribution to TFC.

Here, the formula to find out Contribution Margin is:

$$\frac{\text{TR} - \text{TVC}}{\text{TR}} = \text{Contribution Margin}$$

Thus:

$$\text{BEP} = \frac{\text{IFC}}{\text{Contribution Ratio to Sales}}$$

As per information in Table 1 the firm attains BEP by Sales Value Method when its sales value is ₹ 1200 at 300 units

i.e. ₹ 300/0.25 = ₹ 1,200/-

Further Explanation:

Total Revenue	.....		₹ 1,200
TFC	.....	₹ 300	
TVC	.....	₹ 900	
Total Cost	.....	₹ 1200	TR = 1,200
Net Profit/Loss	.....	Nil	

Assumptions of BEP Analysis

The evaluation of BEP is hypothetical. The main assumptions of BEP analysis are:

1. It is assumed that the *volume of sales* and the total output are equal *i.e.* all that is produced is sold in the market. Thus, there is no *inventory*.
2. The price per unit or the AR remains constant.
3. Revenue rises or falls with a rise or fall in the quantity of production.
4. The costs of production are *perfectly variable* or *perfectly fixed* throughout.

In the real world of business the facts may differ from these assumptions. There is often no uniform price per unit. It may be reduced for bulk purchases. Even the costs are not fully fixed in the long run. Even the assumption of perfect competition is *mythical* and *Utopian*.

However, let it be said that the concept of BEP serves very many useful purposes. (1) It gives a '*worm's eye-view*' of a firm's business condition. (2) It is an *indirect guide* to the assessment of *profitability zone* of a business firm. (3) It also reveals the strength or otherwise of a business firm. (4) Lastly, the concept helps the firm to adopt decisions to changed conditions or *dynamism* is lent by it to *decision-making* regarding *Safety Margin*.

Thus, in spite of its limitations it is useful.

Limitations of BEP

The basic limitations of BEP stem from its unreal assumptions. They are:

1. The calculation of BEP is static.
2. It tries to foresee the future trends on the basis of past sales which is *incorrect*.
3. It overlooks the fact that *selling costs* are unstable in the long-run.
4. The calculation of BEP becomes unreal in the long-run (*i.e.* beyond a year)
5. It neglects factors other than output which influence profits and cost.
6. It neglects the errors arising due to estimates of costing and cost-price relations, over-simplification of dynamic market forces into passiveness.

In short, the concept of BEP is unsuitable to long-run conditions of business. At best it can project only roughly, the short-run guidelines to profit-policy. The fact remains that estimation of BEP is significant to short-term projections of a business firm.

LINEAR PROGRAMMING

Application of Linear Programming to Business Economics

'Linear programming' also called 'Activity Analysis' was first developed by George Danting in 1947. He made use of it to prepare a mathematically planned programme for the diversification of the American Air Force's supplies. It is thus a mathematical device. It is now developed and available to Business Economics and it is liberally applied to the thoery of the firm—its problems of cost minimisation or *diet problem* and profit maximisation.

Meaning

Mathematically speaking it is a quantitative method or technique applied to the problems of analysis of optimum decision subject to constraints of *linear inequalities*. It is applied to problems requiring solution to maximisation or minimisation stated in terms of a set of variable of linear inequalities.

Thus, if a and b are the *linear variables* and if they are the "*function*" of C then the "*value*" of C is maximised when a "*movement*" from that point causes a "decrease" in the value of C. Its value is minimised when its value increases even due to a minute movement from the point.

Now the important question is, what kind of a change is "*linear*" and what kind of a change is "*non-linear*"? The answer to this question in plain language is that (for instance) if output is accompanied with a change in price and cost per unit it is *linear* and if cost and price remain constant when output change then it is *non-linear*.

Therefore, linear programming may be defined as:

> *"A method to decide the optimum combination of factors to produce a given output or the optimum combination of products to be produced by a given plant and equipment."*

It can be used to determine the choice of technique of production for producing a commodity. The technique of linear programming is akin to that employed in industry input-output analysis.

Conditions and Generalisations in Linear Programming

There are certain aims and objectives of linear porgramming. The basic aim of linear programming is to find out and offer optimal solutions to decision-making and study their significant features. However, linear programming cannot proceed without certain conditions and generalisations. Let us try to know what these conditions and generalisations are.

1. Objective Function: First and foremost we must set before ourselves the objective of linear programming. This is known as the '*Objective Function*' of linear programming. The objective as to whether it is profit maximisation or output maximisation or cost minimisation should be determined at the outset itself. It is also known as '*Criterion Function*'. If maximisation of output is the objective minimisation of cost is its dual problem. Quantity maximisation is called the original problem or '*primal*' problem while cost minimisation is its '*dual*' problem and *vice-versa*.

2. Process or Method of Task: There should be an alternative process for achieving the objective or task before the linear programmer. For doing anything in a particular manner, be it manufacturing, storing, consuming, selling, pricing or even throwing something away, there is a specific process and a method for doing it. Linear programming shows the way of performing that task efficiently and economically so that the end objective is attained scientifically.

3. Constraints or Limitations: Problems must have constraints or limitations. The programmer should know *what can be done, what cannot be done and how it can be done.*

4. Choice Variables: Having set the objective and identifying the restraints the programmer has to choose the *numbers* to suit maximisation or minimisation.

5. Feasibility and optimality: Each problem has a number of solutions and there maybe only one optimal and feasible solution to a specific problem on hand. In terms of the theory of consumption, if there are two goods x and y before a consumers choice, a number of combinations lie to the left of the '*Budget Line*'. The consumer has to maximise satisfaction and minimise sacrifice. To do so, he has to choose the '*feasible solution*'. That is, the solution has to satisfy all the restraints. Besides the solution must also be an '*optimal solution*'. That is, it must be the 'most feasible' solution and not merely be *feasible*. The '*Simplex method*'* may be applied to choose the optimal solution.

Output Maximisation and Linear Programming

Decision-making on production based on one or two variables is hardly effective. Various obstacles and capacity constraints of production must be taken into account to minimise cost, and maximise output and profit. This has to be done for a short-run purpose. Although long-run programming can also be done it is beset with very many hazards and is less objective.

Based on certain very necessary assumptions the problem of output maximisation can be programmed meticulously.

The problem: Production of cars.

Objective: Output maximisation and profit maximisation.

Alternatives: Labour intensive and capital intensive techniques.

---

* For detailed information on 'Simplex Method' consult W.J. Baumal. *op. cit.*, Chs. 5-6; and H.H. Liebhatsky, *op. cit.*, Ch. 17.

Assumptions:

1. There are constraints of credit, raw-materials and accommodation.
2. There are linear relations among variables *i.e.* proportional relation between inputs and output.
3. Prices and Co-efficients of inputs and outputs are constant and given.
4. The resources of all firms put together equals the sum of resources of each firm.
5. Products and factors of production have continuity and divisibility.
6. Institutional factors are given and constant.

The solution: It can be explained diagramatically as in Fig. 12.3.

In Fig.12.3 the Units X inputs and Y inputs per unit of output are plotted on OX and OY axes respectively per period. If process C requires 2 Units of Y per unit X to produce 1 unit of cars that will produce 50 cars (ac).

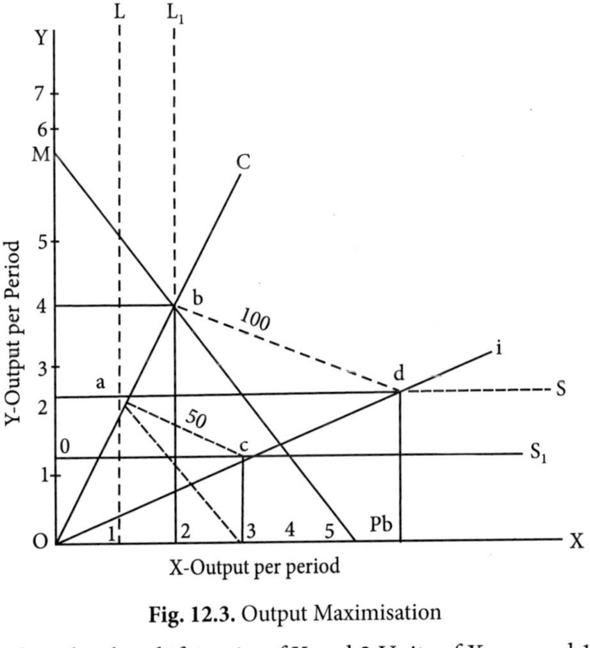

Fig. 12.3. Output Maximisation

On the other hand if 4 units of Y and 2 Units of X are used 100 cars can be produced (bd).

Ray OC is the *capital intensive* technique represented by combinations a and b.

The same quantity of cars (50) can be produced with process L by combining 3 units of X with 1 unit of Y which is *Labour intensive i.e.* Ray OL. As in the other case, 100 cars can be produced with 6 units of X and 2 units of Y. Input combinations c and d represent these alternative combinations of labour intensive technique.

By joining a and c an *isoquant* is caused. The isoquent is Laes, in the diagram at the output level of 50 cars. The isoquant for output level of 100 cars is L, bds.

The isocost curve MP determines the output capacity of cars as permitted by the *cost constraint*. Thus, the firm can produce cars within the area of the Δ^{le} Obd which is called the '*Feasible Region*' in linear programming language.

The Linear Solution: Output will be maximised by using capital intensive technique and combining 4 units of input Y and 2 units of input X and producing 100 cars (where isocost curve touches isoquant at point b).

Revenue Maximisation: Suppose a firm is engaged in producing two products tooth paste and tooth brush and the process has 4 stages A, B, C and D whose capacity is fixed. Let us suppose that the objective function is realisation of maximum revenue. The process of realisation of this objective is illustrated in Fig 12.4

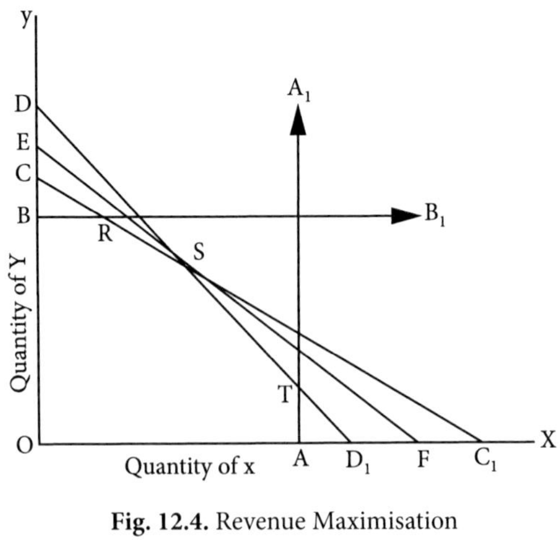

Fig. 12.4. Revenue Maximisation

In Fig. 12.4 output of commodities X and Y are plotted on OX and OY axes. The constraints of their production are A, B, C and D.

Constraints A and B limit production of X and Y respectively to OA and OB respectively. Constraint C limits production of both X and Y to OC_1 and OC respectively while constraint D limits production of X and Y to OD_1 and OD.

The area OSTRB is the '*feasible zone*' for the production of X and Y.

Q: How do we find out the optimal solution? This can be done by taking an '*isoprofit line*' within the feasibility zone. The isoprofit line shows all the combinations of X and Y output with equal profit. The highest isoprofit line *viz.* EF within the feasibility zone OATSRB yields the highest profit.

Cost Minimisation and Linear Programming*

The problem of cost minimisation is also known as '*Diet problem*'. This is the earliest problem to which linear programming was applied.

Let us analyse how this is done, suppose a consumer has two commodities Bread and Butter whose market prices are given. The problem before the consumer is to attain maximum nutrients from different quantities of Bread and Butter.

Let x and x_1 represent bread and butter respectively. Bread contains 1,000 calories and 50 gms of protein per ½ kg. The market prices of bread and butter are ₹ 2 and ₹ 6 per ½ kg respectively.

The standard diet should contain 3,000 calories and 200 gms of proteins per day for balanced '*diet*'.

The total cost of standard diet Z is

$$Z = 2x_1 + 6x_2$$

Which is a minimum subject to

$$x_1 + 2x_2 \geq 3$$
$$2x_1 + 8x_2 \geq 8$$
$$x_1 + 0x_2 \geq 0$$

and the cost to be minimised is Z which is the Linear function of the two variables x_1 and x_2. The side relations (3 and 8) are inequalities of the given diet. The problem is linear since the *non-negative* variables are to be minimised subject to linear inequalities.

The solution to this lies in any two of the 3 available conditions.

Cost Z can be minimised subject to one side relation:

$$x_1 + 2x_2 = 3$$

* 'Advanced Economic Theory'. M.L. Jhingan: "The Diet Problem-Cost Minimisation", p. 420, Ch. 28.

By solving it we have:

$$x_1 = 3 \text{ and } 2x_2 = 3/2 = 1.5$$

In terms of Fig. 12.5 this is shown by the line AB

Where:

$$OA = 1.5x_2 \text{ and } OB = 3x_1$$

The second side relation is —

$$2x_1 + 8x_2 = 8$$

When solved it gives:

$$x_1 = 4 \quad \text{and } x_2 = 1$$

In terms of Fig. 12.5 this is shown by line CD where –

$$OC = 1x_2$$
$$OD = 4x_1$$

In Fig. 12.5 x_1 and x_2 (or bread and butter) are plotted on OX and OY axes respectively. Line AB represents the combination $z_1 + 2z_2 = 3$ and CD represents $2x_1 + 8x_2 = 8$. The *feasible solutions* lie on or above the *dotted line* AZD and *optimal solution* is at point Z.

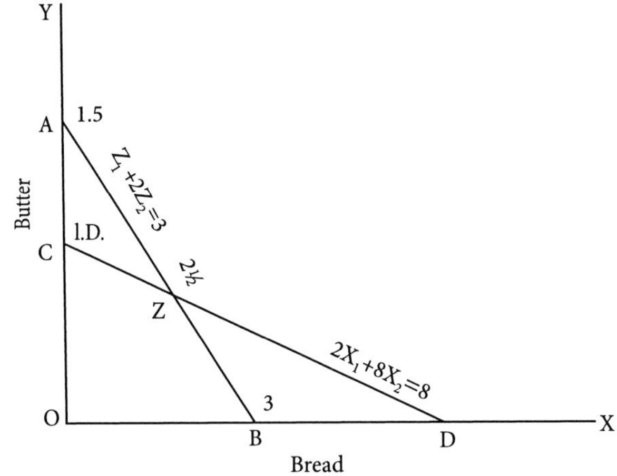

Fig. 12.5. Diet Problem—Cost Minimisation

When we treat the equations (1) and (2) as simultaneous equations and solve them we can find out whether Z is the actual feasible solution.

Limitations of Linear Programming

The business executives lean heavily on linear programming in modern days due to its managerial uses and specially in cost-input-output shall and Pigou take production as the basis of National Income n. A totally different criterion was adopted by Irving Fisher in tion. According to Fisher:

*he national dividend or income consists solely of services received by consumers, whether from their material from their human environments. Thus, a piano or an ercoat made for me this year is not a part of this year's come, but an addition to the capital. Only the services ndered to me this year by these things are income."**

er's definition is less cumbersome, more practical and simpler. it is not free from some defects. Firstly, it is difficult to calculate ey value of consumption. Besides, the value of a durable ty like a piano or a raincoat has to be excluded in the next and nt years in Fisher's terms.

Iodern Approach: *From the modern point of view national or any year consists of the money value of goods and services during that year and taking at the current sale price plus addition k of capital minus depreciation of capital.*

rding to Prof. Kuznets national income is "*the net output of ties and services flowing during the year from the country's e system....*"

V.K.R.V. Rao gives a clear definition of national income. g to him,

Iational income may be defined as the money value of e flow of commodities and services, excluding imports... thin the period, the value being reckoned at current prices inus the sum of the following items: (1) The money value;) the money value of the flow of goods and services used in the course of production; (3) The money value of the w of goods and services used to maintain the existing ck of capital stock....; (4) receipts of the state from direct taxation; (5) favourable balance of trade including insactions in treasure; (6) Net increase in the country's eign indebtedness...."

---

of Capital and Income', Irving Fisher, p. 104.

analysis. In the field of domestic trade, equilibrium analysis and growth problems its utility is enormous.

Yet, linear programming is not an unmixed boon to Business Economics. It has its limitations. The chief limitations are:

1. The chief objective function is difficult to define.
2. The various constraints of the objective function cannot be found out easily as there are so many of them.
3. It is not always possible to express the constraints directly in the form of linear inequalities.
4. A number of constant coefficients enter into a linear programming model and it is a problem to estimate their relevant values.
5. The relation between inputs and outputs is not always linear so that they can be added, divided and multiplied. Most relations are actually non-linear.
6. The assumption of perfect competition is a myth rather than a reality.
7. The technique of linear programming is highly complicated and mathematical which require modern equipment such as computors, desk calculations and a team of trained and efficient experts.

PART II

1

Problems and Concepts of National Income Accounting

National Income statistics are by and large the best indicators of the performance of an economy. The economic welfare is reflected by the National Income Estimates made annually in a country. The estimates not only bring out the relative performance of the different sectors of an economy but also form the guide to the economic plans and policies of a nation's government.

In the words of prof. Samuelson:

> *"By means of statistics of national income, we can chart the movements a country from depression to prosperity, its steady long-term economic growth and development, and finally, its material standard of living in comparison with other nations."*

The National Income Committee also holds the same opinion when it observes that,

> *"National income statistics enable an overall view to be taken of the whole economy and the relative position and inter-relations among its various parts."*

An acquintance with the basis of national income is therefore necessary. In this chapter the broad meaning of the concepts of national income are dealt with. A distinction is drawn between Gross National Product (GNP) and Net National Product (NNP) for clearer

understanding. A brief discussion of the n
Measurement and the difficulties encou
of national income are also brought out i
manner.

Definition: There are two different appr
National Income: (1) The Traditional Appı
Approach.

While Marshall, Pigou, Fisher and their
a traditional way Simon Kuznets and others g
Let us find out the broad distinction betweeı

1. The traditional Approach: Marshall is
traditionalists of national income concept. A

> *"The labour and Capital of a country*
> *resources produce annually a certa*
> *commodities, material and immateri*
> *of all kinds.... This is the true and n*
> *revenue of the country or National div*

Marshall excludes 'capital depreciation' a
from abroad to arrive at the 'Net' annual inc
His definition is simple and concise. Howev
innumerable types of goods and services w
consuming process. A correct figure cannot b
danger of *'double counting'* being committed.
value, raw-material and that of the finished
This will give us an inflated figure of no u
goods produced for one's own consumption
the case of small farmers.

A.C. Pigou gave a simpler, more pre
definition. However, it is full of paradoxes. H
under criticism. He distinguishes between go
be and cannot be exchanged for money an
former kind in national income. Pigou's defi
UDCs.

This is evident when he defines national

> *"National income is that part of obje*
> *community, including of course income*
> *which can be measured in money".*[**]

* 'Principles of Economics', Alfred Marshall, p. 434.
** 'The Economics of Welfare', A.C. Pigou, p. 31.

Ma
estimati
his defi

Fis
Howev
the m
comm
subseq
2. The
income
produc
to the s
Ac
comm
produc
Pr
Accor

* 'Na

Measurement of National Income

The measurement of National Income is very significant from many angles. It is the only macro indicator of economic development and throws a flood of light on various economic variables and their tendency. The planners rely hugely on the national income estimates in preparing the economic plans. In this section let us briefly discuss the three methods of measuring national income *viz.*: (1) The Income Method; (2) The Product Method; and (3) Production-cum-Income Method.

1. The Income Method: This method is based on the statistics of income earned by firms and individuals during a given year. The statistics are obtained from the income-tax department and these are supplemented by figures of average income of various groups of workers.

The Income Method is highly suitable to the developed economies where the income-tax payers are many and where information can be easily obtained regarding the income of individuals from records readily maintained. However, in UDCs the number of income-tax payers is negligible and except in the organised sector ready and reliable information is not available about income of many categories of workers. Moreover, farm labour and farmers do not maintain proper records. Thus, this method does not suit the UDCs.

Under this method national income is arrived at by adding up the incomes earned by firms, institutions and individuals during a period of one year.

2. The Product Method: This method is also known as the *inventory method*. By this method the National Income is arrived at by taking into account the sum total of goods and services consumed in a year calculated at '*market prices*'. ('Market price' is the price which ruled in the market at the time of production.)

The method needs accurate census of production and wages. The '*Net output*' and not '*Gross output*' is taken into account. That is known as Net National Product at market prices. The '*Final Value*' of goods and services are arrived at and the intermediary goods and services have to be excluded along with depreciation charges.

In India the product method gathers information from statistics published by the Government on agricultural production, mining, diary farming, forestry and industrial output.

However, in the primary sector the small farmers do not maintain regular books of accounts of farm produce as most of the output is consumed on the farm itself. This reduces the reliability of information of the product method.

3. The Income-Cum-Product Method: As the name itself indicates, this is a combined method of National Income Accounting. This was evolved and tried in UDCs with a high degree of usefulness. It overcomes the lack of total and reliable data for any one method. The combined method was successfully tried by Prof. V.K.R.V. Rao in India. He made use of Government published data, income-tax statistics and records of wages in industries and other establishments and supplemented this with 'ad-hoc' inquiries.

The three methods are only major methods of measurement of national income. There are also two other methods which are not of practical importance today. They are:

(a) *The Expenditure Method; and*

(b) *Ad valorum or Value-added Method.*

(a) *The Expenditure Method:* When the total expenditures incurred by different individuals, institutions and firms during a given year are added up we arrive at the national income by the Expenditure Method. The expenditures incurred must cover the following groups:

1. Personal consumption expenditure *i.e.* of persons;
2. Net domestic investment *i.e.* investment during the current year within the country in the public and private sectors;
3. Government expenditure on goods and services through various ministries; and
4. Net foreign investment *i.e.* both private foreign capital and investment of foreign Govt. at home.

However, this method implies that the national income equals national expenditure. The method can also be combined with the Income Method whenever necessary but care should be taken to avoid 'duplication' of accounting since one man's expenditure becomes another man's income in the process of transactions.

(b) *Ad Valorum or Value-Added Method:* By this method we arrive at the Gross National Product (GNP). One must calculate the difference between the value of materials produced at each stage of *output* and the value of '*inputs*' used at each stage to find out the value added. The sum total of all values added gives the national income ('GNP') by Value-added Method. Thus, while employing this method one must discount the value of cotton yarn at the stage of cotton cloth output to find out the value added. For an example:

In India National Income estimates were started by Sri Dadabhai Naoroji in 1867 and the names of Lord Curzon, Wadia and Joshi, Findlay

Shirraz and Dr. V.K.R.V. Rao are also associated with it. The *Committee on National Income Estimates* was constituted in 1949 by the Indian Govt, with Prof. P.C. Mahalanobis as its chairman and Prof. D.R. Gadgil and V.K.R.V. Rao as members. The Committee published the Report of N.I. Estimates for 1948-49 which is the first scientific estimate and put the N.I. of India at ₹ 8,830 crores for 1948-1949 subject to corrections (and *per capita income* at ₹ 265). The method adopted was the *Income-cum-Product Method.*

National Income—Some Basic Concepts

A number of concepts are used in the theory and estimation of National Income. A great technical difference lies in these concepts in the Jargon of the economist. It is well nigh impossible for a student to understand the theory of traditional income unless acquainted clearly with the meanings of these concepts. This section is dedicated to introduce the various concepts of national income to the students.

1. Gross National Product (GNP): Gross National Product or GNP is the '*total value*' of goods and services produced in an economy during a given year at '*Market Price*'. It includes the output of farming, mining, forestry, fishing, industries, etc., and services of transport & communication, banking and insurance, services of lawyers, doctors, teachers and a hoast of others.

The GNP is the '*money value*' of goods and services produced in an year measured at '*current prices*' (*i.e.,* price taken belongs to the year or period when calculation is going on). Therefore, any increase or decrease in the prices over the 'market price' will increase or reduce the real value of such estimates as the case may be.

To avoid such an error a '*Base Year*' is taken and the estimates are made on the basis of the '*price index*' of the *Base Year.* The Base Year should be a '*Normal*' period (*i.e.* it should be free from abnormal prices, war, famine, depression, etc.).

The GNP is then adjusted in accordance with the Base Year's index number. For instance, if the Base Year is 1960 for estimation of national income of 1990 the National Income estimate is stated as "National Income for 1989-90 at market/current prices with Base Year 1960."

Further, GNP should always, be calculated only at market prices and only the '*final value*' should be taken to avoid '*Double Counting*'. Care should be taken to exclude services rendered free of cost (*e.g.* services of a house-wife). Similarly, value of stocks and shares transacted of *old companies* and production of the past year should be excluded while computing GNP. Besides these, we should exclude receipts of '*social security*' such as unemployment benefit, old age pension, etc. from GNP. So also the profits and losses due to fluctuations in the market price are excluded. Lastly, windfall profits or anti-social earnings and illegal income such as income from bettings, gambling and smuggling are not a part of GNP.

However, depreciation of value of machinery, plant and equipment should be included in GNP.

2. Net National Product (NNP): Net National Product or NNP is the 'net money value of final goods and services produced at current prices during a given year with the co-operation of Labour and Capital.' The NNP is obtained by deducting '*depreciation of capital*' (*i.e.* wear and tear of machinery) from the GNP.

Thus, NNP = GNP – Depreciation

NNP at Market prices = Personal Consumption Expenditure
+ Net Domestic Investment
+ Net Foreign Investment
+ Government expenditure on goods and services.

If NNP is calculated by adding up the remuneration of factors of production it is called NNP at '*factor price*' or at '*Factor Cost*'. It is the sum total of Rent, Wages, Interest and Capital earned by land, labour, capital and organisation during a given year.

3. Personal Income: The 'Concept of Personal Income'was invented by J.M. Keynes while analysing the '*Consumption Function*'.

Personal Income is the sum total of incomes received by individuals of a country during a given year. Personal Income is never equal to national income simply because personal income includes '*transfer earnings*' like pensions, old-age pension, unemployment benefit, etc.

To find out Personal Income some items are added to National Income and some other items are deducted out of national income.

Thus, Personal Income = NNP + Transfer Payments

— Income Tax

— Social security contributions such as P.F., life insurance premium and E.S.I. contributions.

4. Disposable Personal Income (DPI): The concept of DPI is also a Keynesian discovery. It was introduced by Keynes to show how the '*Propensity to Consume*' is affected by *compulsory savings*. DPI is defined as *the net personal income available for consumption expenditure by individuals and families after meeting compulsory obligations such as payment of income-tax, profession tax, insurance premium*, etc.

Therefore, DPI is naturally less than Personal Income (PI).

5. Real National Income: Real National Income is the natural income expressed in terms of the general price of the '*base year*'. In other words, national income in money terms does not give us the actual condition of the economy. The money income of a nation in 1990 may be high as compared to that of 1989 because the price level in 1990 is higher than in 1989. However, in real terms the economy may not have progressed because of the high price level. Therefore, we should compare the two levels of '*Real National Income*' to get the exact economic picture of the economy. This is why '*Real Income*' is calculated every year.

Real National Income (RNI) is calculated by taking a particular normal year as base year. The 'Index Number' for the base year is assumed as 100 and the Real National Income of the current year is determined by applying the following formula:

$$\text{Real national Income} = \frac{\text{NNP in money terms}}{\text{Index No. of base year}} \times 100$$

Thus:

If 1960 is the Base Year and NNP of 1980 is ₹ 40,000 crores while the index number of 1980 is 500.

Then:

$$\text{Real national income of 1980} = \frac{40{,}000}{500} \times 100 = ₹\ 8{,}000 \text{ crores}$$

Difficulties of Measurement of National Income

The measurement of national income is a Himalayan task. The enumerators have to overcome these hurdles successfully and patiently to make their results useful. The significant difficulties with which they are beset are discussed briefly below.

1. Difficulty of Evaluating in money terms: National Income is measured in terms of money. The difficulty arises when a commodity or services does not lend itself to assessment in terms of '*money proper*'. The '*intrinsic value*' of such items and '*money value*' are two different entities. For instance, hobby painting or a proprietor of a firm marrying his Lady-secretary who renders service as secretary without wages after marriage. These services or products of hobby are a part of national income but they have to be excluded. When they are excluded the N.I. appears smaller.

2. Difficulty of Obtaining Reliable Data: Availability of adequate and reliable data of agricultural output and other allied occupations, consumption expenditure, savings of rural and urban population, etc. mar the task of national income estimates especially in developing countries. Lack of full time and trained personnel at the rural level is the main cause for it.

3. Difficulty of Assessment of unorganised sector: In the developing economies the chunk of agricultural and industrial sector is unorganised. Small and scattered farms and subsistence farms do not maintain proper records output. Even small industries and cottage industries do not have proper Books of Accounts. Most of the information is guess work This reduces the reliability of National Income estimates.

4. The Difficulty of Duplication of Counting: The danger of '*double counting*' can be suicidal to N.I. estimation, guarding against which is a tough task. For instance, the wheat flour that is produced by a flour-mill is a 'final product' but it becomes an '*intermediary product*' at the bakery level. If flour is taken into account at both levels the '*error of double counting*' occurs; the result is a larger N.I. than what it really is. This has to be carefully avoided.

5. The Difficulty of Imputation of Value: This is a peculiar problem arising out of existence of a '*non-monetised sector*'. In countries such as India, agriculture is a partially monetised sector. Many farmers pay 'wages in kind' (*i.e.*, payment in grains it) exchange for services rendered) or much of the produce of small farms are consumed by the farmer himself and the output does not enter the agricultural market. The value of such output or payment is to be 'imputed' and then added to the value of the monetised sector.

6. Difficulty of addition of Transfer payments: Transfer earnings like pensions are the income of recipients of expenditure of the governments. They should be or should not be added to the NI is a problem. To overcome this they are safely deducted from NI.

7. Difficulty arising out of capital gains and losses: Assets such as machinery and buildings gain value or lose value due to 'unpredictable' causes and 'anticipated' causes. When the cause is *unpredictable* it is included in NI and when it is *predictable* it has to be excluded from NI.

8. Difficulty of Inventory valuation: Negative and positive inventory charges are included in NI. The '*Negative*' or '*positive*' inventories are taken in *physical units* and then multiplied by '*current prices*'. The product is then added to the output of the firm and it goes into N.I.

The problem is that the firms record their '*Inventories*' (unsold output of the previous year) at '*original costs*' and not at '*replacement costs*'. Hence, a rise in prices, gives a rise in the '*Book Value*' and when prices fall it gives a loss of *Book Value*. Thus, the book value of inventories is fictitious. Valuation adjustments have to be made in the calculation of GNP. That is, Negative adjustment for gains and Positive adjustment for losses have to be made. Such adjustments are a laborious job.

9. Difficulty of Estimation of Depreciation of Capital: Calculating depreciation of value of capital is a tough task. It is specially so when the capital has a long life (say) 50 years or more. Firms calculate depreciation value of machines and other assets on the original cost of assets. If their prices are changing the cost of using these assets for 50 years or more will be taken as annual rate of depreciation at *market price* of capital (and not at *current price* of capital). Value adjustments of capital depreciation has to be made accordingly in computing GNP. To make such adjustments is a great difficulty.

10. Difficulty due to Price Fluctuations: Money price is the measuring rod of NI. The general price level itself is unstable over a short period. A rise in it gives an inflated figure of NI even though the level of output has actually decreased. Although the Real Income method solves this difficulty, the problem nevertheless persists.

The foregoing analysis of hazards of national income computation can be overcome with the application of care and diligence. A well established and trained army of statistician guided by experts can compile N.I of great practical and theoretical utility which is discussed elsewhere in a separate section.

2

The Business Cycles: Their Fundamentals

Meaning

The level of Economic Activity undergoes cyclical fluctuations from time to time. These cyclical changes manifest themselves in fluctuating national income, employment investment, etc. These fluctuations that are more or less regular in time sequence are called "*Business Cycles*" or "*Trade Cycles*". These are the ebs and flows of economic activity. They are the *ups* and *downs* of an economy which follow like day and night.

Prof. W.C. Mitchell defines Business Cycles thus:

> *"Business cycles are a species of fluctuations in the economic activities conducted on a commercial basis. The noun "cycles" bars-out fluctuations which do not recur with a measure of regularity."*

J.M. Keynes has the following to say about business cycles:*

> *"A trade cycle is composed of periods of good trade followed by rising prices and low unemployment percentages, alternating with periods of bad trade characterised by falling prices and high unemployment percentages."*

Prof. Fredrick Benham has a simpler definition for a business cycle:

> *"A trade cycle may be defined, rather badly, as a period of prosperity followed by a period of depression."*

---

* J.M. Keynes: 'A Treatise on Money', Vol. I, p. 78.

These definitions point to one important fact *viz.*, that, the trade cycles are '*rythmical changes*' or cyclical movements in the level of aggregate economic activity. Further, that the trade cycles refer to changes in the levels of employment, income, output and prices.

Classification of Trade Cycles

Different economists have defined trade cycles from different points of view. A general definition calls a trade cycle as "an alternation of periods of prosperity and depression of good and bad trade" (Prof. Haberler). Some definitions are explicit and some are implicit in meaning. The definitions conform to one or another of the causes or characteristics of the trade cycles. This diversity implies that there are different kinds of Trade Cycles or Business Cycles. Let us therefore acquaint ourselves with the most important kinds of trade cycles in this section.

It is apt to quote F.S. Brooman before classifying the Trade Cycles:

> *"No cycle is perfectly regular with uniform frequency and amplitude, and that is, the time taken to move from one peak level of output to the next would always be the same, and the level of output and employment would always vary in the same proportion between the upper and lower turning points. But such cycles have never occurred."**

Thus, trade cycles are classified on the basis of their *intensity, periodicity, length, regularity* and so on. The commonly known types are the following.

1. Major and Minor Cycles: American economists have identified trade cycles as *major* and *minor* cycles. Fluctuations between major recessions are known as '*Major Cycles*'. Clement Juglar, a French Economist identified these cycles in the 19th century and hence they are called '*Juglar Cycles*'. The recession of 1929 was a major one and the cycle followed was a major cycle. There were 20 major cycles between 1837 and 1937—10 of which had an average duration of 8.33 years and 10 cycles of 8 years duration.

The cycles that interrupt the *recovery stage* are called '*Minor Cycles*'. Prof. Hansen identified 27 minor cycles between 1837 & 1937 in the economic history of the U.SA. The average duration of these minor cycles was 3.48 years.

Recently, Profs. Kitchin and Crum have discovered minor cycles of 40 months duration known as '*Kitchin Cycles*'.

---

* F.S. Brooman: 'Macroeconomics', 1967 Ed.

According to J.A. Estey "*minor oscillations are not dramatic...but major cycles are dramatic and have serious results.*"*

The major cycles have significant impact on economic policy and economic activity.

2. Kondratieff Cycles: These are cycles of very long duration and length. They are long cycles consisting of at least 6 Juglar Cycles whose total duration is more than 50 years according to N.D. Kondratieff, a Russian economist. They are long-wave cycles.

3. Building Cycles: Cycles of a fairly regular duration occurring in construction activity are called '*Building Cycles*'. Their duration is two times that of a major cycle—18 years on an average. These were identified by two American economists Warren and Pearson in 1937. Their duration is between 15-20 years. There were at least 6 Building Cycles between 1830 and 1934.

4. Kuznets Cycles: Another American economist Prof. Simon Kuznets identified Cycles of 16-22 years duration of very pronounced nature. These are named after him as Kuznets Cycles.

5. Very Long Wave Cycles: Cycles of 50-60 years duration have also occurred in the past between 1790 and 1930. These fluctuations in the level of economic activity have been confined to '*whole-sale prices*' in the U.S.A. and the U.K. Such fluctuations were due to fluctuations in the supply of gold *vis-a-vis* the level of production of gold. As such these cycles have very long wave lengths. There is doubt, whether they can really be called true cycles. Since these fluctuations in wholesale prices reflect themselves in fluctuations in general level of economic activity and the general price level they may also be regarded as trade cycles.

General Features of Trade Cycles

A general observation of different trade cycles has been conducted by economists. In addition to individual inquiries the *American Economic Association* has also revealed some general characteristics of Trade Cycles. The chief characteristics are as follows:

1. Synchronic Character: A trade cycle is synchronic by nature. The prices, production and employment contract or expand in all industries at the same time. The effect of a trade cycle is uniform on all firms. Just like in the human body the effect of a trade cycle is felt in other parts of the body-economic. The phases of a trade cycle appears in every field of activity though the degree of its intensity may vary.

---

* J.A. Estey: 'Business Cycles', p. 15.

2. Periodic Nature: Periodicity is observed in the occurrence of trade, cycles. The occurrence is in fairly regular intervals. Though the period of the interval may be unpredictable the degree of regularity is clearly seen. Besides, the expansion and contraction in a trade cycle follow one another with definiteness.

3. International Character: Trade cycles have a certain amount of international character. That is, the fluctuations in the level of economic activity of one country easily spread to that of other countries through exports and imports. The Great Depression of the 1930s was of this nature. In this context Prof. Samuelson said that '*if the U.S.A. coughs the entire world catches pneumonia*'. That is, if the level of economic activity fluctuates it spreads to other countries through international trade from the U.S.A.

4. Uniformity of pattern: Each cycle may differ in its details but the general pattern that can be observed is the same in all cycles. Prof. Pigou notes that "*All the recorded cycles are members of the same family, but among them there are no twins.*"

According to the 'American Economic Association' a standard Business Cycle exhibits the following characteristics:

A. Prices and production move in the same direction of expansion and contraction.
B. Capital and durable goods industries are subject to a more severe fluctuation than the non-durable consumer goods industries.
C. Large changes in aggregate output, employment and prices are followed by corresponding changes in currency, credit and velocity of circulation of money in the same direction.
D. The agricultural prices are flexible while prices of manufactures are rigid.
E. Income from profits are more fluctuating than the income from other sources.
F. Lastly, fluctuations spread from industry to industry since all industries are related in some way or the other to each other. Moreover, such fluctuations attain an international character also.

Phases of a Trade Cycle

A typical trade cycle has '*four*' phases or stages. Each stage distinct from the rest of the stages.

Profs. Burns and Mitchall have noted the following four phases of a business cycle or trade cycle:

1. Recession stage
2. Contraction stage
3. Revival stage
4. Expansion stage.

The analysis of these phases is interesting and *brain-teasing* as well. It would be helpful to analyse these phases with the help of a simple but useful diagram of an imaginary Business Cycle as in Fig. 2.1.

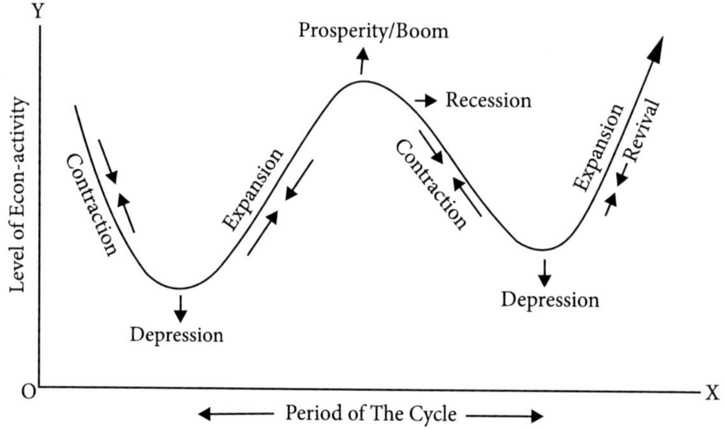

Fig. 2.1

1. Recession Stage: Contraction begins after the *prosperity* or *boom* suddenly ends and *recession* has just set in. In this phase, business *optimism* ends and business *pessimism* begins. The producers and traders cannot realise the anticipated rate of profits. The Marginal Efficiency of Capital (MEC) suddenly decreases. There will be '*panic sales*' and many firms shut down. Credit facilities from banks will suddenly decrease. Unemployment begins to show its face in capital goods industries. This shows signs of spreading to the other industries also. Recession then gives place to '*contraction*'. The upper most part of the wave in the diagram is '*prosperity*' or boom which is very short and Recession sets in as soon as *boom* ends.

2. Contraction Stage: Economic activity will be low during this stage but would be going on at a low rate. Employment, incomes and prices will be falling continuously. Pessimism becomes stronger and stronger as profits fall continuously. Agricultural prices fall more quickly than that of others. Construction activities almost come to a standstill. The lowest point in the diagram is also short like that of boom. It is called *depression.*

3. Revival Stage: This stage begins after the depression ends suddenly due to many *Monetary* and *Fiscal* measures taken by the state to end the depression. The level of employment, income and prices begins to increase. *Pessimism will give place to gradual optimism.* The capital goods industries will begin to invest more as they are receiving more orders from the manufacturers who are receiving more orders from the ratailers. In short, revival becomes cumulative as profits go on increasing. The MEC begins to rise. These induce the banks to come forward to lend readily for investment. Now, the stage is all set for *expansion.*

4. Expansion Stage: Revival or '*Recovery*' begins after the depression ends. Generally, revival takes a longer time than contraction and '*Expansion*' begins after the revival has germinated the '*seeds of optimism*'. The MEC reaches its highest level in this phase. Investment in all sections attains the '*Multiplier Effect*'. The rate of increase in employment, output and prices becomes very rapid. '*Redevelopment*' becomes rapider and rapider as profits reach the peak level as in Fig. 2.1.

Thus, according to Prof. Heberler, a business cycle is a crisis between *Prosperity* and *Depression.* The economy then experiences stresses and strains of all types.

THEORIES OF BUSINESS CYCLES

Business Cycles or Trade Cycles, as is often called, are a special feature of modern capitalist economics. There are cyclical movements or rythmatic ebb and flow of economic activity from time to time. These movements in the level of aggregate employment, income, demand, output and prices are termed as "*Business Cycles*" or "*Trade Cycles*" in Business Economics.

Multitudinous factors and circumstances underlie cyclical fluctuations with far reaching effects on trade, commerce and banking and production. Many attempts have been made to formulate a satisfactory theory of trade cycles. Some theories treat them as monetary phenomenon and others as a non-monetary phenomenon. Yet another version of the trade cycle is the saving-investment-spending variation approach. In the succeeding pages an attempt is made to present some of the major theories of Business Cycles in simple terms.

The Monetary Theory of Trade Cycles (Hawtrey)

The Monetary Theory of Trade Cycles was formulated by Prof. R.G. Hawtrey on a purely monetary basis. He contends that "*Trade Cycle is a purely monetary phenomenon*".

According to him, non-monetary factors can cause only partial depression but not a general depression; the main cause of a general depression is to be found in the expansion and contraction of Bank Credit or money-mechanism. The producers and traders alter their demand for money in accordance with the changes in bank credit.

Bank credit is the main source of transactions in the trade world. When commercial banks expand or contract credit through lower or higher rates of interest the prosperity or boom and depression are caused.

Let us suppose that commercial banks lower the lending rates of interest. In terms of this theory, the banks will offer more credit by buying securities. Producers and merchants are able to borrow more now. Cheap credit will increase the stocks or inventory of merchants. There will be a chain reaction from the merchants onwards to the owners of factors of production. That is to say, more orders for supply from wholesalers to producers will increase investment and output by producers. To produce more they need more factors of production. Increased demand for these factors will increase employment of factors of production and their incomes increase. This in turn increases consumption expenditure and the effective demand in the '*Commodity market*'.

Then the inventories begin to diminish and the merchants and traders place more orders with the producers. This sets in motion a cumulative process of increase in output, employment, income and demand. The result is: *boom*.

This cumulative process of higher prices will encourage more borrowings for more stocks leading to higher profits until the optimum point is reached.

Trade optimism and economic prosperity cannot go on indefinitely according to Prof. Hawtrey. Banks are experts in sensing the inevitable end of boom and the onset of recession. They become cautious and contract credit as their funds are decreasing. The consumers also begin to "hoard savings". On the other hand, high domestic price level increases export of gold because imports exceed exports. The banks are forced to increase lending rates of interest and also recall previous loans. This marks the end of boom and the beginning of *recession phase*.

To pay back borrowings stocks are sold by traders and merchants. Prices begin to fall due to flooding of commodity markets. The negative process begins and output, employment, income and prices crumble till the lowest level is reached which is "*Depression*".

Businessmen and traders are pessimistic and even the lowest lending rates fail to attract borrowers. The "*deadlock of credit*" is reached.

According to Prof. Hawtrey the deadlock has to be broken to initiate "*Recovery*" and it is a painfully slow task. The task is to be achieved through "*cheap-money policy*" by the Central Bank. Thus, the solution also lies in monetary measures.

An Assessment of the Theory

The Monetary Theory of Trade Cycles has both its supporters and critics. The theory has found good support from Prof. Milton Friedman. At the same time the theory has been subjected to severe criticism by D. Hamberg. According to Hamberg *the theory is logically correct but suffers from empirical defects.*

The major defects are as fallows:

Firstly, according to Hamburg there '*appears to be a great exaggeration of importance of the wholesaler in causing fluctuations in the level of economic activity*. According to him after 1914 the wholesaler has lost his important place in countries like the United Kingdom.

Secondly, according to A.C. Pigou the actual cause for boom is not the expansion of credit. At best it can be the cause for expansion of business activity. In this context Pigou says "*Variations in the bank money supply is a part of the business cycle*, it is not the cause of it." In other words, though credit is cheap during Depression the revival does not start as much as a contraction of credit during Boom does not cause recession.

Thirdly, Heberler has objected to Hawtrey's contention that the boom breaks down due to monetary contraction. According to Heberler, "The *contention that the reason for the breakdown of the boom is always a monetary one and that the prosperity could be prolonged and depression staved off indefinitely, if the money supply were inexhaustible*" is highly objectionable.

Fourthly, Hamberg disagrees with Hatwrey on the influence of rate of interest on the borrowings by traders. According to Hamberg borrowings increase only if the reduction of interest rate is permanent. However, during depression traders expect a further reduction in interest rate and borrowings do not increase. Further, the rate of interest will have no impact at all if stocks or inventories are financed out of traders own funds.

Fifthly, according to Hamberg, changes in stocks cause cumulative changes in employment, output, income and prices. On the contrary, fluctuations in stocks can only lead to *minor cycles* which are not cycles at all. Moreover, the Hawtrian Theory fails to explain the periodicity of a cycle.

Lastly, it ignores non-monetary causes of trade cycles but they may be more nonrmonetary by nature than monetary. In this context J.A. Estey says:

> *"......Changes in real demand, changes in cost, inventions, and so on, which, too, may be powerful contributions to cyclical fluctuations. These... suggest that the monetary is not always 'sufficient' and that other explanations will have to be given considerations."**

Innovations Theory of Trade Cycles (Schumpeter)

The Innovations Theory of trade cycles was propounded by Joseph Schumpeter in 1939.* He developed his, theory on the basis of Juglar's statement that the "*cause of depression is prosperity*." Schumpeter maintains that the '*innovations are the source of fluctuations*.'

He defines innovation as '*the introduction of a new product or a new process of production or a discovery of a new market or new source of raw-materials or changes in business organisation*.'

Schumpeter distinguishes between *two* stages of innovations: (1) The *first stage* deals with the '*initial impact*' of innovations while the *second stage* deals with '*reactions*' to the initial impact.

First Stage: Schumpeter's theory is explained in terms of the assumption of '*Full employment equilibrium*'. According to him, every capitalistic economy attains a "*stationary state*". The Stationary state is also called the "*Circular Flow Economy*." *A Circular flow economy is one which is producing itself year after year, neither expanding nor contracting*. Variables like 'New' investment, 'Net' investment, Net Savings and Capital Stock will all be constant. Costs of production equals revenue. Average and Marginal costs are equal to price. Therefore, profits as well as interest rate are '*Zero*'.

In short, according to him *circular flow economy* is characterised by stagnation and products are produced year after year in the same manner without any variety in the same manner as circulation of blood in an animal organism.

---

* James Arthur Estey: 'Business Cycles', p. 206.

At one stage "Innovation" breaks this 'circular flow'. Innovations are defined by him as "*such changes in the production of goods as cannot be affected by infinitestimal steps or variations on the margin.*"*

According to the Theory of Innovations these innovations are not cyclical in occurrence. There is a continuous improvement of existing products and new products find their way into the markets. These changes are introduced by the entrepreneur and not by the capitalist. The entrepreneur is not a man of ordinary ability; he is an "*Innovating Entrepreneur*" and he is always searching for something new to break the circular flow.

The innovations of the entrepreneur are different from '*inventions*'. The inventions are simply discoveries of a new techniques of production or a new model of a product by a genius. They do not affect the circular flow in themselves and by themselves. It is their actual adoption by the entrepreneur in production that does the breaking of the circular flow.

To innovate the entrepreneur has to be dynamic. He requires two essential factors, *viz.:* (1) readily available fund of technical knowledge and (2) bank credit.

The first is always available in a Capitalist economy, according to Schumpeter—a reservoir of untapped technical knowledge.

The second, 'bank credit' should be obtained from banks at a rate of interest as investment of such funds is 'risk-bearing'.

With the funds that he has obtained from banks he is "*bidding away resources*" from other industries.

This leads to increased incomes and prices. Further investment is stimulated and the flow of a new set of goods begins. Then there is an excess of supply over demand.

The surplus supply causes a fall in costs and prices. Recession ultimately sets in and the producers curtail output. Then there is a decline in credit, prices and interest but the aggregate output is now larger than that of the previous level the level previous to recession.

Thus, in his theory, in the first phase the economy begins with the full employment equilibrium, reaches boom and begins sliding down through recession and goes on till a new equilibrium is attained.

A very noteworthy point in his theory is that the '*new equilibrium*' is higher than the earlier equilibrium level. This is because of the innovation of a new product.

---

* Joseph A Schumpeter: 'Business Cycles', 1939.

Second Stage: As already noted the second stage is the stage of the reactions of the impact of the First Stage or of the '*initial innovation*'. In this stage the entrepreneur follows the successful initial innovation in "Swarm-like Clusters". That is, the initial innovation induces innovations in other related fields. There will be an around '*cumulative*' increase in money income, prices and demand. The products of old industries find more demand but their supply is lagging behind demand. As a result, the prices of old products and the profits on them increase. Old industries expand with the aid of bank credit.

There is now a '*Secondary Wave*' of credit inflation. This is superimposed by the *primary credit expansion*' due to initial innovation. In the second phase there begins over-optimism and speculation adding to boom.

After some gestation, new products will replace old products. Old products will either *readjust or liquidate or get absorbed* as the demand for old products decreases. Their prices fall and declining profits lead to repayment of loans. Uncertainty and pessimism replace *optimism*. The impact of innovation becomes weak and eventually ends. The depession sets in.

According to Schumpeter, the 'painful' process of readjustment to the previous neighbourhood of equilibrium begins.'

Then, *Recovery*' is started by natural forces and '*Revival*' is brought about. According to him, the cyclical fluctuations are a permanent feature of capitalism and it is the cost of economic development under capitalism. In short, Schumpeter's theory of business cycles is centred round the *entrepreneur and innovations, capitalism and circular flow economy.*

An Assessment of Innovations Theory

No doubt the theory is an integrated theory of business cycles, and the treatment of business cycles and their turning points is logical and novel. It is certainly unique as compared to the other theroies. However, the theory has been criticised for its overemphasis of the entrepreneur and innovations as the sole factors. Hamberg is the most vehement of the critics of the theory.

Firstly, according to Prof. Hamberg the process of economic changes may be the result of various socio-economic factors. There may be even psychological, natural and financial causes for a trade cycle. Schumpeter relegates all of them to the background and stresses the role of the innovating entrepreneur in his theory. Besides, the innovations were found largely in the Eighteenth and Nineteenth centuries as a separate class of entrepreneurs. In the modern dynamic world innovation is a '*routine task*' of an entrepreneur and not a '*distinct task*' as made out by Schumpeter. In this context Hamberg points out that:

*"Placing so much importance on the role of the entrepreneur results in too great a role for the element of chance in the process of technological progress.... history is the net product of great underlying socio-economic forces"**

Secondly, bank credit is also given undue importance. Bank credit maybe sufficient only in the short-run but that alone will not be enough in the long-run. In fact, it is the '*capital market*' that finances expansion in the long-run through sale of shares and debentures. The theory is hence weak.

Thirdly, according to Prof. Hamberg again, innovations are only a common cause of trade cycles and not a special cause. He maintains that:

"*Innovations in the history of modern capitalism have undoubtedly been one of the great driving forces behind the major cycles of the past*" and not the only cause.

Fourthly, not every innovation is financed by bank credit; some of them may be financed by voluntary savings or '*plough-back profits*' internal funds. In that case, in an economy working below full employment equilibrium there will be no trade cycle at all for some time.

Fifthly, the assumption of full employment is unreal. At the revival stage there will be unemployed resources and if an innovation is introduced unemployment of labour will not occur but more employment is created and costs and prices will not increase.

Lastly, according to Prof. Frederick A. Hayke it is the credit 'mechanism which causes a trade cycle and real factors or innovations do not explain the causation of a trade cycle.

Keynesian Theory of Trade Cycles

According to Lord Keynes, trade cycles are caused by cyclical changes in the Marginal Efficiency of Capital (MEC). His theory of trade cycles is a part and parcel of his General Theory of Income, Output and Employment. The periodic fluctuations in income, output and employment result from fluctuations in MEC and these may be called the trade cycles in his theory.

---

* Hamberg: 'Business Cycles', p. 242.

The depression in a trade cycle is due to lack of *aggregate demand.* Revival is possible only by increasing aggregate demand. Demand can be raised only by increasing consumption and investment.

In the short-run, consumption is stable. Hence, investment should expand in order to increase the demand so that revival from depression takes place. Conversely, recession is due to decrease in investment.

Thus, fluctuating rate of investment due to fluctuations in MEC are the cause for trade cycles according to him. Investment rate may fluctuate even due to changes in the rate of interest but they are less important in his opinion.

Role of MEC in causing Fluctuations: According to Lord Keynes trade cycles occur due to fluctuations in the rate of investment caused by the instability of MEC. He states trade cycles occur "*mainly due to the way in which marginal efficiency of capital fluctuates.*"* The fluctuations in the rate of investment are associated with changes also in the rate of interest but the rate of interest is not an important factor of trade cycles because the former is more or less stable. Similarly, the propensity to consume is also relatively stable.

Thus, given the rate of interest and the *consumption function*, MEC is the sole determinant of the levels of income, employment and prices, according to Keynes.

By MEC is meant, '*the rate of prospective returns on capital invested.*' In plain language, MEC is the expected rate of profit of addition to investment. The expected rate of profit itself depends upon the business environment. According to Prof. Hansen, "*The Cycle consists primarily of fluctuations in the rate of investment,*" and fluctuations in the rate of investment are caused mainly by fluctuations in the marginal efficiency of capital.**

The role of MEC in the course of a trade cycle can be more easily understood by beginning with the '*Expansion Phase*".

During the expansion the MEC is high. There is optimism everywhere and investment expands rapidly. Expansion of investment causes an increase in output, employment and income through the "*Multiplier Effect*". The boom is ultimately reached.

Recession and contraction will soon set in because of a decline in MEC. The MEC declines because businessmen's expectation of future profits changes for two vital reasons. *Firstly*, competitive investment and

* John Maynard Keynes' 'General Theory of Employment', Ch. 22.

** 'A Guide to Keynes', A.H. Hansen, p. 213.

secondly, risking cost of capital because of higher demand for capital. Pessimism sets in as supply in the commodity markets is higher than demand due to overproduction in a boom. This collapse of MEC is responsible for the succeeding phase of the trade cycle viz., the *contraction*. In this phase, according to Keynes, "*the prevailing optimistic estimate of future yields of capital goods is increasingly displaced by disillusion. The collapse of marginal efficiency of capital precipitates a sharp increase in liquidity preference. This causes a sharp increase in the rate of interest ...But the cyclical swings in the marginal efficiency of capital are made more violent than the facts justified by the uncontrollable and disobedient psychology of the business world.*"*

During the contraction phase there is a cumulative fall in employment and income because of the '*negative multiplier effect*'. The depression worsens. Thus, Keynes became the "*Prophet of Boom*" by attaching a great importance to MEC in ending the Boom or prosperity.

Revival is slow and painful because the MEC is slowly increasing. Revival begins only after the surplus stock of output is exhausted and optimism sets in.

Thus, the falling MEC is the sole cause of depression in his theory. The emphasis has often lead Keynes to be dubbed as the '*Depression Economist*'. However since he felt that "*inflation is just and deflation is expedient*" and in abolishing slumps and keeping permanently in a quasi-boom we may call him '*anti-deflation economist*'.

Keynes Theory of Trade Cycles and Its Policy Implications

Keynes theory of trade cycles had a profound influence on '*social philosophy*' and '*Fiscal policy*'. Keynes argued in favour of 'State Interference' to revive the economy from depression. This is known as 'Socialisation of Investment'.

He advocated public works programmes to stimulate investment during depression. He wanted the state to take up the task of inducing investment since '*voluntary privte investment*' does not take place due to losses. Every effort should be made to step up government expenditure on road-building, railway lines and bridges and dams so that more and more money is pumped into the hands of people which rises the effective demand and causes a rise in prices. In this context he pointed out thus:

> "*If the treasury were to fill old bottles with bank-notes, bury them at suitable depths in disused coal-mines which are*

---

* *Ibid.*

then, filled upto the surface with town rubbish and leave it to private enterprise ....to dig the notes up again, there need be no more unemployment and.... the real income of the community, and its capital wealth too would probably become a good deal greater than it actually is."

He even believed that a progressive taxation policy will revive the economy through redistribution of income in favour of the poor whose *propensity to consume* is high. Surprisingly, but not senselessly, he believed that 'wasteful expenditure' would go a long way in stimulating investment during depression. He noted in this context thus:

"Ancient Egypt was doubly fortunate, and doubtless owed to this its fabled wealth, in that it possessed two activities, namely, pyramid-building as well as the search for the precious metals....The Middle Ages built Cathedrals and sank driges. Two pyramids, two masses for the dead, are twice as good as one; but not so two railways from London to York" (New York).*

Thus, to Keynes '*digging up notes*' and '*vainful search for wealth*' in pyramids by paid labour would do the trick of reviving income, employment and output if it could really be done through '*deficit finance*'. As Gerhard Colm has rightly remarked, "*It is almost impossible to think of fiscal policy in the modern world, without thinking of John Maynard Keynes.... In fact, he gave the concept of fiscal policy a new meaning, and the operations of government finance a new perspective.... Keynes thought of survival of liberal capitalism in terms of fiscal policy correctly understood and broadly carried out.*"

Not only that, his theory ushered in a generation of '*New Economics*' whiciHias witnessed empirical and theoretical research.

A Critical Note on Keynes' Theory of Trade Cycles

Though Keynes' Theory of Trade Cycles in particular and the General Theory of Employment in wide terms has had a profound influence on the *New Deal Policy* in the U.S.A. during the Great Depression of 1930s and during the establishment of the I.M.F. and the I.B.R.D. it has been criticised by Profs. Hart, Saulnier, Dullard, Hazlitt and Knight. For instance, Prof. Knight commented on the General Theory that, "*We must simply forget the revolution" caused by Keynes and "read the book as a contribution to theory of business oscillations.*" But in the opinion of

* 'The General Theory of Employement, Interest and Money', J.M. Keynes, p. 131.

Hazlitt the concept of MEC is vague and ambiguous. The crisis of MEC is either '*useless tourism or an obvious error*'.

The others feel that the theory overemphasises the *role of expectations* in determining MEC. The concept, according to Prof. Hart, is superfluous and *unrealistic*. Prof. Oza remarks:

> "*No expectations need ... be taken into account. The businessmen are supposed to behave as if they are adjusting their positions not to their expectations but to observable data.*"

It is also said that Keynes' theory is not in any way different from A.C. Pigou's Psychological Theory of Trade Cycles since according to Keynes investment depends on the psychology of businessmen or producers regarding MEC.

Besides, according to Saulnier, his theory of trade cycles lacks factual proof and its deductions are not tested with facts. The same opinion is held by Prof. Dillard when he says that Keynes "*does not examine closely the empirical data of cyclical fluctuations.*"

According to Prof. Dillard, "*It is less than a complete theory of the business cycles because it makes no attempt to give a detailed account of the various phases of the cycle.*"*

Lastly, according to Prof. Estey, "*...the stress that he (Keynes) puts on the importance of investment indicates that he would accept the underconsumption theory*", *that we would "progress only while we are filling up our shelves.*"**

---

* 'The Economics of J.M. Kenes', p. 267.

** 'Business Cycles': A.J. Estey, p. 270.

3

Trade Unionism

The role of Labour in the process of production is such that no firm can be successful unlesss it gives to labour its rightful due. Any greed on the part of the employer is certain to end up with ample labour problems. Indeed, the period, specially the post-industrial Revolution years of growth of labour discontentment has witnessed rapid growth of trade union movenment. Its popularity has been marked during the post-war years due to mounting inflationary tendency the world over. In the present chapter we shall acquaint ourselves with some of the important aspects of trade union movement. We shall also see how trade unions have an important bearing on the performance of a business. An effort is also made to introduce the student to the birth, problems and the history of the Movement in India. Towards the end of the chapter some suggestions are also given for strengthening the Movement.

What is a Trade Union: A Trade Union is a voluntarily organised association of workers formed to protect the welfare of its members through better bargaining power. Thus, it endeavours to secure to its members better wages, conducive working conditions, improved welfare measures to the families of its members and in a broad sense better efficiency of labour and cordial employee-employer relationship for mutual benefit.

Thus, the trade unions are useful both to the workers and employers in the long-run if they function in a healthy manner and free from external influences.

In the West, trade unions have a broad-base covering all catagories of workers—agricultural, mining, small and large scale manufacturing and trading. Unfortunately in the South-East Asian countries its base is very narrow both in terms of coverage and membership. The movement is still wanting in quality in countries like India.

Its suffice for the present to know that trade unions, when conceived broadly, are voluntary organisations and that they are charged with the responsibility of securing a better bargaining power to the workers and promote better efficiency and productivity in the long-run.

Objectives of a Trade Union

The main objective of a trade union is protection of the interest of its members through '*militant*' and '*welfare*' measures. The militant measures are a method of forcing the employer to meet the genuine demands of workers when all peaceful means have failed. They may take the form of strikes of various sorts like *go-slow tactics, pen-down* and *tool-down strikes* or violent strikes of boycot of work. By definition, the militant action of unions results in loss of output due to loss of '*man-hours*' of work. It is neither desirable nor productive in the long-run as it leads to friction and deterioration of employer-employee relationship which may culminate in retaliation and counter-retaliation on both sides with all attendent consequences detrimental to the very objectives of the trade unions.

Thus, the proper method is to adopt methods and measures to promote give-and-take attitude between the employers and employees. Negotiations, liaison and workers representation in management, etc. would go a long way in promoting the growth of both firms and employers.

Trade Unions are organised ultimately to secure the following objectives:

1. Security of Employment: The foremost objective is to ensure security of employment to the workers. Often, the worker is thrown out of his job on flimsy grounds by greedy and unscrupulous employers. Victimisation is also common in some undertakings. Trade Unions therefore treat security of employment as their basic objective.

2. Better Bargaining Power: Labour is subject to exploitation. Wages are often uneven and very low. Unions strive to improve the wages of workers. Fair Wages, Minimum Wages and wages compensatory to the job are their aim. This objective is very significant as wages are 'sticky' during inflation. While the cost of living increases due to rising prices, wages do not rise compensatorily unless the unions demand better wages and dearness allowance to off-set the rise in the cost of living.

3. Improvement of Standard of Living: Wages and standard of living of workers are interlinked. Better wages may improve the living standard but it is not solely enough. The Unions therefore work towards securing welfare schemes like education, health and recreational facilities to the children of workers from their employers. Better housing schemes and sanitation for workers go a long way in improving their lot.

4. Promotion of Workers' Unity: Workers are generally disorganised and stand divided on linguistic, regional and communal grounds. This is the major bottleneck in achieving their own interest. Trade Unions bring together the disorganised and ununited workers. Divided, they fall and united they rise. In the wake of lack of unity the strength of the Movement will be lost.

5. Betterment of Working Conditions: The conditions of work have a great bearing on the health and efficiency of labour. Ill-ventilated, ill-lit and conjusted factories are *treasure houses of deceased workers, inefficiency and industrial accidents*. Labour unions in the early 20th century played a pivotal role in forcing the employers to provide healthy working conditions. In recent years, the various legislative measures have enforced strict norms to provide good working conditions all over the world but in stray cases the unions are even today called upon to improve the working conditions.

6. Uniform and Minimum Work: In some industries labour is exploited through long and tedious hours of prolonged work. Labour is often unpaid for extra work performed by it. Only organised resistance of such exploitation can remove this ill. Trade Unions have been able to force the employers to fix the working hours and over-time allowances for any extra work rendered by labour.

7. Other Objectives: The objectives of trade unions discussed above are only the broad ones. There are innumerable other minor, but by no measure negligible, objectives also such as resistance against victimisation of workers, demand for bonus, regularisation of employment, housing facilities and recreation, compensation to victims of industrial accidents and so on which are necessary.

Impact of Trade Unions on Firms

Whether a producing unit or a business firm, it has to take cognisance of the trade unions. They are influenced both directly and indirectly by the actions of the trade unions. Any neglect of labour welfare leads to friction between them, their ultimate goals and labour. Disputes between managements and workers reduce productivity and production or turnover. Irregular supply during strikes or lock-outs have a tremendous influence on the market. The consumers may change over to the other competitive products resulting in loss of revenue and good-will of customers. All this will strengthen the market hold of newer firms and regaining the lost reputation may take a long time, and sufficient damage would already have been caused.

Besides, *discontented labour* is a liability to a firm as any amount of rectification of its causes by the firm may not heal the wounds and the scars of discontentment and exploitation of labour will have long lasting effects.

Firms which take best care of their employees have been found to do well in business by experience in the world. This is the secret of high profitability and stability of the U.S. firms like the Firestone Units both at home and abroad. Well-paid and cared for, labour will certainly protect the interests of their employers at all stages. This is a significant hint that every businessman and producer needs to bear in mind while taking decisions on wage policy and other labour welfare schemes.

It is the '*give-and-take policy*' that stands in good stead. Thus, a business economist who is also an expert on matters of labour should advise the management on these matters.

Managements which provide comfortable housing, recreational facilities to their employees and sufficient welfare schemes to the families of labour such as schools and colleges, hospitals and consumers' stores etc. relieve the domestic tensions and pre-occupation. Then alone the workers can work whole-heartedly and turn out standard work. All these would ensure better profits, revenue and long and stable existence of firms.

In short, contented labour force is the '*sine-qua-non*' of stability and prosperity of business in the longer perspective.

LABOUR DISPUTES-CAUSES AND CURES

'Labour Disputes' or Industrial Disputes arise due to a number of reasons in the modern business and industrial world. These are unfortunate and undesirable to both the employees and the employers. These are like a *double-edged blade* which cuts on either side and harm both the parties to the disputes.

Basically, the causes of labour disputes, either in the field of production or trade and commerce, are to be looked for in the neglect of the interests of labour. Disputes arise and may even become violent causing loss of business or production and may even lead to lock-outs and victimisation of labour or strained relations between labour and managements.

The most common source of such disputes is low wages. Majority of the disputes originate due to exploitation of labour through low wages. Next in line is inadequate and unhealthy working conditions in which labour is made to work. Labour strikes work to attract the attention of the management to the improvement of working conditions.

Demand for bonus and for higher bonus, reinstatement of victimised workers, regularisation of wages of casual labour, reduction of working hours, participation of labour in management, recognition of workers' unions, resistance to over-mechanisation and computerisation and others are also found to lead to labour disputes.

Mechanism of Settlement of Disputes

We have seen the causes and effects of disputes. A number of measures have been taken by the states in many countries to solve these disputes. In this section we shall restirct our attention to the machinery available for the settlement of labour disputes in India due to sheer necessity and utility. Now, a brief summary of the machanism of settlement of disputes in India as envisaged by the Industrial Disputes Act 1947 and the subsequent amendments to the Act from 1956 onwards.

1. Work Committees: Under the provision of the Industrial Disputes Act 1947 all undertakings with a work force of 100 or more should constitute a 'Work Committee'. A work committee comprises of members drawn from the employees and the management. The novel idea behind it is to bring about sound co-ordination between the workers and managements. These committees negotiate and come to a mutually acceptable agreement on the demands of workers. This is more a comfortable arrangement to avoid disputes than to settle them after they crop up. Their range of operation is limited to the day-to-day problems of labour while at work.

2. Conciliation officers: As per the provision of the same Act conciliation officers are appointed for every undertaking by the Government. The officer is a full time representative of the Govt. He brings together the representatives of workers and the management and acts as an important link in bringing about settlement of a dispute. He is liaison officer in short. If his efforts fail to bring about an amicable settlement of the dispute, he must report to the government the details out of the dispute, and his efforts thereof. Based on his report the Government initiates further steps in this direction.

3. Conciliation Board or Committee: This committee is constituted by the Government. It is headed by an independent officer as the Chairman not below the rank of a High Court Judge. Its members are drawn from among workers and the management. The committee resolves the disputes after threadbear discussions and the verdict is binding. The results are then reported by the Chairman to the Government. In case the committee fails to resolve a dispute the Government is informed to take further steps to resolve the dispute. Disputes arising out of victimisation, retrenchment and suspension fall within the jurisdiction of these committees.

4. Inquiry Committees: An Inquiry Committee is headed by a Chairman and one or more independent members nominated by the Government. The committee is headed by the senior most judge of the High Court. It comes into picture only where the earlier measures fail to resolve disputes. The Inquiry Committee conducts a thorough enquiry into the cause of the dispute and fixes responsibility for the dispute. A detailed report is then submitted to the Government for referring the dispute to the '*Industrial Tribunal*'. It is a step prior to the tribunal taking up a dispute. Dispute arising out of dearness allowance, wages, etc. are enquired into by these committees.

5. Workers' Courts: These courts are set up by State Governments. Unresolved disputes of employers' action and retrenchment, suspension of workers, strikes and lock-outs fall within their jurisdiction. The verdict of these courts are binding on the parties to the disputes and are final.

6. Industrial Tribunals: There are two types of Industrial Tribunals; one each at state level and one at the national level. State Level Tribunals deal with disputes which affect only the state concerned and do not have any repercussions on the other state or states. The National Industrial Tribunal resolves disputes which arise in any state but have far reaching implications or effects on other states as well. These disputes may be in the Railways, Posts and Telegraphs Department, Life Insuarance Corporation of India, public sector industries with branches and the like. It is headed by the senior most Justice of the Supreme Court. Its verdict is final and binding on the employees and employers.

7. Workers' Participation in Management: The Government of India has constituted special Administrative Boards in industrial undertakings on the recommendation of an Enquiry Committee. These Administrative Boards promote cordial and congenial relationship between the workers and the management. They implement workers' participation in management and administration of the undertakings. The objective is to make labour feel responsible for decision-making and profitability, productivity of the undertakings and also to ensure proper share in the fruits of labour.

8. The Code of Discipline: A conference of All India Industrial Workers was held in 1957 to prepare a 'Code of Discipline' to be observed by labour. The resolution adopted at this conference was unique. As per the '*code*' the employees and employers should endeavour to resolve all disputes by mutual cooperation and negotiation. All available steps must be fully exhausted by the workers before striking work. They should not indulge in damage or destruction of property and indulge in wastage of time and resources of the undertakings. They should keep national and public interest above all considerations in their actions. Though the code had lukewarm response in practice in the initial stages it has now been very effective and has aroused favourable response from the workers.

The above measures to solve industrial and other disputes have been supplemented by a number of industrial security Acts and labour legislations such as Compensation Act, PF Act, ESI Act, Payment of Bonus Act, Minimum Wages Act and many more.

A SHORT HISTORY OF INDIAN TRADE UNION MOVEMENT

The Trade Union Movement in India is roughly about Seventy Years old. At a time when the West had a very strong and well organised workers' unions India had still to make a beginning. Early attempts to organise workers met with resistence from the employers. The task was hindered by ignorance and illiteracy of workers also. There was lack of appreciation of the benefits of the movement on the part of both employees and the employers. Even the British rule was unsympathetic to the Movement.

It was under these circumstances that B.P. Wadia attempted to organise the workers in 1918 in the then Madras Presidency. The World War I had caused severe inflation and wages were utterly low.

We may trace the history of the development of the Movement in three stages *viz.*: 1. Pre-war period (2) Post-war period and (3) Post-independence period.

We shall briefly analyse each one of these stages.

1. Pre-War Period: This period covers from 1875 to 1914. Though industrial development began in 1850 in India there were no efforts to improve the lot of industrial labour until 1875 in India. In 1875 Mr. Sohrabjee Shapurjee drew the attention of the British Empire to the plight of Indian industrial labour. The first Labour Union was organised in Bombay in 1890 consisting of the Bombay cotton textile workers. In 1897 the united committee of the Indian and Burmese workers was constituted. In 1905 the Calcutta Printers' Union was organised in Calcutta. The year 1907 saw the birth of the Bombay Dock Workers' Union. Following these attempts the Workers' Welfare Society and the Social Service Leagues were organised in 1909 and 1910 respectively.

2. Post-War Period: The outbreak of the First World War brought about the awakening of the working class in India. Industries had been earning very high profits during the World War by exploiting workers. The *war flame inflation* and the *Post-War inflation* affected the workers adversely as the wages remained more or less stagnant in the absence of labour movement. This gave a shot in the arm to the Trade Union Movement in India.

Besides, the '*October Revolution*' of 1917 was started by the workers in the U.S.S.R. Its success was a morale booster to the trade union movement in India. In 1918 the Madras Trade Union was organised. The cotton textile workers were brought into the mainstream of the movement. With this a real beginning was made by the movement.

From then on upto 1947 there was no looking back for the Movement. The All India Trade Union Congress (AITUC) was organised in 1920 at the national level. Mr. M.S. Joshi a noted unionist strongly pleaded for according recognition to trade unions. In 1921 the All India Railwaymen's Federation and the All India Post and Telegraph Union was organised. 1926 was red letter day in the history of Trade Union Movement in India. In 1926 trade unions achieved legislative recognition with the enactment of the Indian Trade Unions Act.

The outbreak of the Second World War caused severe galloping inflation and the movement received further impetus. Between 1945 and 1947 many strikes were successfully organised. These enlightened the workers regarding the strength and need for a well organised movement.

3. Post-independence Period: The Government of India, after independence, amended the Trade Unions Act of 1926 in 1948. The amended Act made it mandatory on the point of employers to recognise the trade unions and stop harassment of workers. It granted permission to the Unions to collect membership fee from the workers. Further, the amended Act empowered trade unions to act as mediators between the workers and managements to settle disputes.

At present all catagorises of workers except agricultural workers have been organised into unions. The mining and plantation workers who were left outside the movement have been brought under its wings. Labour engaged in small-scale units also are well organised now.

Yet, the trade union movement suffers from a number of defects. These defects are responsible for the failure of the movement on many fronts. Defects like poor membership, lack of unity, political interference through outside leadership and neglect of paternal functions have been plaguing the alround development of the Movement and urgent remedial measures on a war footing are required to increase its strength.

Measures to Strengthen the Movement

The Trade Union Movement has a history of over 100 years and yet it has not been able to achieve a significant degree of development in India. There are about 26,000 registered trade unions with above one crore membership on its rolls. Of these, the INTUC alone accounts for 2,400 unions with a total membership of over 26.1 lakhs and the AITUC accounts for 4,800 unions with a membership of 26 lakhs. The Hind Mazdoor Sabha (HMS), established in 1951, has 4 lakh membership.

The above figures only exhibit the numerical strength and do not speak for qualitative achievements.

There are a hoast of ills in the Movement. A cursory look at some of these ills or defects is necessary to know the graveness of the defects before we can venture to suggest remedial measures.

For instance, the basic defect is its very small membership with over 70% of the unions registering less than 500 members. The primary cause being the voluntary nature of membership. Added to this is the multiplicity of unions at the unit level and national level that cause lack of unity and strength. The poor membership has left the movement wanting in financial strength. With the result, it has not been able to either bargain effectively or take up paternal functions. Similarly, the illiteracy of majority of members and their narrow communal, linguistic and regional outlook fosters internal squabbles and disunity which only helps the selfish interest of the employers and outside leadership. There is political interference and a devilish grip of political parties over the national unions. This is glaringly evident from the hold of INTUC, AITUC, HMS and others by national political parties. Thus, according to Sri. V.V. Giri the Movement is still in its infancy.

Let us now consider if there is any panacea or cure for the ills of the Movement.

It is rightly observed by the Planning Commission of India that '*the Labour Unions instead of concentrating merely on the improvement of standard of living of their members should come to play a pivotal role in the development of the economy*'. *The time has come when they should come out of their shell.*

Remedies to Defects

A number of constructive suggestions are made from time to time by academicians and experts to remedy the defects. Let us briefly go quickly over these suggestions.

1. *Education of workers* regarding the need for enrolment as members, unity, broad-mindedness and active participation in the movement.
2. *Enhancement of membership* fees so that effective action and paternal functions can be taken up.
3. *Implementation of the 'principle of one union-one Industry'* so that better co-operation and co-ordination at the unit and national levels are ensured.
4. *'Deniocratic principle'* of election of Union leaders to remove outside leadership and political interference, so that those who lead the movement are from the rank and file of workers who know intimately the sufferings and problems of the workers.
5. *Promotion of better employer-employee relationship* such that a cordial atmosphere prevails to solve the problems of workers without friction or coercive action.
6. Instil the much wanted sense *of responsibility* among the members so that they can play a very constructive role in building up an industrially strong economy.
7. *Gaining 'public sympathy' through disciplined and non-violent strikes* and demonstrations so that the society and themselves benefit by the movement.
8. Strict self-*adherence to the 'code of discipline'* of 1956, so that they gain sympathy of the employer.
9. Greater state patronage through better and newer legislative measures to promote the movement.

These suggestions, when sincerely implemented, will certainly put the movement on a strong edifice and ensure better bargaining power of labour and the economy would witness around development.

A Case of Multiplicity in the midst of Unity

Indian trade union movement is unique at least in one sense; that is though they are supposed to unify the working class they stand divided on ideological grounds and political and religious fanaticism. That it is so is evident from the existence of a multiple number of Federations of trade unions at the national level such as, the AITUC, INTUC, ABHMS, UTUC, CITU and a hoast of others. These unions or Federations of unions were established at a time when labour unions at the unit level were no more than '*Strike Committees*' with temporary aims and existence. The Federations were to co-ordinate and unify the activities of the '*Units*'. The Trade Unions Act was passed in 1926 to support these unions. The constitution of the INTUC in 1910 was a major step.

However, the Federations could not hold themselves together for long. The AITUC got split in 1928-29 into two blocks. While one block passed into the hands of the '*Communists*' the other came to be controlled by the '*moderates*'.

After the Second World War INTUC was constituted by the followers of the National Congress of India and its objective was to check the spread of the influence of communism among workers rather than strengthen their bargaining power.

Later, the Hind Mazdoor Sabha (HMS) was organised by the '*Socialists*'. This is under the control of the BJP, the erstwhile Jan Sangh.

The AITUC is the oldest of the Federations which was established in 1910 under the control of the leftist communists with a membership of 43,000 unions and 26 lakh workers. It is the most strengthy of all the Federations and has a great record of achievements and occupies the second place.

The CITU is under the control of the Marxists and occupies the third place among the Federations.

The Akhil Bharathiya Maha Sabha (ABMS) came into existence in 1951 with the backing of the Jan Sangh and has a membership of 4 lakh unions. It is dominated by capitalist, communal, superstitious and antisocialist ideologies and is unpopular.

The Extent of Man-hours Lost

Industrial peace is absolutely necessary for a stable and sustained growth of production and productivity. This is however lacking in India. Industrial peace breaks down frequently due to strikes, demonstrations and lock-outs resulting in loss of output and fall in productivity. Hence, peaceful relations between labour and capital is highly essential to avoid loss to the employers and labour. The Planning Commission has remarked that, "*The employer-worker relationship has to be conceived of as partnership in a constructive endeavour to promote the satisfaction of the needs of the community in the best possible manner.*"

India was free from industrial unrest for a long time in the 19th century. The modern industries began to develop in the 19th century itself and for about 50 years there were not any significant industrial disputes.

The First World War saw the quick awakening of workers to fight for their rights. The Second World War injected a number of disputes during the post-war years.

The incidence of industrial disputes and the loss of man-days was quite low during 1951-1954. However from 1956-1963 the loss of man-days was high. It was the highest in 1958. In the years that followed, it was considerably low and touched the lowest figure of 32 lakh man-days in 1963. Again, from 1964 there was a sharp increase but fell to some extent 1965.

1967 was full of strikes, lock-outs and bundhs. The Code of Discipline was thrown to winds in 1967 and the incidence of disputes and the resultant loss of man-days was an all time high.

However, in 1968 was a relatively peaceful year but the situation became worse again in 1970. In 1970 there were 2889 disputes involving 18.3 lakh workers and 205 lakh man-days were lost as compared to 190.5 lakh man-days in 1969,172.4 lakh man-days in 1968 and 171.5 lakh man-days in 1967.

If we compare these figures with that of 1961,1962,1964 and 1965 when the loss of man-days was hardly about 49 lakhs, 61 lakhs, 77 lakhs, 64.4 lakhs respectively, the loss is alarming.

In 1963 there were hardly 32.7 lakh man-days lost due to disputes. In 1973 loss declined to about 178 lakh man-days.

Between 1961 and 1973 there was a two-fold increase in the incidence of disputes. In 1975 the number of disputes and man-days lost was 52, 997 and 1.92 crores respectively. The loss of man-days once again declined in 1976 to just 80 lakhs.

A closer and thorough analysis of the pattern of industrial disputes shows that it was higher in the public sector than in the private sector. The number of disputes and loss of man-days was higher in the public sector due to irresponsible strikes and lock-outs.

Thus, industrial disputes are detrimental to the productivity of the industrial sector and affect the welfare of one and all. A careful scrutiny of the occurrence of disputes and the loss of man-days reveals a more accute and devastating trend than it otherwise appears on the surface. A glance at the following table reveals the serious dimension of the problem.

Table showing No. of Disputes & Loss of Man-days*

Year	No. of Industrial Disputes	No. of man-days lost (in lakhs)
1961	1,357	49.2
1962	1,491	61.2
1963	1,471	32.7
1964	2,151	77.2
1965	1,835	64.7
1966	2,556	138.5
1967	2,815	171.5
1968	2,776	172.4
1969	2,627	190.5
1970	2,889	205.6
1971	2,752	165.5
1972	3,243	205.4
1973	2,924	177.9

The United Trade Union Congress (UTUC) was organised by T.K. Shah in 1949 and is under the control of the Revolutionary Socialists with over 500 unions and 4 lakh members.

Apart from the above Federations of divergent unions and interests that are conflicting there are smaller groups like the P & T Employees Union, the All India Insurance Employees Union, The Railway Employees Union, The Tea and Coffee Plantation Workers Union and so on.

The above account depicts a sorry state of affairs of the Trade Union Movement in India. It is a replica of a house divided and subdivided. In short, it has become akin to a bus that every body tries to drive when the driver is absent. It is a ship without anchor drifting in the ocean of workers. It is time to set it in the right direction and consolidate these federations in the interest of the workers.

SOME CONCEPTS OF WAGES

Maintenance of a certain minimum standard of living requires a fair minimum wage level. This has been recognised in the advanced countries of the West. In India also there has been a lot of debate and discussion on the question of evolving a workable integrated wage policy. At a seminar in 1974 "A rational and national wage policy" was favoured by many

* Source: India-1974, p. 312 upto 1971 figures. For 1972 and 1973 India-1975, p. 294.

participants. It was felt necessary to remove anomalies and irrationalities in the wage structure. It is the duty of the state to ensure adequate wages to labour so that labour can enjoy a decent standard of living.

Therefore, a machinary was set up to fix a "*minimum wages*" specially in '*Sweated*' trades without organised unions.

Minimum Wage: As a step in this direction the Minimum Wages Act, 1948 was enacted in India. The Act covers platation workers, rice mill and flour mill workers, oil mills and tannery workers, motor transport, road construction, building workers, quarries, agriculture and the like.

The minimum wage applies to even the clerical labour and covers men, women and children working at home and in factories. The minimum wage is fixed at (1) Minimum time-rate (2) Minimum piece-rate (3) Guaranteed time-rate and (4) over-time rate in accordance with: (a) the occupation (b) location (c) nature or class of work done.

It may consist of: (1) Minimum Wage plus cost of living allowance or (2) Basic Wage with or without the! cost of living allowance or (3) money value of essential commodities supplied at a concessional rate or (4) an all-inclusive rate.

The minimum wages are applicable only to industries with a total labour force of 1,000 or more only and is implemented by state governments. Thus, industries with less than a labour force of 1,000 remain outside the purview though the need for minimum wage is very high.

Need-based Wages: "Need-based Wage" may be defined as that *wage that is sufficient for the worker's subsistence and maintenance of his efficiency*. It is the rate which enables the worker to provide the necessities to himself and his family and also enjoy some basic comforts such as education, health services, essential social requirements, insurance, etc.

According to the Indian Labour Conference 1957 certain norms or standards were accepted for determining the Need-based Wage. They are:

1. Income of women, children and adolescents should not be counted.
2. The net intake of food should be calculated as per the recommendation of Dr. Aykroyd;
3. Clothing requirement of 18 yards should be calculated per head per annum per worker's family;
4. Rent should be taken on the basis of minimum provided by the Govt. Industrial Housing Scheme; and

5. Lastly, fuel, lighting, etc. should constitute 20% of the total minimum wage.

Theoretically and on grounds of social and economic justice the minimum wage concept is justifiable but practically unfeasible in the opinion of the Pay Commission and the Wage Boards. The National Pay Commission rightly observes that,

> *"There simply was not enough milk, fruit, eggs, fish or meat to go round for everybody when there is not enough for all, the sacrifice must also be from all."*

Moreover, the implementation of minimum wages is inflationary if there is no corresponding increase in productivity.

Productivity-linked Wages: The Second and Third Plans have emphasised the need for linking wages to productivity of labour. The Second Plan observed as follows:

> *"Improvement in wages can result mainly from increased productivity" while "No real advance in their (workers') standard of living was possible without steady increase in productivity, because any increase in wages generally, beyond certain narrow limits, would otherwise be nullified by a rise in prices."*

The implementation of productivity-liked wages abounds in many difficulties. In many industries the actual wages are many times higher than productivity (textiles, chemicals and leather goods). Moreover, labour is not inherently less productive but it is due to lack of modernisation and poor capital, etc. If wages are linked to productivity, labour suffers in these industries. Besides, it is not favoured universally by either the employers or the employees. It creates disparity in wages.

The conclusion is that there is a dilemma in arriving at an all-acceptable wage policy. The wise course would be to contain inflation, link wages to productivity and follow it up with appropriate modernisation of technology and supply efficient capital to labour.

4

International Trade

National or domestic trade and International or Foreign Trade are entirely two different entities. The two types of trade take place on different scales and under different conditions. As long as Business Economics extend to international trade so long will we be concerned with its formalities and methods.

There have been a number of attempts in economic theory to explain the factors leading to international trade—from the classical economists upto the modern day. However, in this chapter we shall restrict ourselves to the discussion on the basic differences in the *terminology* used in International Trade and be content with the methods of correcting an *'Adverse Balance of Payments'*.

Balance of Trade

International trade consists of exchange of both *goods* and *services* across countries.

Thus, basically there is a need to distinguish between 'trading in goods' and 'trading in services' such as shipping, insurance, etc.

Hence, a fundamental distinction is made in international trade between *material* and *immaterial* imports and exports.

The *material* imports and exports are referred to as *Visible* and those of services as *Invisible* by importers and exporters.

In terms of Business Economics, they may be addressed to as *'Trading on Goods Account'* and *'Trading on Services Account'* respectively.

In pure theory of International Trade a distinction is made between *'Balance of Trade'* and *'Balance of Payments'* for the sake of convenience of understanding.

Thus, '*Balance of Trade*' is the net difference between the values of goods or merchandise imports and exports of a country during a given year. To be more specific, *Balance of Trade* refers to trading between countries in goods only.

The balance of Trade maybe either *(a) favourable (b) unfavourable or (c) inquilibrium.*

It is said to be favourable when the net difference between commodity exports and commodity imports is positive (+) and unfavourable when the net difference is negative (—).

It is said to be in 'Equilibrium' when the two values are just equal.

Balance of Payments

As already noted, Balance of Payments refers to the overall difference between *visible* and *invisible* imports and exports of a country during a given year.

Thus, Balance of Payments is an *aggregation* of a country's foreign trade position.

'*Balance of Payments*' is, therefore, the over-all difference between the value of *visible* and *invisible* imports and exports.

Just as balance of trade could be favourable or unfavourable or could be just self-balancing so could be the Balance of Payments.

Measures to Correct Adverse Balance of Payments

As we already know, the '*Balance of Payments*' is a systematic record of *all exports* and *all imports* between countries. Further, it throws full light on a country's final strength in foreign trade. In maintaining the account of Balance of Payments we follow the '*Double Entry Method* of book-keeping.

On observation, we may find that it is either *unfavourable* to the country (or *Adverse* to the country) or *favourable* or it is just in *equilibrium*.

If the Balance of Payments is *adverse* to the country, it has to be rectified soon. However, it should be noted that a continuously favourable Balance of Payments is not desirable in the long-run.

There are at least *five* measures to combat an Adverse Balance of Payments *viz.*,

1. Deflationary Measures;
2. Exchange Depreciation;

3. Exchange Control;
4. Export Promotion and Import Restriction; and
5. Devaluation of Currency.

It would be apt to know how these measures help to correct the adversity of balance of payments of a country.

1. Deflationary Measures: Very often *disequilibrium* in balance of payments is caused by excess demand for a country's imports. In that case, it is wise to reduce or '*deflate*' the prices of domestically produced goods so that they become more attractive than the imported goods. Simultaneously, the export prices could be reduced and exports will increase as they become less dearer to the importing country. This policy has, therefore, the double-effect of reducing imports and increasing exports at the same time.

However, this measure requires '*fixed exchange rates*' which is not in vogue now. Further, this policy aims at reducing wages or incomes which is not attainable as *collective bargaining* has become a force now. Moreover, this measure has fallen into disuse today as it causes unemployment.

2. Exchange Depreciation: Exchange Depreciation as a method of correcting adverse balance of payments refers to a reduction in the Rate of Exchange of a country's currency in terms of the currency of other countries with whom there is an adverse balance of payments. To put it more simply, it is a method of *making a country's currency cheaper in terms of foreign currencies.*

When a currency is *depreciated* the importing country or countries will be able to get more imports for each unit of their currency than before. Hence, the demand for exports will rise so that the deficit is reduced.

Exchange Depreciation should not be mistaken for '*Devaluation*' of currency. For, the latter means a reduction in the value of currency in terms of gold.

Depreciation of currency suffers from some limitations. *Firstly*, it is *inflationary*. *Secondly*, it may turn the *terms of trade* against the country.

3. Exchange Control: Total regulation over all international transactions refers to exchange control. The monetary authority controls all transactions of receipts and payments arising out of international trade. Prior permission has to be sought from the Central Bank for all international payments or receipts. Further, transactions when permitted have to conform to the prescribed rates of exchange.

> According to Enke and Salera, "*An exchange control or exchange restriction is any interference by government with the freedom of the market in which one currency may be exchanged for another.*"*

This method was extensively used by many countries during the *Great Depression.* It was universally practised during the Second World War. Even today, it is in practice all over the world.

While it ensures essential imports, it secures better bargain and prevents export of capital, gold and essential commodities at the same time.

There are a number of methods of Exchange Control. The following chart sums up the various methods of Exchange Control.

4. Export Promotion and Import Restriction: The deficit balance of payments can be reduced by encouraging exports and restricting unnecessary imports. Better methods of marketing, import substitution, subsidising exports, etc. also go a long way in reducing the deficit.

TYPES OF EXCHANGE CONTROL

- **Direct Methods**
  - Intervention (Pegging)
  - Exchange Restriction
  - Exchange Clearing Agreements
  - Transformation of Units
- **Indirect Methods**
  - Interest Rate Changes
  - Import Duties
  - Export Subsidies

5. Devaluation: It is found to be the most effective of all remedial measures for correcting an adverse balance of payments. However, it is also an extreme measure. It is resorted to only in case of acute deficit.

'*Devaluation*' means reducing the '*external value*' of a country's currency in relation to the currency of other countries. When this is done, imports become costly and the demand for imports decreases. Contrarily, the exports of the country become cheaper to other countries and hence exports increase. Thus, the disequilibrium is removed.

However, devaluation has some *demerits* in the long-run. They are:

1. Devaluation increases the prices of imported raw-materials and essential machinery. Thus, *it hinders the development of UDCs.*
2. Devaluation is also *inflationary* because in course of time thc rise in price level within the country is imminent.

* 'International Economics': III Edn., pp. 172.

3. Then the favourable effect of a rise in exports will be neutralised by the rise in the domestic price level.

Despite these disadvantages, devaluation has been practised by many countries like India (1949 and 1966), England (1949 and 1967) and U.S.A. (1972). The devaluation of currency will be successful only when the *elastic demand* for exports and imports is given and on whether the other countries do not devalue their currencies in retaliation.

FOREIGN EXCHANGE

Purchasing Power Parity Theory (Gustav Cassel)

Gustav Cassel, a Swedish economist developed the 'Purchasing Power Parity Theory' (PPP Theory). According to the PPP theory the rate of exchange between any two currencies depends upon their relative purchasing power in the countries in which they circulate. In simple language, the theory states that exchange rate of a country's currency is determined by the '*purchasing power parity*'.

According to H.E. Evitt, "*The purchasing power parity between any two countries is that amount of currency of one country which endows the holder with the same amount of purchasing power i.e. command over goods and services.*" Thus, purchasing power parity is the ratio between two currencies which would equalise their relative purchasing powers over goods, according to Prof. Whittlesey.

Gustav Cassel held that the rate of exchange falls exactly in the same proportion as the price level rises and *vice versa* and consequently the value of the home currency will fall and its value in terms of foreign currencies will also fall. In other words, according to the PPP theory, movements in domestic price levels will cause changes in the external purchasing power of the currencies (*i.e.* in exchange rates).

A simple example will help clearer understanding of the theory. Suppose, a unit of commodity x costs £2 in the U.K. and ₹ 30 in India. Then the rate of exchange is £2: ₹ 30 (as determined by the internal purchasing power of the £ and the ₹). The reason is simple: the Britishers want ₹ to purchase Indian goods and Indians want the £ to purchase British goods. The rate of exchange between £ and ₹ is determined by the price of x in the U.K. and India.

When there is a change in the purchasing power of the £ and ₹ there will be a change in the rale of exchange and a new '*equilibrium rate*' will be established.

The theory has 'two' forms of interpretation; the '*Absolute*' form and the '*Comparative*' form.

In its '*Absolute Form*' it deals with the mechanism of determination of exchange rate at a '*point of time*' (*i.e.* short-term rate of exchange). Therefore, the '*absolute rate of exchange*' does not take into account the movements in the exchange rate caused by changes in price levels of the current and past dates. Thus, there is no time sequence.

In its '*Comparative Form*' it takes into account movements in price levels (of domestic and foreign price levels) in the current period relative to a previous date. Therefore, the '*Relative Approach*' is more useful than the '*Absolute Approach*' to the theory.

Prof. Scammel has applied the following formula for obtaining the '*equilibrium rate of exchange*':

$$R_1 = R_2 - 1 \times \frac{P_1}{P_2}$$

Where,

$R_1 \rightarrow$ New rate of exchange

$R_2 - 1 \rightarrow$ The change in index number for the currency of the country in terms of another country's currency for which exchange rate is expressed.

$P_2 \rightarrow$ The changes in index number of the value of the other currency.

Prof. Scammel arrives at the new equilibrium rate of exchange by multiplying the previous or old equilibrium rate of exchange by the relative change in price levels of the two countries concerned from the date on which the old exchange rate ruled. The movements in price levels are expressed in the form of Index numbers in the formula.

Let us take a numerical example: Suppose in 1980 the exchange rate of ₹ to $ was 10:1 which is the normal rate of exchange. If the price level in India doubles in 1981 and if the price level in America remains constant then rate of exchange in comparative terms will be calculated as under:

$$\$ \text{ in } 1981 = \frac{200}{100} \times 10$$

Therefore, the rate of exchange of $ in 1981 = ₹ 10

or

The exchange rate of ₹ in 1981 will be

$$₹\,1 = \frac{200}{100} \times 10 \text{ Cents.}$$

Thus, the rate of exchange is determined by comparing the purchasing power of two currencies. When the two purchasing powers change the rate of exchange of the currencies will necessarily change. This is the norm round which actual rates of exchange will vary. According to Cassell, "*This is easily seen or reflect on the fact that the price paid in a foreign currency is ultimately a price for foreign commodities, a price which must stand in certain relation to the prices of commodities on the home-market. Thus, we arrive at the conclusion that the rate of exchange between two currencies must stand essentially on the quotient of the internal purchasing powers of these currencies.*"*

Critical Assessment of the PPP Theory

The purchasing power parity theory of exchange rate determination is an essential tool for understanding the process of 'monetary adjustment' in spite of its several weaknesses.

According to Prof. Whittleasy, it cannot fully and satisfactorily explain the entire phenomenon of exchange rates and "*It is hardly realistic that relative price levels perfectly control international trade*" through their influence on the rates of exchange. "*Nevertheless, in the absence of unsettling influences such as sudden movements of capital, commodity trade does constitute the most important factor of the supply and demand of foreign currencies*".

Further, according to Prof. Elseworth the concept of equilibrium rate owes much to the Purchasing Power Parity Theory.

CRITICISMS

We may now note the important grounds on which the PPP theory is attacked and how far the assumptions of the theory are unrealistic and what qualifications are required to make it useful.

The basic objections raised by the critics are as follows:

1. The Theory compares index numbers of prices in two countries to arrive at the rate of exchange but the *price-indices so compared are incomparable for reasons of innumerable problems in constructing such indices.* It involves the assumption of a Base Year. If the relationship between two price levels changes in that year the rate of exchange will change in the same proportion.

* Gustov Cassel, "Foreign Exchanges." Article 'Encyclopaedia Britannica, Ed. 13: First Supplementary Volume, p. 86.

However, usually, price levels of different countries remain at different levels. Even the question of what commodities should be included and what weights should be given to each commodity in each country is a cumbersome task as different goods have different degrees of importance in the two countries in question.

2. *The theory maintains that domestically demanded types of goods are to be included while taking the domestic price level.* Many have suggested that only exported goods must be considered as the supply of and demand for foreign exchange depends on the demand for imports and exports.
3. *Even if the price level of two countries may not change there may be a change in the rate of exchange.* This may occur when the 'conditions of currencies' in the two countries has an influence on the demand for currencies. For instance, a rumour of speculation that the currency will '*depreciate*' due to over-issue of notes the demand for it will decrease since none wants to transfer one's funds into that currency whose value is likely to depreciate. There will be 'hot money movements' or flight of currency and the rate of exchange will go up. That is also the case if there arises political instability.
4. *The Theory neglects the influence of invisible exports and imports on exchange rates.* Repayment of loans, payment of interest on loans from abroad, purchase of and sale of foreign securities etc. involve conversion of domestic currency into foreign currency. Hence, the demand for foreign currency increases and the exchange rate moves against the domestic currency.
5. *The theory neglects Banking influences also.* Purchase and sale of banker's drafts, travellers cheques, letters of credit, orbitrage operations, etc. affect the demand for foreign currencies and in turn affect the exchange rate. Even the 'Bank Rate' has its influence on the Exchange
6. *Trade conditions i.e. the relative value of imports and exports affect exchange rates which is neglected.*
7. *The theory neglects grossly the presence of restrictions to the flow of imports and exports.* There are frequent changes in '*Tariff Policies*' of countries in the wake of "Restricted Trade" and '*Free Trade*' is assumed in the theory. Restrictions such as import and export duties and exchange control affect the exchange rates

in reality. A country can successfully stabilise its exchange rate even though the purchasing power has fallen.

8. Lastly, the theory does not foresee that changes in the price of '*specific*' commodities may affect the rate of exchange even though the 'general price levels' have remained constant.

Despite the several criticisms there is an element of utility in the theory. It guides the fixation of 'parity rates of exchange during a postwar period when the post-war inflation has affected the rates of exchange of pre-war period.' In the words of Prof. Ham, "*Purchasing power parities cannot be used to compute equilibrium rates....Nevertheless, the purchasing power approach may be used with advantage when we are entirely in the dark as after long periods of exchange control or violent inflation.*" It enables us to come nearer the area of equilibrium if not to the exact equilibrium rate ofexchange.

Exchange Control - Meaning and Objectives

The war, all over the world as a common measure to fight inflation and balance of payments arises here. As a peace-time measure it came to be adopted after the '*Great Depression*' of 1930s.

Exchange control may be defined as 'a system of *government intervention to maintain a rate of exchange* which is quite different from the one that would have prevailed in its absence'.

Exchange control thus refers to 'a complete control overall transactions of international nature involving foreign payments and receipts. It bans any receipts from foreigners and payments to foreigners without prior permission from the monetary authorities.' In other words, the entire *extent, direction and rate of exchange* are all controlled by the monetary authority.

According to Enkey and Salera:

> *"An exchange control or exchange restriction is any interference by government with the freedom of the market in which one currency may be exchanged for another."**

H.E. Evitt States that:

> *"Any form of official interference with the freedom of dealings in foreign exchange is ....a form of exchange control."***

---

* Enkey and Salera:'International Economics' (3rd Ed.), p. 172.

** H.E. Evitt: "Manual of Foreign Exchange", p. 189

According to Fredric Benham exchange control is—"*a method of preventing a deficit, in the balance of payments.*"*

Lastly, George N. Halm gives the following definition:

"*By 'exchange control' we refer to measures which replace part of the equilibrium functions of the foreign exchange market by regulations alien to the pricing process.*"**

Objectives of Exchange Control

Exchange control obviously has many broad objectives in the modern set up of international trade. Some of the purposes or objectives may be underlined in brief as follows:

1. Counteracting Balance of Payments Crisis: Recourse to exchange control checks imports in general or of specific types as the case may be and encourages exports to specific countries. According to Prof. Salera '*Exchange control protects the balance of payments and limits the drain on foreign exchange reserves in the absence of controls.*'

2. Ensures Better Bargaining Power: Better bargaining power can be ensured in international markets through exchange control. It can be excercised to limit the export of scarce exports only to selected countries on favourable terms of trade. Some essential imports can also be secured at lower prices. It even helps a country to secure a monopoly power to exploit a foreign market.

3. Encourages Effective Centralised Planning: Exchange control can be effective in the planning process of a country. Essential goods can be obtained, scarce resources can be conserved and foreign private capital can be attracted all of which are essential for successful planning in UDCs.

4. Prevents Flight of Capital: When a large amount of capital flees from the country, economic crisis will set in. Exchange control checks the *flight of capital* in the form of '*Over-valuation*' of the currency to retain domestic capital at home.

5. Protects Domestic Industry: Unfair and cut-throat foreign competition kills 'infant industries' at home. Exchange restriction in the form of import quotas and import duties protects such industries.

6. Checks Internal Inflation: Internal inflation can be arrested by over-valuing the currency and the adverse effects of inflation can be overcome.

* Fredric Benham: 'Economics' (6th lid.), p. 5534

** George N. Halm: 'Monetary Theory' (Ed. 1968). p. 237.

Thus, it can be used not merely to correct international circumstances that exchange control is needed but also for domestic inflation.

7. Checks fluctuations: Fluctuations of a temporary nature can be checked at home if they are due to speculative transactions without affecting respective values of different currencies. The long-term equilibrium rate can be firmly established thereby.

8. Ensures Essential Imports: Foreign exchange resources can be conserved by restricting non-essential imports and permitting essential imports through *import licensing policy*. This ensures supply of essential goods and their stable prices.

However, exchange control has *three* different sets of objectives according to Prof. Geofey Growther *viz.*: (1) *Over-valuation*; (2) *Under-valuation*; and (3) *Avoidance of fluctuations*. But it should not be forgotten that exchange control can at best be doubtful in neutralising or eliminating temporary or speculative ups and downs in the exchange rates. Therefore, Prof. Growther remarks:

> *"It is a game that everyone can play. If everyone plays it and currencies enter upon competition to see which can be pushed furthest below its real value, it quickly develops into a race to render all currency worthless." And in the ultimate analysis all stand to lose. It is an immoral game and utterly selfish too.*

5

International Financial Institutions

INTERNATIONAL MONETARY FUND (IMF)

The International Monetary Fund (IMF) was established in December 1945 with the recommendation of the '*Bretton Woods Conference*' of July 1944. The initial membership of the IMF was 44. Its total membership at present is 146. The Fund is a comprehensive and determined step of international monetary co-operation. It is a deliberate and an honest effort to mutually aid the fulfilment of international goals of member countries.

The IMF incorporates the broad outlines of the '*Keynes Plan*' and the '*White Plan*' prepared by Lord Keynes and Harry White respectively. According to W.M. Scammell, the Keynes plan was more daring and objective than that of Mr. Harry White and "*The proposal still bears the stamp of Keynes' personal genius.*"*

The IMF is one of the "twins of *Bretton Woods*", the other being the IBRD or World Bank.

Resources and Organisation: The IMF began operating in March 1947 with an initial capital of $8.8 billion. The quota of each member was determined on the basis of its national income and its share in international trade. The quota is divided into two parts *viz.*, partly in gold and partly in home currency in the ratio of 25%: 75% respectively.

The Fund is organised on the following lines: The '*Board of Governors*' is the General Body of the Fund. It consists of a Governor and one Alternate Governor from each member country.

* 'International Monetary Policy': W.M. Sammell, p. 129.

'The Executive Directors' (20 of them) are responsible for the day—to-day affairs of the Fund. Twenty of the '*Board of Executive Directors*' are appointed by the largest members of the Fund *viz.*, the U.S.A., the U.K., West Germany, Japan and France. The Chief Executive Director (appointed by the Board of Executive Directors) is the Chief Executive of the IMF.

Objectives: The objectives or functions of the IMF are laid down in Article I of the Fund's Agreement as follows:

1. Promote international monetary co-operation.
2. Expand and promote balanced growth of international trade and high level of employment.
3. Promote stable exchange rates.
4. Promote multilateral system of payments.
5. Eliminate restriction of foreign exchange.
6. Aid settlement of balance of payments through the resources of the Fund.
7. Assist the members to avoid a consistently adverse balance of payments crisis.
8. Promote a system of fixed exchange rates.
9. Provide consultancy to UDCs on matters of credit and finance, aid and assist in foreign exchange policy, expansion of tax-base and actively provide technical assistance to UDCs.

In substance, the Fund was established, according to J.L. Hanson, "*To encourage multilateral trade, and so stable exchange rates and free convertibility of currencies were the ultimate objectives. The aim was to secure the advantages of gold standard without its rigidities, together with the greater measure of freedom over internal policy which free exchange rates give.*"*

The IMF and International Liquidity: International liquidity may be defined as '*the resources or reserves at the disposal of the various countries of the world for settling trade and other obligations arising out of international trade*'.

The international trade may not always be favourable nor be in equilibrium. Thus, an unfavourable balance of payments may arise; a nett balance has to be paid to other countries. Prior to the inception of the IMF such international payments were settled either through gold or through internationally accepted currencies viz. Pound and Dollar

* 'Monetary Theory and Practice': J.L. Hanson, p. 155.

as they were treated as '*hard currencies*' (*i.e.* currencies whose exchange rates were stable).

The IMF provides the third method of settlement of international payments viz., the Fund's reserves of currencies of members. This enables members to retain their own resources of *hard currencies* and earn interest on them. The drawings from the IMF facilitates smooth conduct of international trade.

The problem of *International Liquidity* has assumed alarming proportions recently. The world trade has outgrown the monetary and gold reserves of free countries.

The problem of international liquidity has been severe due to:

1. Slow growth of gold reserves and stable currencies.
2. High demand for gold while its world production has been low.
3. Uneven distribution of gold and foreign exchange reserves among the countries of the world.
4. Weakening of confidence in key-currencies like the Pound and the Dollar.

The IMF has increased its capital over years but the reserves are insufficient to finance the enormous growth of world trade. Hence, the IMF created the *Special Drawing Rights* (SDRs) to tide over the problem of international liquidity.

Special Drawing Rights: The Special Drawing Rights (SDRs) was created on July 28, 1968 to supplement the resources of the IMF for providing international liquidity. Ten leading members of the IMF are the leading contributors to the special fund of the SDRs. They are: (1) The U.S.A., (2) The U.K., (3) West Germany, (4) France, (5) Japan, (6) Canada, (7) Belgium, (8) Holland, (9) Italy, and (10) Sweden.

As many as 121 out of the 129 members of IMF had become participants of the SDRs by 1976 itself. The SDRs can be used by the participant members in the following manner:

1. Foreign exchange can be obtained from SDRs to redeem balances of a country's own currency held by other countries.
2. Obtain foreign exchange from other participants '*Designated*' to receive the SDRs. That is, under '*Transactions with Designation*' arrangement the '*user-country*' should request the IMF to arrange for conversion of its SDRs into foreign exchange and the IMF then instructs the participants (one or more of its members) to provide the required currency by the user-country.

The 'participants', in turn have a right to use their own '*holdings*' in SDRs to obtain foreign exchange for their use.

3. *Lastly*, the members can use SDRs under "Operations and Transactions" to operate their '*General Account*' with the IMF (The General Account is the account with which the IMF conducts its transactions with its members. It is thus different from the SDRs).

Thus, the IMF, through the SDRs has introduced a unique international medium of exchange made of paper which has no linking with gold. This has given the advantage of the Gold Standard *minus* gold. This is actually an incorporation of one major proposal of the '*Keynes Plan*' at Britton Woods Conference wherein J.M. Keynes proposed the introduction of an internationally acceptable currency to be called as '*Bancor*'. Incidentally, the U.SA. did not accept Keynes' proposal as it was a bit harsh. Eventually, the introduction of the unique SDRs succeeded in reducing the importance of gold in international transactions to the advantage of all participants of IMF. The SDRs units are now rightly described as '*paper gold*'.

We now conclude with the words of A.C.L. Day thus: It is "*the most ambitious so far of the post-war monetary institutions*". J.L. Hansen has also rightly remarked that "*the scheme (SDRs) weakens the position of gold in the international monetary system, and some people regard this new development as the first step towards freeing the system from any sort of dependence on gold at all*" for providing international liquidity.

INTERNATIONAL BANK FOR RECONSTRUCTION AND DEVELOPMENT (IBRD) OR WORLD BANK

Established in June 1946 the International Bank for Reconstruction and Development (IBRD) is also known as the '*World Bank*' (WB). It is an outcome of the '*Britton Woods Confereance*' of July 1944. The major objective of the IBRD is to 'facilitate and promote' long-term 'foreign investment' into productive channels.

The IBRD consisted of only 40 member countries and now all the members of the IMF are automatically the members of the IBRD or world Bank.

Prof. W.M. Scammell has summed up the task before the IBRD in the following words:

> *"Brought to birth in a war-shattered world its immediate task was to aid in reconstruction by promoting loans for*

rebuilding of productive machinery. From this it was to pass, in due time, to developing the resources and productive capacity of the world's backward regions."*

(A) Objectives: The Article of the IBRD has stated its functions very clearly. Its objectives may be summed up as follows:

1. Reconstruction and development of member countries through promotion of investment of long-term 'capital of other members'.
2. Promotion of 'private foreign capital' through participation in loans and investments or through 'guarantees' of loans and investments of private foreign sources.

   The Articles of Agreement of the IBRD reads thus: "*The International Bank does not replace private investments abroad; rather, its purpose is to promote private foreign investment by means of guarantees or participation in loans and other investments by private investors; and when private capital is not available on reasonable terms, to supplement private investment by providing ...... finance for productive purposes out of its own capital, funds raised by it and its other sources.*"**
3. Promotion of long-term '*balanced growth*' of international trade and ensure '*equilibrium*' in balance of payments of member countries—through international investments.

   Thus, the assistance of the IBRD or World Bank is mainly for development of infrastructure of economic development and reconstruction.
4. Technical assistance to member countries such as advice on technical and managerial problems that may arise in preparation of projects, modification of projects, determination of priorities, etc. The World Bank has established permanent Missions at Nairobi and Abidjan for this purpose and they work in cooperation with the '*African Development Bank*'. Besides, it has constituted the '*Economic Development Institutes*' with the assistance of the *Ford and Rockefeller Foundation* to train government officials in programmes and techniques of development.

(B) Resources: The IBRD started with an initial capital of $10 billion of 1 lakh shares of 1 lakh dollars each. Of this, $9.4 billion were subscribed by members. These shares are transferable only to the IBRD.

* 'International Monetary Policy': W.M. Scammell, p. 227.

** Quoted in 'Monetary Theory': George N. Halm, pp. 290-91.

The subscription of each member is payable as follows:

1. 2% in gold or U.S. Dollars freely available to the IBRD for lending.
2. 18% in local or domestic currency available to the IBRD for lending with the consent of the holder member.
3. Remaining 80% is subject to *call* by the IBRD as and when required and it is not readily available for lending.

(C) Membership: Any country which subscribes to the *Charter* of the IBRD is eligible for membership. However, membership of IBRD is granted only to those countries which are also members of the IMF. Withdrawal of membership is open to the members on giving prior notice in writing. A member country may be suspended when it fails to fulfil its obligation towards the Bank.

(D) Management: The IBRD has a *three-tier* system of management. *Firstly*, there is a 'Board of Governors' that deals with only the *broad issues*. It consists of one Governor from each member-nation who is usually the Finance Minister. The Board of Governors meets once a year.

Secondly, there is a 'Board of Executive Directors'. It meets once a week at Washington, DC. Five of the members of the Board of Executive Directors belong to the largest subscribers *viz.* the U.K. the U.S.A. France, West Germany and Japan. The rest of the Governors are elected by the member countries.

Lastly, there is a President who represents the important level of management who is responsible for the overall administration of the IBRD and for negotiations with the borrowers.

The Executive Directors have voting rights at the rate of 250 votes per Director '*plus*' one vote per $100,000 of subscribed capital. The operational structure is on regional basis since 1972.

(E) Process of Granting Loans: The IBRD follows a predetermined process and principles while granting loans. The procedure adopted begins with the "*End-use Supervision*" of the loan. The member nation applies for a loan to the IBRD. A preliminary investigation is made regarding the '*merit*' of the application. A special investigation team or mission visits the applicant country to assess the technical viability of the proposed project and submits its report to the President of the IBRD.

The president and his staff scrutinize the report and submit the findings to the Board of Executive Directors which finally grants the loan or rejects the loan application.

The loans are granted subject to certain conditions. The important conditions are that:

1. The borrowing country must have repaying capacity.
2. The project or projects are economically and technically viable and require priority.
3. The member-borrower meets the *non-foreign exchange content* of the project with domestic resources.
4. The borrowing country maintains a continuing relation with the IBRD for evaluation of the project financed.

(F) Working: As per the broad objectives of the IBRD the UDCs are given assistance for economic development. A broad spectrum of projects are financed by it. The sectors financed include:

1. Agriculture and power;
2. Industry, transport and telecommunication;
3. Education; and
4. Urban development and water supply.

Accordingly, about 90% of the financial assistance of the IBRD has been to finance specific development projects. Military and politically motivated projects are therefore not assisted by the IBRD. During the first three decades the loans committed by it was $29 billion. It is a *tougher* and *harder lender* than any other financial institution.

In short; the IBRD has an unstinted record of achievements. According to Enkey and Salera, "*The Bank has gone on to achieve an enviable record in contrast to the case of the Fund.*" Further, according to Scammell, "The record of the Bank is one of quiet success." It has contributed modestly to the flow of international investment since the war and the volume of its transactions is increasing.

INTERNATIONAL DEVELOPMENT ASSOCIATION (IDA)

No doubt the international financial institutions meet a number of requirements of countries for their economic and industrial development. Thus, the projects which are financed by the IBRD and IMF are productive projects which fulfil the technical requirements. Their financial accommodation follows '*rigid*' terms.

The developing countries require certain amount of financial assistance for technically less viable projects which are essential for social and economic development. They may be construction of bridges, dams, roads, etc., public utility works such as those that require huge funds which are not readily available to the infant economics. Reduction of *regional imbalances* in UDCs also requires huge investments in technically less productive projects. The International Development Association (ADA) was established to provide financial assistance for such projects on '*flexible*' terms.

(A) Objects: The IDA was established in 1960 with the broad objective of providing '*Soft-loans*' to the developing countries for economic development. The loans are called '*soft-loans*' because the rates of interest and the period of repayment are liberal as compared to those of the IMF or IBRD.

The IDA grants loans repayable over 50 years at 3/4% of interest per annum. Thus, the IDA has come to be known as '*The World Bank's Soft-loan Window*',

The '*end-use*' conditions of the IDA are as stringent as that of the IBRD. It insists on credit worthiness while granting loans to its members. The '*softness*' is limited to the rate of interest and period of repayment.

(B) Membership: Its membership is open to all the members of the World Bank or the IBRD. The present membership strength of the IDA is 130. Of this 22 are Part-I members and 118 are Part-II members. The basic distinction between the two types of membership is that while the *former* have subscribed to the IDA in gold freely convertible currencies in full, the *latter* have subscribed 10% in gold and 90% in their domestic currency. Besides the currencies of the latter are convertible into other currencies by the IDA.

(C) Capital: As on 30 June 1981 the subscription of Part-I and Part-II, members stood at $ 27,400 million and $12,00 million respectively. The former is from the highly industrialised countries. The IBRD has also provided $1.02 billion in the form of 'grants' to the IDA.

(D) Management: The IDA has a 'Board of Governors'. It is headed by a president. It also has a Board of Executive Directors. All these bodies are manned by those of the World Bank as '*ex-officios*'. However, financially and legally the IDA has an independent entity. Its assets and liabilities are maintained separately.

(E) Working: The credit policy of the IDA is very flexible. Countries which are unable to get credit from the IBRD and the poorest of the poor are given priority. Where terms are altered interest-free loans are also granted for housing, water supply, sanitation, hospitals, urban development, etc. The range of projects financed by it are wider than that of the IBRD. Sometimes loans are granted to individual industries which have no state guarantee but they must be '*development-oriented*'.

India is the largest beneficiary of the loans from the IDA. Some highly indebted countries are given interest-free loans to generate resources to reduce the burden. The funds granted up to the end of 1975 was $11.5 billion and rose to $27 billions by June 30,1982 and the total number of loans stood at 1176 in all as on the same date.

Thus, the IDA as the 'soft-loan window of the World Bank', has been of great help to the Third World Countries in particular and to the developing countries in general. It has been functioning satisfactorily. Its funds are meagre as compared to the tasks ahead of it and there is an urgent need to augment its resources. Probably, the advanced West can supplement its resources through voluntary subscriptions to its funds.

THE ASIAN DEVELOPMENT BANK (ADB)

We have already seen how the IMF and the IBRD are world bodies catering to the financial needs of all the members of the world as one single unit. The Asian and the Far East Asian Countries which are more backward have to find a separate or special arrangement to attract priority in international monetary co-operation on a '*regional basis*'.

The founding of the Asian Development Association (ADB) in November 1966 was a hallmark in this direction. The ADB was set up on the recommendation of the Ministerial Conference of the UNO's agency at Manila (Philippines).

The ADB bagan functioning in December 1966.

(A) Objectives: The ADB is a regional bank for monetary cooperation among Asian and Far East Asian Countries and as such its prime objective is promotion of economic growth and economic cooperation among countries. Thus, it provides funds, promotes investments and lends technical assistance to these regions. However, it should be remembered that the ADB is not purely a Regional Bank at the global level because there are '*non-regional members*' in it. The bank's capital is partly drawn from these non-regional members.

(B) Membership: The members of the United Nations Economic Commission for Asia and the Far East (ECAFE) are the members of the ADB. Besides, countries which are members opt the UNO or Associate Members of the ECAFE are also its members. There were 20 "regional members" on its inception with 13 other non-regional members. As on 31st December 1975 the regional membership and non-regional membership increased to 41 and 27 respectively. Japan, India and Australia are its prominent members while the U.SA. is the leading non-regional member.

(C) Capital Resources: The ADB began with an initial capital of $1000 million. The total '*subscribed capital*' of the ADB as on 30th June 1975 stood at $107.22 million. Each member country subscribes in proportion to its subscription to the I.F.C. The subscriptions are paid partly in gold and partly in domestic currencies. Besides, the ADB is authorised to raise '*Special Fund*' by increasing capital, issuing Bonds or accepting contributions to the special fund out of which it can grant *soft-loans* like the IDB does. About 10% of its '*paid-up capital*' is in the Special Fund.

(D) Management: The management vests with the 'Board of Governors', Board of Directors and the President. Each member country is represented by one Governor and one Alternate Governor. Policy-making rests with the Board of Governors but it can delegate some of its powers to the Board of Directors. The former meets at least once a year. The Board of Directors is responsible for the day-to-day affairs of the ADB and consists of 10 Directors. At least 7 of them are regional members and 3 are non-regional members of the ADB. The term of the Directors is 2 years and they are eligible for re-election.

The ADB is thus organised on lines similar to that of the IBRD and supplements the efforts of the IBRD and IDB.

(E) Working: It has progressed remarkably (going by its achievements) in mutual co-operation, interdependance, complementary efforts and strength. The ADB has furthered the efforts of its members in systematic development. Its lending activities are remarkable in the field of social significance. There is 41.9% increase in loans from the Special Fund. Upto 1978 it provided $ 5,404 million to 21 members.

The ADB has financed construction of highways, harbours, airports, schemes of electricity and water supply, irrigation projects and a hoast of other allied projects of social importance and technical importance.

The reputation of the ADB is growing and it has a bright future and international backing. It stands out as yet another successful venture in regional monetary co-operation, vigour and confidence of the non-regional members. Its *ordinary lending and specialised lending* operations are highly significant.

THE INTERNATIONAL FINANCE CORPORATION (IFC)

The IFC was established in 1956 as an affiliate of the World Bank or IBRD. It was to fill the shortcomings of the IBRD in providing '*equity capital*' to member countries. It is open to all members of the IBRD. There were 100 members as on 30th June 1975.

Its objective is to step in where the IBRD cannot. That is to finance or guarantee loans to its members and bring together investment opportunities.

The aims and objectives of the IFC are stated in its *Articles of Agreement* as under:

1. To encourage private enterprises;
2. To establish a link between those enterprises which have managerial skills and no finance and those which have finance only—from world over; and
3. To encourage private foreign capital to come forward to invest in other countries in productive projects.

The IFC is managed and organised on lines similar to that of the IBRD. Thus, the 'Board of Governors' of the IFC consists of the representatives of member countries in the IBRD. The President of the IBRD is the Chairman of the IFC. The President of the IFC is appointed by the Chairman.

The identity and funds of the IFC are independent though it is an affiliate of the IBRD.

The working of the IFC was rather slow to begin with and now it has picked up tempo. It has been lending to Asian and African countries in addition to Latin American and Central American countries of late out of its subscribed capital $373 million and borrowed funds of $310 millions from the IBRD. Its total resources in June 1975 was $700 million.

The IFC has financed a number of projects in the private sector in developing countries like India. Its total investment commitments have increased manifold and there is diversification in the area of its financing operations. It is sure to play a more dynamic and responsible role in the development of its member countries during the years ahead.

6

Public Finance

TAXATION

Taxation is an important aspect of *Public Finance*. The revenue of the state is, for the most part, derived from taxes. Moreover, taxation has a great impact on the various aspects such as consumption, production, distribution and price level. Similarly, the *ability* of the people to pay a tax (*Taxable Capacity*) determines the tax revenue of the state. Further, *Public Expenditure* depends partly on taxes and plays a dynamic role in an economy.

Therefore, in this chapter the students are introduced to these concepts in a brief manner.

Distinction Between Tax and other Terms

A 'Tax' is a compulsory contribution made by the people and firms to the state for the general services rendered by the government or state without any '*quid-pro-quo*' (*i.e.* without any promise of equivalent service by the state).

According to Dalton:

"*A tax is a compulsory charge imposed by an authority*"* namely the government.

Prof. Seligman gives a clearer definition of 'Tax' when he defines a tax as:

"*A compulsory contribution from a person to the government to defray the expenses incurred in the common interest of all without references to special benefits conferred.*"**

---

* Hugh Dalton: 'Principles of Public Finance', *op. cit., p. 17.*

** E.R.A. Seligman: 'Essays in Taxation', p. 432.

Thus, a tax is compulsory and inescapable, unobjectionable and does not confer any preferential benefit but only common benefit to all.

Prof. Taussiq states that, "*The essence of a tax, as distinguished from other charges by government, is the absence of a direct quid-pro-quo between the tax-payer and the public authority.*"

On the other hand '*Fee*' is also a compulsory payment but it is for the definite service in return from the state. It covers only a part of the cost of the service and not fully. Fee confers a "*special advantage on the fee-payer*" according to Prof. Seligman. Thus, there is *quid-pro-quo in fee* while it is absent in tax.

Similarly, tax is different from '*price*' and '*fine*'. While 'price' is paid for services of business character the '*fines*' are paid only by the lawbreakers to the state.

DIRECT AND INDIRECT TAXES

Now that we have clearly differentiated taxes from other forms of payments, we, can proceed to distinguish between '*Direct*' and '*Indirect*' taxes.

It is a tradition in public Finance to classify broadly the taxes as (1) *Direct taxes* and (2) *Indirect taxes.*

The simplest distinction between them is that while '*Direct Taxes*' are levied on and intended to be paid by the persons or firms on whom they are levied, '*Indirect Taxes*' are paid by someone else though it is levied on a particular person or firm.

Technically, the '*impact*' and the '*incidence*' of a direct tax are on one and the same person or firm. Theatre on different persons or firms in the case of indirect taxes.

'*Impact*' is on the *first bearer* of the tax and '*incidence*' is on the *final bearer* of the tax.

Further distinction is that direct taxes are *not shiftable* while indirect taxes are shiftable both *forward* or *backward* and *vertically* or *horizontally* and partly or fully. ...*As Prof. Dalton puts it, "...A direct tax is really paid by the person on whom it is legally imposed, while an indirect tax is imposed on one person, but paid partly or wholly by another..... Thus, an indirect tax....can be shifted or passed on; a direct tax....cannot (be).*"*

J.S. Mill makes the distinction as follows:

> A direct tax is "*demanded from the person whom it intended or desired should pay it*" and an indirect tax is "*demanded*

* Hugh Dalton: 'Principles of Public finance'; op. cit., pp. 23-24: The word 'be' in brackets in mine.

*from one person in the expectation and intention that" he himself pay "at the expense of another."**

Prof. Charles M. Allen makes an administrative distinction between the two types of taxes as follows:

> *"Each tax has a set of administrative arrangement for its collection. Income-tax is paid direct by the tax payer to the authorities, while sales taxes are paid by the consumer of goods and services but reach the government indirectly through the retailers who act as a collecting agency."*

Lastly, we can conclude with Prof. Allan William's distinction that direct taxes are levied as per the economic status *progressively* while indirect taxes are levied as per *proportion of expenditure* of the consumer with no reference to economic status of tax-payers.

Merits of Direct Taxes

There had been a long controversy about the choice of taxes. However, the controversy has been resolved now. Yet, it is customary to discuss the merits and demerits of Direct and Indirect taxes in the Economics of Public Finance. We shall presently note the major merits and the demerits of direct taxes in this section.

Direct taxes have the following merits.

1. Direct taxes fulfil the *equity principle i.e.* they can be made *progressive*. The rate of tax may be increased according to the ability of the tax-payer. Thus, the rich pay higher percentage of income-tax than others.
2. They are useful in reducing the inequalities of income and wealth.
3. Direct taxes are *certain i.e.,* the amount of tax is known beforehand to the tax-payer.
4. These taxes are *economical* as the cost of collection of direct taxes is relatively less. Taxes like income-tax on salaries is automatically recovered at source.
5. They are highly *elastic* as the rates can be increased by the *stroke of a pen* to obtain additional revenue during emergencies. They can also be decreased during deflation.
6. They *arouse civic consciousness* of the tax-payer. The tax-payer takes keen interest in the affairs of public finance. The tax-payer becomes a watch-dog of government's expenditure.

* J.S. Mill: 'Principles': Book, V, Ch. III.

7. Direct taxes therefore satisfy a maximum number of *cannons of taxation*. They make the system of taxation *diverse* and *productive*.

Demerits of Direct Taxes

Those who support Indirect taxes on the other hand pin point the following demerits of Direct Taxes:

1. Direct taxes are *unpopular* as they need probing into personal and private affairs of individuals as in the case of income-tax.
2. They are *arbitrary* since the ability to pay the tax is calculated without reference to factors such as whether one is a bachelor or married, one's dependents are many or less, cost of living is low or moderate or high.
3. They are really *inconvenient* since the tax burden is high and payable in lump-sum in the case of firms.
4. They are a *tax on honesty* as those who honestly declare the income pay more than those who *falsify* accounts and *evade* the payment of the direct taxes. For instance, an employee who earns his income only by salary (inescapably pays the income-tax) while a businessman evades tax partly or wholly.
5. The *cost of collection* is virtually high rather than being low if we consider the huge army of administrators and their fat salaries. Hence, they are *uneconomical* in relation to indirect taxes.
6. They are unjust since '*they rob Peter to pay Paul*' *i.e.* rob the rich man's fruits of hard earned income to spend on the benefits to the poor.
7. They are *severe* in effect on employment, savings and investment after a limit.

However, we must remember that these demerits are not inherent in nature. Most of them are put forward just *argumentatively* by the opponents of direct taxes. Some of these are purely *capitalistic* arguments. The defects or demerits of direct takes can be overcome by careful planning of administration of these taxes. They are both useful and necessary; not unjust.

Merits of Indirect Taxes

The other camp which supports Indirect Taxes points towards some major merits of Indirect taxes. They are:

1. Indirect Taxes are *broader than* Direct Taxes. They involve one and all in the payment of taxes. They are, therefore, '*equitable*' in this sense.
2. They are *unevadable*. Any one who buys the goods must pay the tax. Thus, they are also *justifiable*.
3. They are *less unpleasant* and do not "*make the goose*" (the taxpayer) *queek under the weight*" of the tax. To be more humorous, they are like a *sugar coated quinine pill* which is bitter after the coating wears out or melts but yet serves the purpose.
4. Indirect Taxes are *convenient* as they are paid in small amounts as and when a commodity is bought (and if bought) *i.e.*, they are not burdensome.
5. They can be made *elastic* depending on the nature of the taxed commodity. That is, depending on whether it is a necessity or a comfort or a luxury.
6. They are as *equitable* as direct taxes on luxuries are higher than on the necessities and comforts of the less rich or the poorer classes.
7. Indirect taxes have a '*reformatory effect*' on the people when they are levied on goods like liquors and tobacco products.

Demerits of Indirect Taxes

These taxes are also said to have some limitations or demerits. The chief of them are:

1. They are *unjust* and *inequitable* since the tax on necessaries like *salt* and *matches* make even the poor and poorest of the poor pay them. They become 'inequitable' when the rate of an indirect tax falls heavily on the luxuries. However, this part of the argument is narrowly conceived.
2. They are *relatively uneconomical* especially in the case of *Customs Duties* as it is necessary to maintain a huge fleet of *white-collared* personnel.
3. They are *regressive* as the burden is heavy on the poorer classes (*i.e.* on necessities).
4. They *lack civic consciousness* as they are concealed in the price.
5. They are *shiftable* and hence their burden falls on the consumers.

A sound system of taxation must contain both types of taxes. There has to be *diversification* in the *tax structure*. As Hugh Dalton puts it, "*The* *best system of taxation, from the economic point of view, is that which has the best, or the least bad, economic effects*".* Thus, as long as any tax fulfils this criteria must contain the best of both taxes. Hence, J.S. Mill may be said to have been misled when he said, "*A Graduated income-tax was an entirely unjust mode of taxation and, in fact, a graduated robbery.*" Prof. Charles has resolved the controversy about the choice between the two types of taxes by comparing them to '*two attractive sisters having an ample fortune and the same percentage, differing only as sisters may differ*'. The difference is purely *genetic* and not of kind. They are equally attractive to the Finance Minister due to their ampleness of "fortune".

TAXABLE CAPACITY

Of all the confusing concepts in Public Finance the concept of '*Taxable Capacity*' can be said to be the most confusing concept. Hence, it would be better if the students of Business Economics are given an unambiguous introduction to this concept.

In a very broad sense let it be known that '*Taxable Capacity*' is the ability of the taxed person to bear the burden of the tax in relation to his source or sources of income without experiencing a reduction in the standard of living or margin of profits and investment in the case of firms.

Broadly, the taxable capacity is of two categories, viz.:

1. *Relative Taxable Capacity*, and
2. *Absolute Taxable Capacity.*

'*Absolute Taxable Capacity*' does not consider factors other than the level of gross income while '*Relative Taxable Capacity*' relates the *ability to pay* the tax to all factors that determine the *ability to pay* the tax. It was Prof. Hugh Dalton who made this distinction in a rough manner when he said that the former refers to the '*extent that a community can be taxed without producing unpleasant effects on the economy*' and the latter as the comparative '*taxable capacity of two or more commodities*'.

Let us also revise what other leading economists have in store to say about Taxable Capacity.

Sir Josiah Stamp states that the taxable capacity of a country is the maximum amount which the citizens of a country can contribute "*without having a really unhappy and downtrodden existence and without dislocating the economic organisation too much.*"**

Prof. Findlay Shirras says that, "*Taxable Capacity is the limit of squeezability... standard of living remaining constant.*"

* Hugh Dalton: 'Principles of Public Finance', p. 72.

** Sir Josiah Stamp: 'Wealth and Taxable Capacity', p. 134.

Thus, Taxability is a *relative concept* rather than an absolute concept as per experience. It differs from section to section of a nation's communities. Hence, it also guides the *degree of taxation*.

The Determinants of Taxable Capacity

According to the 'Taxation Enquiry Committee' of India there are three major determinants of Taxable Capacity and they are:

1. Ratio of total tax revenue to national income of the nation;
2. The benefits of public expenditure out of tax revenue; and
3. The efficiency of administration of taxes.

However, the noted Indian economist Prof. Bhargava states in this context that the, "*Absolute taxable capacity is just another name for optimum taxation and its limit is indicated by the principle of public finance.*"

Further, according to him, the taxable capacity depends on the following factors:

1. Per-capita income,
2. Employment level and Efficiency of Labour.
3. The Stock of Natural Resources.
4. Capital formation.
5. Technological status of the country.
6. The pattern of income distribution.
7. The morality of the Nation's Government.

CAUSES FOR INCREASE IN PUBLIC EXPENDITURE

A number of causes may be cited for the recent increase in public expenditure all over the world. The alarming expansion in public expenditure is generally due to the concept of the '*Welfare State*'. In other words, modern States no longer follow Adam Smith's concept of the role of a '*police state*'. They act and regulate activities of individuals *from the cradle to the grave*'.

Therefore, in this concluding section of this book it is befitting to state in brief the causes for the expansion of the horizons of public expenditure in recent years.

The most consequential causes for the increase in public expenditure are:

1. General Inflation: All countries of the globe are strained by the rising price level. Hence, the national governments' public sector investments have been rising. Moreover, the salaries and '*Dearness Allowances*' are revised upwards due to inflation.

2. Increase in Defence Expenditure: The Defence Expenditure is rising due to the global deterioration of political relations in the wake of *aggressiveness* of the neighbourhood.

3. Social and Political Causes: Socially, governments of the nations have been giving '*Social Security*' to their citizens. These programmes cost non-developmental expenses. *Politically*, modern governments spend a huge sum on visiting foreign dignitaries, embassies, etc. in order to maintain cordial international relations.

4. Granis-in-Aid: During emergencies like floods the national government is under obligation to come to the rescue of the states in terms of finance which is non-refundable.

5. Planning for Economic Growth: There is a keen race for economic growth among nations and hence, public expenditure is rising on account of Economic Planning by nations.

6. Growth of Population and Urbanization: The pattern of population growth has been very alarming and often worse in some countries of the '*Third World*' than the "*Atomic Explosion*" according to Dr. Chandrashekar, a noted Indian demographist.

Hence, population control has been costing heavy public expenditure.

The growth of population has much to do with migration from villages to cities and towns. Thus, overcrowding in towns and cities causes a burden on state finances in the form of housing, drainage, water supply, etc.

In short, public expenditure is no more '*passive*' but '*dynamic*'. It is *corrective* and has an economic and socio-economic relevance. It is '*functional*' as well as '*formal*'.

7

The Reserve Bank of India

A Short History: In every country the central bank has emerged over the process of evolution over a number of years. Before the emergence of a Central Bank the "Issue of currency —" and the "Banker-to-the-Government Functions" were undertaken by what was known as "*The General Bank of Bengal and Bihar*" in India (1773). It had a short span of life. Towards the end of the 19th century and the beginning of the 20th century there were three "*Presidency Banks*" operating as central banking authorities in the erstwhile Presidency states of Madras, Bombay and Bengal. These Presidency Banks were discharging independent functions of a Central Bank in India. As a result there was lack of co-ordination and the monetary system was defective.

In 1921 these Presidency Banks were amalgamated and the '*Imperial Bank of India*' was established to function as a Central Bank. But it was entrusted only the power to control credit while issue of currency remained in the hands of the government. This was defective as there was always a danger of over-issue of currency. The Imperial Bank was also acting as Banker to the Govt. The need for a full-fledged Central Bank remained unfulfilled until 1925.

In 1925 the British Govt, appointed the famous "*Hilton Young Commission*". This Commission recommended strongly the need for a separate Central Bank in India. It proposed nationalisation of a Central Bank to be named "The Reserve Bank of India". However, the proposal fell through the Legislative Assembly in 1927.

In 1931 The 'Central Banking Enquiry Committee' in its report strongly submitted a proposal again to set up a Central Bank.

Accordingly, the '*White Paper*' issued on Constitutional Reforms in 1933 provided for setting up the Reserve Bank of India. The British India

Finance Minister, Sir George Schulster introduced the "*Reserve Bank of India Bill*" on 8th Sept. 1933 in the Legislative Assembly. It was passed duly and attained the status of an Act on 6th March 1934 with the consent of the Governor-General.

The Reserve Bank of India (RBI) formally came into existence on 1st April 1935 as a a *Joint-Stock Bank* with limited liability. It was thus a private sector bank with an initial *share capital* of ₹ 5 crores (the share capital of ₹ 6 crores has remained unchanged up to this day). It was divided into 5 lakh shares of ₹ 100 each.

For better and effective co-ordination of monetary and credit policies the RBI was nationalised after independence on 1st January, 1949 as per the Reserve Bank (Transfer & Ownership) Act, 1948. With this the instability of the Indian Banking System ended. The maintenance of external and internal value of the Rupee became easier and effective. And the implementation of Govt's policy and co-ordination of monetary, economic and fiscal policies became smooth.

Organisation of RBI

The RBI's affairs are managed by the '*Central Board of Directors*' as per the directives of the Govt, of India. The Board consists of 20 directors. It consists of:

1. '*One*' Governor/Chairman of the Board.
2. '*Four*' Deputy Governors (Nominated by the Central Govt.).
3. '*Ten*' Directors (Nominated by the Central Govt.).
4. '*One*' official (Nominee of the Govt. of India).

The Central Board of Directors issues regulations from time-to-time. The Governor is the Chairman of the *Board of Directors*. The Governor and Deputy Governors have a full term of 5 years on full-time basis subject to re-appointment at the discretion of the Govt.

The *ten* Directors have a term of 4 years who can be re-elected on retirement. *Two* directors retire every year and in their place *two* new Directors are nominated or elected.

Apart from the Central Board there are 4 *Local Boards*, one each for Western, Eastern, Northern and Southern Regions with headquarters at Bombay, Calcutta, Madras and New Delhi respectively. There are 5 members on each Local Board with representation for different sectors *viz.* agriculture, industry, banking, etc. Their term is 4 years and are eligible for reappointment on retirement. *The Chairman of the Local Board* is elected from among the members of the Local Board.

The Central Board meets at least 6 times in an year subject to a minimum of one meeting per quarter. The Deputy Governor has no voting rights (one of them can vote in the place of the Governor if the Governor is absent at a meeting). The official nominee does not have voting rights but can attend the meetings. In the absence of the Governor the Deputy Governor acts on behalf of the Governor.

Administration: For the purpose of administration the R.B.I. has its Head Office at Bombay. The administrative structure consists of 16 departments such as, Personnel and Administrative Dept., Agricultural Dept., Banking Dept., Exchange Control Dept., Inspection Dept., Issue Dept., Legal Dept., etc.

The RBI operates an office at London and the State Bank of India acts as the '*Agent*' of the RBI where the RBI has no office.

The following chart represents the Administrative set up of the RBI:

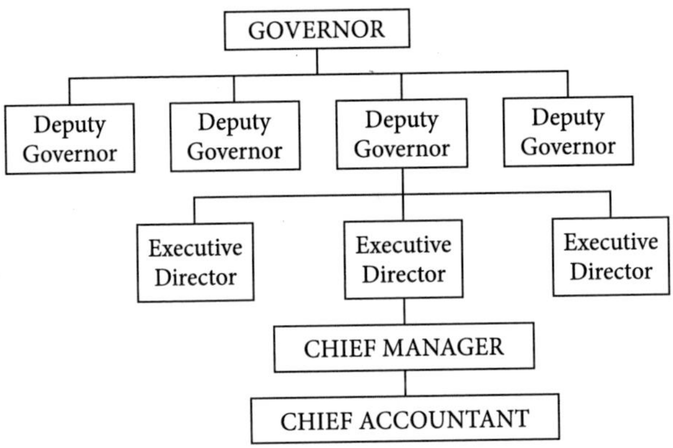

Functions: The functions of the RBI are broadly grouped under *two* heads, viz.:

1. Central Banking Functions; and
2. General or Non-Banking Functions.

The Banking functions are sub-divided into the following catagories in order of importance:

A. Issue of currency.

B. Banker to the Govt, of India.

C. Bankers' Bank.

D. Last-resort lending to Commercial Banks.

E. Control of Credit Creation by Commercial Banks.

F. Custody of Foreign Exchange and gold reserves.

G. Promotional functions such as expansion of banking facilities and establishment of special agencies to cater to the expanding needs of various sectors of the economy. These are general in nature.

A Note on S.B.I.

The SBI (State Bank of India) was constituted on July 1, 1955 by nationalising the Imperial Bank of India, the unofficial leader of the Indian banking system till then. Today, the SBI is the largest public sector commercial bank.

The broad concept behind the establishment of the SBI was elimination of competition from the European controlled Imperial Bank of India. The SBI was set up, therefore as "*one strong, integrated, state-partnered commercial banking institution with an effective machinery of branches spread over the whole country for stimulating banking development....without departing from canons of sound business*".*

The SBI has an authorised capital of ₹ 20 crores of 20,00,00 shares of ₹ 100 each. Its paid up capital is ₹ 5.265 crores. Of the issued capital of ₹ 5.265 crores 92% is owned by the RBI.

The SBI affairs are managed by:

1. *One* Chairman and Vice-Chairman.
2. *Two* Managing Directors.
3. *Six* elected Directors of share-holders.
4. *Eight* Directors nominated by the Govt. of India (in consultation with the RBI).
5. *One* Director independently appointed by the Govt. of India.
6. *One* Director nominated by the SBI.
7. *Two* Directors representing the employees of the SBI.

The S.B.I. Group has a strong network of Branches spread over India and abroad. The SBI group had 8860 Bank offices by June 1982. It covers 1/3 of banking industry with 23.1% of total deposits of Commercial Banking sector.

Its total deposits increased from a meagre ₹ 188 crores (1955) to ₹ 10,514 crores by the end of June 1982.

The SBI is the single largest source of finance to large scale private and public sector industries, small industries, co-operative sector, rural

* All India Rural Credit Survey Report, 1952.

industries, etc. It also renders general assistance in the form of remittances, village adoption schemes, agro development branches, IRDP and so on. It also finances foreign trade arising out of trade agreements, Exchange-clearing Agreements, etc. Its export finance was ₹ 437 crores by 1981 (outstanding) and was 1/3 of total export credit.

A Note on Lead Bank Scheme

The '*Lead Batik Scheme*' was invented by the SBI for the development of the most under-developed and inaccessible districts of the country. It takes primary initiative in planning and development of such districts as are entrusted to it as the '*Leader*'. Hence, the name '*Lead Bank Scheme*'.

It co-ordinates all activities in the district adopted under the scheme. It conducts objective surveys of economic activities and finances those feasible activities which the survey report identifies as necessary.

Its activities are closely linked with the *Community Development Projects* (CDPs). The scheme aims at utilisation of indigenously available resources for the development of the districts concerned. By 1980-82 there were 77 '*Lead Districts*' with a plan outlay of ₹ 718 crores of which the SBI accounted for ₹ 159 crores (39%) and commercial banks shared ₹ 405 crores.

Regional Rural Banks (RRBs)

The RRBs were set up on the recommendation of the Working Group on Rural Banks 1975. A modest beginning was made with the setting up of 5 RRBs at the following places:

(1) Moradabad, (2) Gorakhpur, (3) Bhiwani, (4) Jaipur, and (5) Malda. They are sponsored by SBI, PNB, Syndicate Bank, United Commercial Bank and the United Bank of India.

The share capital of each RRB is contributed by the Govt. of India, sponsoring banks and state govts. Its authorised and paid capital is ₹ 1 crore and Rs. 25 lakhs respectively. They enjoy the status of scheduled banks and mobilise rural savings also.

The Regional Rural Banks are those special banks which are set up to cover those rural areas of the country that are not covered by the commercial banks and co-operative banks in India. Their twin objectives (1) to bring about development of rural unbanked areas by providing credit facilities to small and marginal farmers, rural artisans and weaker sections of society in villages; and (2) reduce the dependence of these sections on '*Indigenous Bankers*' for credit needs.

The RRBs are an entirely new agency for rural credit. They overcome the inherent weaknesses of the commercial banks and cooperative banks. While the co-operative banks are not competitive and suffer from huge over-dues, the commercial banks are urban-oriented and are not able to understand the peculiar credit requirements of small and marginal farmers of the country.

The RRBs are established to realise the advantages of commercial banks and the co-operative banks; that is, the strength and competence of commercial banks and the easy reach of the co-operative banks and their spirit.

The introduction of the Integrated Rural Development Programme (IRDP) has given a great phillip to the RRBs. The RRBs are a boon to the small and marginal farmers, artisans and village industries. They are expected to fill the void in credit supply to these sections of borrowers.

The RRBs only '*supplement*' and not '*supplant*' other lending agencies. They correspond in regional language. Though they finance only productive activities they provide some per cent of total advances for religious ceremonies, medical and educational purposes. The rate of interest on loans is on par with that of co-operative banks. To block other sources of borrowing the loans are granted against security of the entire property of the borrower in his own interest.

By 1981 there were 102 RRBs operating in 172 districts in 18 states with 3598 branches. At the end of June 1981 deposit mobilisation was ₹ 253 crores and advances stood at ₹ 302 crores.

Their multi-agency approach has made them popular. The '*Dantwala Committee*' has rightly observed that the RRBs are a superior rural credit agency over rural commercial banks due to the former's low cost of operation, simplicity, local participation and low profile. They certainly provide a great sign of relief to the rural sector which is debt ridden and caught up in the cob-webb of the rural money-lenders.

A Note on NABARD

The National Bank for Agriculture and Rural Development (NABARD) was established on July 12,1982 on the recommendation of the special committee appointed by the RBI.

The NABARD has taken over the Agricultural Refinance Corporation (ARDC), refinancing functions of the RBI and the RRBs.

The initial capital of the NABARD is ₹ 100 crores raiseable to ₹ 500 crores in future. The capital is shared by the RBI and the Govt. of India in 50: 50 ratio.

The short-term funds for its operation are provided by the RBI while long-term funds are from the Govt. of India. Besides it draws from the National Rural Credit Fund (NRCF) and raises funds through Bonds. It accepts deposits for not less than 1 year from Central and State Govts., scheduled banks and local boards.

The NABARD provides refinance credit for the following purposes:

1. Marketing of agricultural produce.
2. Marketing and supply of agro-inputs.
3. Production and marketing of small industries, village and cottage industries, handicrafts and other rural crafts.

The NABARD extends credit for these purposes to Co-operative Banks and RRBs and institutions specified by the RBI for not more than 18 months. The terms of the loans can be extended up to 7 years under draught and famine conditions.

ANNEXURE

MODEL QUESTIONS

(As per model of the Bangalore University Question Paper)

MODEL QUESTION PAPER-1

Section A (16 Marks)

I. Answer to these questions in not more than 'Four' sentences each. Each question carries 'Two' marks. Answer 'Eight' questions.

1. (1) Define 'Business Economics'.
   (2) Define 'Consumer's Surplus'.
   (3) Define 'Consumer's Sovereignty'.
   (4) State the 'Law of Maximum Satisfaction'.
   (5) Distinguish between 'increase' and 'decrease' in demand.
   (6) Mention the types of elasticity of demand.
   (7) What is meant by 'Indifference Map'?
   (8) What are Iso-costs?
   (9) Distinguish between GNP and NNP.
   (10) What is Demand Forecasting?
   (11) Distinguish between 'prime costs' and 'real cost'.
   (12) What is meant by 'full-cost pricing'?
   (13) Define 'group equilibrium'.
   (14) What is meant by 'price-leadership'?

Section B (24 Marks)

II. Answer to these questions should not exceed 30 sentences each. Each question carries 'Eight' marks. Answer 'three' questions.

2. With the help of the data given below use the 'total outlay method', find out the 'price elasticity' of demand for oranges. Also represent it graphically:

	Price per Kg of oranges ₹	Demand for oranges (in Units)
(a)	5.00	2000
	4.50	3000
	4.00	6000
(b)	5.00	500
	4.50	1000
	4.00	500
(c)	5.00	2000
	4.50	2050
	4.00	2000

3. With the help of the following data find out the total cost (TC), Average Fixed Cost (AFC), Average Variable Cost (AVC) and Marginal Cost (MC) when Total Fixed Cost (TFC) incurred is ₹ 500 by Thara Chand & Co.

Total output (Units)	TVC
100	300
200	600
300	650
400	800
500	825
600	950
700	1500
800	4000

4. The following is the data pertaining to the Refrigerators produced by Leonard & Co.:
   (a) The cost price of model 'A' = ₹ 4000
   The seller's margin = ₹ 1000
   Find the mark-up-price based on 'cost'.
   (b) The cost price of model 'B' = ₹ 6000
   Seller's margin = 1500
   Find the mark-up price based on 'selling price'.
   (c) The producer's price is ₹ 4,000 per model. 'C' consumers' price is ₹ 8000 per Model 'C'. The difference is distributed in two mark-up as follows:

1. Wholesaler's mark up 20%
2. Retailer's mark up 35%

Find the relation between:

(a) Mark-up on cost price; and

(b) Mark-up on selling price

5. Explain the role of a Business Economist in the modern world
6. Explain the need for demand forecasting

Section C (60 Marks)

III. Answer to these questions should not exceed 'Three' pages each. Each question carries '*Fifteen*' marks. Answer '*Four*' questions.

7. Distinguish between cardinal utility and ordinal utility approaches. Why do you consider the Indifference Curve Technique as superior to the Marginal Utility Analysis?
8. State and explain the Law of DMRS. What are its uses in Business Economics?
9. What is meant by a 'Trade Cycle'? Explain the different phases of a trade cycle.
10. What is 'Trend Projection? What are its uses and Limitations as a method of Demand Forecasting?
11. Examine the importance of 'Time Element' in the Theory of Value.
12. Explain the determination of price and output under perfect competition with illustrations

MODEL QUESTION PAPER-2

I. Section A (16 Marks)

1. (1) Distinguish between 'Stock and Supply'.

   (2) Define price elasticity of demand.

   (3) Define 'Price Effect'.

   (4) What is meant by 'Trend Projection'.

   (5) Mention the different methods of measurement of national income.

   (6) Distinguish between 'Average Cost' and 'Marginal Cost'.

   (7) What is 'Giffen's paradox'?

   (8) Define 'taxable capacity'.

(9) Distinguish between Balance of Trade and 'Balance of Payments'.

(10) Define 'Qptimun Firm'.

(11) What is meant by Opinion Survey Method of forecasting demand

(12) Distinguish between 'Tax' and 'Fees'.

II. Section B (24 Marks)

2. Distinguish between perfect and imperfect competition.
3. (a) In order to determine the demand for T.V. Sets in the Union Territory of Pondicherry the following formula is used by the enumerator:

$$y = 0.2 + 0.118x$$

Where (1) y is the Economic indicator of T.Vs sold in thousands

(2) x = 210 which is the economic index of urban income (as on 31-3-1991).

Find out the total demand for T.V. Sets in the Union Territory of Pondicherry with the aid of the Index Number given.

(b) With the given data find out the Break-even Point for Andrew Yule & Co.:

Total Sales	—	2108 units of fans.
Sales proceed	—	1,02,000 rupees.
Total Fixed Cost	—	30,000 rupees.

4. Explain the general considerations involved in formulating a sound price policy.
5. Describe the role of Iso-costs and Iso-quants in determining costs of production.
6. Defined Taxable Capacity. Explain its determinants.

III. Section C (60 Marks)

7. What is meant by Collective Bargaining? How does it influence wages of Labour?
8. What is monoploy? Explain with illustrations how price is determined under monopoly.
9. Distinguish between going-rate policy and rate-of-return pricing and explain their merits and limitations.
10. What is Price Policy? How are prices of Joint-products and New Products determined?

11. "Trade cycles are purely a monetary phenomenon." Critically examine this statement.
12. Distinguish between GNP and NNP. Explain the difficulties in the measurement of national income and uses of national income estimates.

MODEL QUESTION PAPER - 3

I. Section A (16 Marks)

1. What is price-consumption curve?
2. Define price discrimination.
3. Define a Representative Firm.
4. What is Stackelberg solution?
5. What is skimming price strategy?
6. Define B.E.P.
7. Distinguish between 'internal' and 'external' economies.
8. What is meant by 'Speculative Motive'.
9. Define Life Cycle Pricing.
10. Define national income at factor cost.
11. Distinguish between 'visible' and 'invisible' exports.
12. What is meant by *quid-pro-quo*?

II. Section B (24 Marks)

1. From the information given below find out the nature of elasticity of demand for the Wilson's Stonewear pants, using Total Outlay method.

		Price	**Qty. of demand**
(a)	Initial price	₹ 10	200
	New Price	₹ 6	240
(b)	Initial price	₹ 8	280
	New Price	₹ 7	370
(c)	Initial price	₹ 6	360
	New Price	₹ 5	400
	New Price	₹ 4	480

2. Axium Spares Limited incurs a fixed cost of ₹ 100 during 1989-90. Use the following data and find out:

   (a) Total Variable Cost (TVC);

(b) Average Cost (AC); and

(c) Marginal Cost (MC)

Output (units)	TC (₹)
0	120
1	180
2	200
3	210
4	225
5	260
6	330

3. (a) The following is a schedule of demand of consumers for Vivaldy shirts. Calculate the numerical co-efficient of income elasticity of demand:

Annual income of consumers (₹)	Annual demand for shirts
	0
4,000	1
6,000	2
8,000	3
10,000	4
12,000	5
14,000	6
16,000	7

(b) Construct a diagram from the above schedule taking income on OX axis and shirts on OY axis.

(c) Indicate the range at which the Vivaldy shirts are regarded as:

(1) A Luxury — at ₹ ....

(2) A Normal commodity — at ₹ ....

(3) Inferior commodity — at ₹ ....

4. (a) Define B.E.P. by sales value.

(b) Calculate the BEP by Physical Unit Method when—

Total Fixed Cost (TFC) = ₹ 600, Average Revenue (AR) = ₹ 8 and Average Variable Cost (AVC) = ₹ 6

Apply the formula: $\text{BEP} = \dfrac{\text{TFC}}{\text{TCF / unit}}$

When

$$\text{Contribution Margin} = \text{AR, ABC or BEP} = \frac{\text{TFC}}{\text{AR}}$$

III. Section C (60 Marks)

5. Define price elasticity of demand. Illustrate and explain different types of price elasticity. What are the uses of the concept of elasticity of demand.
6. What is profit planning? Examine the need for profit planning and what are its limitations?
7. State and explain critically the liquidity preference theory of interest.
8. Define price discrimination. When is it possible and profitable?
9. Distinguish between price and income effect. Illustrate and explain the price and income effects on consumer's equilibrium.
10. Explain the concept of Consumer's Surplus. What are its uses and limitations?

FIRST YEAR B. COM. DEGREE EXAMINATION
APRIL/MAY1992

(Revised Scheme -1989-90 onwards)

BUSINESS ECONOMICS

Time: 3 Hours Maximum: 100 Marks

Section A

(16 marks)

Answer any eight sub-questions from the following. Each sub-question carries 2 marks

Answer to each sub-question should not exceed 4 lines.

1. (a) Define Business Economics.
 (b) Mention the two approaches for the study of consumer behaviour.
 (c) What is Giffen's paradox?
 (d) Distinguish between Substitutes and Complements.
 (e) What is income elasticity of demand?
 (f) Give reason for U-shaped average cost curve.
 (g) State the law of supply.
 (h) Mention four factors influencing cost of production.
 (i) What do you mean by market equilibrium?
 (j) Mention four features of perfect competition.
 (k) Distinguish between Favourable and Unfavourable balance of trade.
 (l) Distinguish between Risks and Uncertainties

($8 \times 2 = 16$ marks)

Section B

(24 marks)

Answer any three questions from the following. Each question carries 8 marks.

Answer to each question should not exceed 30 lines.

2. With the help of the data given below calculate total variable cost, average fixed cost and average cost.

Output units:	0	1	2	3	4	5	6	7	8	9	10
Total cost ₹:	120	204	248	288	320	360	408	476	576	720	920

3. (a) Explain the meaning of

$$E_p > 1, E_p - 1 \text{ and } E_p < 1.$$

(b) With the help of the data given below find out the nature of elasticity of demand. (Use total outlay method):

Price per	Quantity (unit) (₹)	demanded (units)
	20	600
(a)	15	900
	10	1400
	20	600
(b)	15	700
	10	800
	20	600
	15	800
	10	1200

4. What are indifference curves? With the help of indifference curve analysis explain income effect.
5. Mention the general considerations for price policy. Explain its objectives.
6. "Selling costs and product differentation are the hallmarks of monopolistic competition." Explain.

(3 × 8 = 24 marks)

Section C

(60 marks)

Answer any four questions from the following. Each question carries 15 marks.

Answer to each question should not exceed three pages.

7. Define, classify and explain the economies of large scale production.
8. Explain and critically examine the Liquidity preference theory of interest.
9. What do you mean by demand forecasting? Explain the important methods of demand forecasting.
10. What do you mean by adverse balance of payments? Explain the measures to correct it.
11. Explain four canons of public expenditure. Give reasons for the continuous increase in public expenditure in the recent years.
12. How does profit emerge? Explain the factors which limit business enterprises in the direction of profit maximisation.

(4 × 15 = 60 marks)